THE JOURNAL JURISPRUDENCE

VOLUME NINE

"LEGAL HISTORIES"

Contributors

Isaac J. Colunga
Ice Miller LLP

George Skouras
The New School for Social Research

Scott Hamilton Dewey
UCLA School of Law

Editor

Aron Ping D'Souza
University of Melbourne

HILARY TERM
MARCH 2011

Elias Clark

PUBLISHED BY THE ELIAS CLARK GROUP

DISTRIBUTED IN CONNECTION WITH THE GALE GROUP,
A PART OF CENGAGE LEARNING

The Elias Clark Group
www.elias-clark.com

GPO Box 5001
Melbourne, Victoria 3001
Australia

First Published 2011.

Cataloguing-in-Publication entry

Editor:	D'Souza, Aron Ping.
Authors:	D'Souza, Aron Ping. Colunga, Isaac. Skouras, George. Dewey, Scott.
Title:	The Journal Jurisprudence, Volume Nine, "Legal Histories."
ISBN:	978-0-9871170-0-7 (pbk.)
ISSN:	1836-0955
Subjects:	Law – jurisprudence. Philosophy –general.

This edition may be cited as

(2011) J. Juris.

followed by the page number

ABOUT THE TYPEFACE

The Journal Jurisprudence is typeset in Garamond 12 and the footnotes are set in Garamond 10. The typeface was named for Claude Garamond (c. 1480 - 1561) and are based on the work of Jean Jannon. By 1540, Garamond became a popular choice in the books of the French imperial court, particularly under King Francis I. Garamond was said to be based on the handwriting of Angelo Vergecio, a librarian to the King. The italics of Garamond are credited to Robert Grandjon, an assistant to Claude Garamond. The font was re-popularised in the art deco era and became a mainstay on twentieth-century publication. In the 1970s, the font was redesigned by the International Typeface Corporation, which forms the basis of the variant of Garamond used in this Journal.

TABLE OF CONTENTS

CALL FOR PAPERS

The field of jurisprudence lies at the nexus of law and politics, the practical and the philosophical. By understanding the theoretical foundations of law, jurisprudence can inform us of the place of legal structures within larger philosophical frameworks. In its inaugural edition, *The Journal Jurisprudence* received many creative and telling answers to the question, "What is Law?" For the second edition, the editors challenged the scholarly and lay communities to inquire into intersection between jurisprudence and economics.

With the backing of our diverse and disparate community, *The Journal Jurisprudence* has now evolved into a more diverse form. We will no longer be setting a question for each issue, but instead designing issues around the articles we received. Therefore, we invite scholars, lawyers, judges, philosophers and lay people tackle the any and all of the great questions of law. Knowing that ideas come in all forms, papers can be of any length, although emphasis is placed on readability by lay audiences.

Papers may engage with case studies, philosophical arguments or any other method that answers philosophical question applicable to the law. Importantly, articles will be selected based upon quality and the readability of works by non-specialists. The intent of the Journal is to involve non-scholars in the important debates of legal philosophy.

The Journal also welcomes and encourages submissions of articles typically not found in law journals, including opinionated or personalised insights into the philosophy of law and its applications to practical situations.

Jurisprudence is published four times per year, to coincide with the four terms of the legal year, in an attractive paperback and electronic edition.

All authors who submit to this edition will be provided with a complementary copy of the journal.

Length: Any length is acceptable, although readability to non-specialist is key.

Presentation Style: Papers must comply with the Australian Guide to Legal Citations, Second Edition published by the Melbourne University Law Review. An electronic edition is available at, http://mulr.law.unimelb.edu.au/PDFs/aglc_dl.pdf

Submission: You must submit electronically in Microsoft Word format to editor@jurisprudence.com.au. Extraneous formatting is discouraged.

Correspondence can also be sent to this address. If you are considering submitting an article, you are invited to contact the editor to discuss ideas before authoring a work.

SUBSCRIPTION INFORMATION

The Journal is published four times per year in an attractive softcover book. Subscription to the Journal can be achieved by two methods:

1) Single issues can be purchased on amazon.com. Our publishers, the Elias Clark Group, set a retail price for each edition, typically AU$40. However, due to their agreement with amazon.com, the price may vary for retail customers.

2) A subscription to the Journal can be purchased for AU$150 per year, or AU$280 for two years. This price includes postage throughout the world. Payment can be made by international bank cheque, but not a personal cheque, to:

   The Journal Jurisprudence,
   C/o The Elias Clark Group
   GPO Box 5001
   Melbourne, Victoria, Australia.

Alternatively, the Journal is available online at www.jurisprudence.com.au and can be read there free of charge.

EDITORIAL: LEGAL HISTORIES

Morton Horwitz of the Harvard Law School famously asked "Why is Anglo-American jurisprudence unhistorical?" in the *Oxford Journal of Legal Studies* in 1997.[1] His claim was not that all Anglo-American jurisprudence was detached from historical fact, but that analytical jurisprudence, particularly of the Hartian tradition, ruled out history as a legitimate source of authority. This, he said, was a response to the historicist value of relativist philosophy.

H.L.A. Hart is well established as the father of modern jurisprudence, at least in the Anglo-American tradition, and his positive approach to legal reasoning, aspiring towards a general theory of jurisprudence, was inherently ahistorical. The unhistorical nature of Hart's work was groundbreaking and was a necessary pre-requisite for his separability thesis.

Hart's notion that law was somehow distinct from morality has been challenged since its publication, most notably by John Finnis. The value of this edition is to highlight the importance of history to legal scholarship. Our trio of authors interact with the living history of law and show how historical events have formed the lifeblood of modern legal thinking. I believe the articles of this edition provide a substantial critique of the notion that jurisprudence can be unhistorical.

Isaac Colunga, who was previously Law Clerk to the Honorable Charles R. Norgle of the U.S. District Court for the Northern District of Illinois and now is in private practice with Ice Miller LLP, dissects ancient Rome's treason laws and how they evolved through Roman history and have been subject to misinterpretation. Mr Colunga's strength is to show us that even in ancient law, there is still scope for original inquiry.

It has been said that the corporation is the dominate form of social organisation in the modern world. George Skouras of the New School for Social Research gives us insight into the formation of corporations, particularly under the Fuller Supreme Court. Using the jurisprudence of the Fuller Court, Skouras shows us how the contemporary American corporatist state emerged and illustrates the connection to the current financial climate. Mr Skouras is a talented author and his article is of importance to current events and will have, I am sure, impact in both academic and professional debates.

---

1 (1997) 17(4): 551-586.

Scott Hamilton Dewey of UCLA tells about the history of the common law's essence, the doctrine of *stare decisis*. Using the state of Illinois as an example, he examined hundreds of cases dating back from 1876 relating to the concept of antagonistic defenses. Dr Dewey's detailed research has broken new ground, and inspires critical reflection on presumption of *stare decisis* granting both legal and linguistic certainty to courts. *The Journal Jurisprudence* is very pleased be able to share *How Judges Don't Think: The Inadvertent Misuse of Precedent in the Strange Career of the Illinois Doctrine of Antagonistic Defenses, 1876-1986* with our global readership.

I am certain that the articles in this issue show that legal history is a thriving field of enquiry, and has genuine relevance to jurisprudential debates. Personally, I am honored to have worked with our contributors in delivering this ninth issue of *Jurisprudence.*

Aron Ping D'Souza
Editor
Valetta, Malta
21 March 2011

UNTANGLING A HISTORIAN'S MISINTERPRETATION OF ANCIENT ROME'S TREASON LAWS

By

Isaac J. Colunga

INTRODUCTION

A prominent feature of Rome's political life was the *maiestas* or treason trial, which persisted for many years throughout the Republic.[1] *Maiestas* generally describes either the sovereignty or the dignity of the Roman people,[2] and thus the *crimen maiestatis* in ancient Rome could include any behavior construed as offensive or otherwise hostile toward the majesty of the State or the emperor. Convictions stemmed from a host of serious acts, such as plotting a rebellion, and even from harmless acts, such as defacing a public image. Indeed, under the broad concept of *maiestas*, prosecutors could convict anyone of a crime so long as their conduct was perceived, in the very least, as a threat to social order.[3]

The laws that governed these trials, the *lex maiestatis*, provided generally that whoever successfully accused and prosecuted someone on *maiestas* charges would be given part of the victim's estate. And, on top of that, in some cases successful accusers attained their victim's political offices, insignia and seniority status in the community. Although harsh, the laws likely had been intended to

---

[1] Olga Eveline Tellegen, *A Short History of Roman Law* [hereinafter, "Tellegen"] (1993), 65-67 (referring to the Principate as "the first three centuries of the republic"). According to Tellegen, the transition from the Republic to the Principate "constituted a political revolution accompanied by "changes in the social structure of the Roman empire."

[2] Clifford Ando, *Aliens, Ambassadors, and the Integrity of the Empire*, 26 LAW & HIST. REV. 491, 499 (2008) (recognizing the importance of maiestas in the age of Roman conquest); cf. Patrick McKinley Brennan, *Against Sovereignty: A Cautionary Note on the Normative Power of the Actual*, 82 NOTRE DAME L. REV. 181, 205 (2006) (describing the term "maiestas" as a "term of art," through which one serves the common good); Michael J. Kelly, *Pulling At the Treads of Westphalia: "Involuntary Sovereignty Waiver" – Revolutionary International Legal Theory Or Return To Rule By the Great Powers?*, UCLA J. INT'L L. & FOREIGN AFF. 361, 369 (2005) ("Sovereignty is the absolute and perpetual power of a commonwealth, which the Latins call maiestas . . . .").

[3] Nathan K. Cummings, *The Counterfeit Buck Stops Here: National Security Issues In the Redesign of U.S. Currency*, 8 S. CAL. INTERDISC. L.J. 539, 543-44 (1999) (stating that maiestas "encompassed a broad range of treasonous activities, from violating civic duties and acts of maladministration by magistrates to the more typical acts against the sovereign or the constitution of the state.") (citing Floyd Seyward Lear, *Treason in Roman and Germanic Law* 119 (1965)).

inspire a patriotic purpose. But given the obvious social advantages for the accuser, they quickly became a vehicle for upward mobility. Using *maiestas* trials, Romans of modest roots could secure wealth and high-rank by subduing their well-to-do opponents through personal attacks and accusations. So much is true; but modest Romans were not the only ones that prospered. Ambitious senators used *maiestas* trials to defeat their political rivals, while emperors used *delatores* – a term that describes both the accuser and the prosecutor[4] – to eliminate anyone they distrusted, to enrich the treasury, to consolidate power and, generally, to keep Romans in check.[5]

According to Tacitus, the malicious use of *maiestas* proceedings escalated under the rule of Tiberius. At first glance, the historian gives the impression that during Tiberius' reign the use of *delatores* was a unique phenomenon, whose central objective was to spitefully accuse others in the interest of profit, power and personal gain. Taken at his word, Tacitus portrays Tiberius as an oppressive leader who sought to reinstitute the use of *maiestas* in an attempt to control and manipulate the Roman populace. But, on closer inspection from an unbiased position, the text reveals a more complex reality from which the evidence that Tacitus presents calls into doubt his own portrayal of Tiberius.

Citing Tacitus' account of the *maiestas* trials in Books I through IV of the Annals, this article posits that Tiberius was not some power-starved monster for whom *maiestas* trials satisfied a lust for seeing people suffer, as Tacitus would have us believe. Rather, Tiberius' disposition during the early *maiestas* trials illustrates an emperor that was, for the most part, detached emotionally from the process and able to intervene when the accusations swelled out of control. Tiberius on many occasions placed limits on the *maiestas* proceedings and exercised a self-restraint that was unexpected in light of the many challenges to his character. It was a tumultuous time, but the facts drawn from the early part of Tiberius' reign simply do not support the cruel and malign portrait of Tiberius that Tacitus describes.

---

4 Steven H. Rutledge, *Imperial Inquisitions: Prosecutors and Informants from Tiberius to Domitian* [hereinafter "Imperial Inquisitions"] (Taylor & Francis, 2002), 9 (stating, "The word delator comes from the phrase *nomen deferre*, meaning either to lay information or to accuse, since the individual who initially denounced another individual before a magistrate could also be the one who conducted the prosecution.").

5 Katharina de la Durantaye, *The Origins of the Protection of Literary Authorship in Ancient Rome*, 25 B.U. INT'L L.J. 37, 42 (2007). Durantaye asserts that writers became targets of suppression after Augustus' death, and that "[m]any members of Rome's ruling class were tried for violation of the maiestas law – the law concerning high treason – and as a result were banished or sentenced to death." *Id.*

In reaching this conclusion, and in rebutting Tacitus' position, this article will first track the evolution of *maiestas* proceedings, starting with their humble beginnings, leading up to and including Augustus' reign. From there, I describe Tiberius' revival, as it were, of the *lex maiestatis*, focusing on the limitations that he placed on the laws early on. Then, using Tacitus' own historical account, this article will recount the facts and events surrounding the various *maiestas* trials that took place during Tiberius' reign. Each case will exemplify that Tiberius, when the opportunity arose, put in place suitable restrictions on the charges that accusers brought and on the evidence accusers used to prove those charges. Through this assessment, we see that at every turn Tiberius urged Rome's senators to consider the evidence without regard to their preconceived ideas as to the guilt of the accused. Tiberius pled with them to undertake their inquiries from a neutral position. He created, in essence, a contained environment in which senators would not only judge the *maiestas* proceedings, but scrutinize them. Tacitus' own writings make this perfectly clear.

I. *MAIESTAS*: EARLY FORMS AND EVOLUTION

In only a few sentences near the end of the Annals' first book, Tacitus provides a cursory definition of treason, while almost parenthetically relating its introduction, or, rather, its reintroduction into Roman law. He does so by describing a conversation between Tiberius and Pompeius Macer. In a short moment, according to Tacitus, the praetor asks Tiberius whether he should revive prosecutions for treason. Tiberius replies rather flippantly that the laws must be enforced.[6] In light of this brief exchange between the emperor and his praetor, Tacitus explains that the law of treason, through Tiberius' cunning, "crept in among" the community, "burst into flame and consumed everything."[7]

Missing from Tactius' sinister description is an admission that treason laws existed for several decades prior to Tiberius. Tacitus hints that it was Augustus who first applied treason laws to combat libelous writings, but he offers nothing to explain treason's lengthy origins. Rather, he speaks only of a single set of laws, the *lex maiestatis*, when in fact at least four treason laws existed in the seventy years before Augustus' reign.[8] Tacitus leaves us, then, with a vague understanding of a complex law so that he, in an attempt to vilify Tiberius, can

---

[6] Tacitus, *The Annals & The Histories* [hereinafter "Ann. book, chapters"] (Modern Library, 2003), 41.

[7] Ann. I, 69-73.

[8] C.W. Chilton, "The Roman Law of Treason Under the Early Principate [hereinafter "Chilton"]," *The Journal of Roman Studies* 45 (1955): 73.

define and outline the upcoming trials according to his own interests and biases.

To illustrate this point, it will be useful to review in brief the law of treason as it was written and adopted during the Republic and in the early part of the Principate. With this background, we can appreciate that neither the economic incentives for the accuser nor the deep social problems driving the broad and uncertain use of *maiestas* charges had changed substantially after Tiberius obtained power. From this we find that the origins of the treason laws themselves cast a serious doubt over Tacitus' contention that Tiberius re-invoked the *lex maiestatis* maliciously, or even carelessly, in an attempt to suppress his constituents.

A. FROM *PERDUELLIO* TO *MAIESTAS*

In the early years of the Republic, the crime *perduellio* was comprised of any offense against the State and its officers.[9] Although it appeared in Roman law as early as the establishment of the State itself,[10] *perduellio* reached a high point at the beginning of the Republic. Historians described it as "the crime of acting with malice towards the Roman people."[11] At the time, it was developed as a civil action through which plaintiffs, or *delatores* (who were often ordinary citizens), would come forth and accuse an individual of malicious conduct. They did so in the private courts, acting as the accuser, witness and prosecutor on behalf of the state. It was a simple proceeding in which the *delator* presented evidence proving that the treasonous act had been performed and that it was punishable. [12] If the prosecution was successful, offenders were subject to a variety of sentences, including fines and occasionally death. More importantly, regardless of the sentence imposed, the State sought to ensure that a sufficient number of *delatores* continued to come forward. Thus, authorities instituted the *praemia accusatoria*, or accusers' rewards, which typically allocated part of the

[9] Iian D. Jablon, *Civil Forfeiture: A Modern Perspective on Roman Custom*, 72 S. CAL. L. REV. 247, 258 (1998) ("The autocratic power of the emperor became more pronounced with time, and the offenses which were classified as perduellio became so broad as to include 'the slightest affront or disrespect to the emperor."') (citing William L. Burdick, *The Principles of Roman Law and Their Relation to Modern Law* 60-61 (1938)).

[10] P.M. Schisas, *Offences Against the State In Roman Law* [hereinafter "Schisas"] (London: University of London Press, 1926), 3-5 ("King Romulus – the legendary founder of Rome – according to Dionysius, took measures to protect his newly established kingdom from the treacherous acts of *perduelles*.").

[11] Chilton, 74.

[12] Jablon, *supra* note 9, at 258 (stating that either the emperor or senate adjudicated heard treason trials, though much went on behind the scenes that made them, in all respects, unfair).

offender's fine to the *delator*.[13] It is important to stress, however, that the *praemia accusatoria* was neither codified nor upheld uniformly; rather, the reward varied greatly, depending on the seriousness of the crime and the trustworthiness of the evidence. And, regardless of the risk that the accuser would receive nothing, prosecutions suddenly became an attractive proposition. With a reward at hand, accusations could provide strong financial gains and give a boost to the accuser's prestige and honor. Now, even for the lowest orders, a successful prosecution could mean freedom, with respect to slaves, or power beyond one's status, as in the case of freedmen.[14]

In approximately 100 B.C. treason received a slight shift in focus, as Saturninus passed the *lex Appuleia de maiestate*. This new law established the crime of *maiestas*, which at first co-existed with *perduellio*. The two crimes differed only in scope, though *maiestas*, with its more extensive reach, encompassed *perduellio*. This meant that if an offender committed *perduellio*, he would likely be tried and convicted for *maiestas*. Saturninus designed the *lex Appuleia* to target specifically the conduct of military commanders, magistrates and other high-profile figures that damaged the State's interests because of their alleged incompetence.[15] Their occupations, Saturninus believed, required the utmost care, and thus he left no room for negligent behavior. This shift in focus, as it turned out, was rather significant. It indeed broadened the crime of treason to reach those that acted without any ill-will. In effect, Saturninus transformed treason from a specific-intent crime into one that accusers could potentially establish by presenting evidence of the offender's negligence or recklessness. And, for the first time in its long history, treason could be applied to any individual, including foreigners, without regard to his or her social or official position.

B. *MAIESTAS* AS ARBITRARY AND ALL-ENCOMPASSING

In 81 B.C. the senate appointed Lucius Cornelius Sulla Felix, or Sulla, as Rome's dictator, thus granting him control of the State and charging him with the duty of establishing its laws and constitution. Drawing from both the *perduellio* and *maiestas*, Sulla passed the *lex Cornelia de maiestate*, which combined the previous two laws into one. This combination cast a wide enough net to ensure that it reached any conduct classified as treasonous. And to determine what conduct fell into this category, Sulla ambitiously established a permanent commission (*quaestio*) comprised of consuls and magistrates to administer the

13 Theodor Mommsen, *A History of Rome Under the Emperors* [hereinafter "Mommsen"] (New York: Routledge, 1992), 144-45.
14 Imperial Inquisitions, 21.
15 Chilton, 73.

new laws.[16] This commission ran the courts and interpreted the criminal statutes. It was Rome's first attempt to codify the *maiestas* laws, though it is unclear whether the commission was successful in this endeavor. Either way, as a committed and decorated former general, Sulla's primary goal for the *lex Cornelia* was to foster a vigorous discipline in the army. Authorities therefore typically prosecuted soldiers that left the province without permission to start a private war, individuals that tampered with the soldiers' loyalty or soldiers that committed the illegal detention of prisoners.[17]

As with the *lex Appuleia*, Sulla's new laws remained broad and arbitrary, despite the new commission. However, one thing was for certain – the penalty for violating the *lex Cornelia* was exile, and nothing more. Several historians note that death remained a possible penalty, but it was never carried out on a citizen. It was generally accepted that if the accused saw conviction as an inevitable outcome, he or she was allowed to escape abroad, never to return to Italian soil.[18] Under Sulla, the self-exiled traitor could choose the place of exile and retain his or her property. Better yet, for high-profile traitors that amassed numerous self-depictions in the form of coins or statues, a conviction did not result in the removal of those depictions from the community – a shameful practice known as *damnatio memoriae* – and thus the traitor's legacy lived on.

Years later, when Julius Caesar obtained control, he did little to amend the *lex Cornelia* or its accompanying statutes, though he did make a significant contribution. Perhaps acknowledging that the death penalty was rarely used, or perhaps using this opportunity to gain political favor, Caesar abolished the death penalty altogether. To appease those senators that favored the death penalty, the official penalty for *maiestas*, exile, now came by order of the State as part of the offender's sentence.[19] This was not to be taken lightly, for Caesar's amendment made exile obligatory even for crimes that previously called for a mere fine. Further, as a State-ordered sentence, Caesar could commute the sentence at his whim and recall an exiled traitor if for some reason he or she could be of use to the State.

---

[16] Schisas, 73-79 (mentioning the use of *quaestio* and *Senatus Consultum*).
[17] Chilton, 74 (noting that Sulla also made it a crime for a governor not to leave his province on time).
[18] *Id.*
[19] Gordon P. Kelly, *A History of Exile in the Roman Republic* [hereinafter, "Kelly"] (Cambridge: Cambridge University Press, 2006), 95-98.

C. *MAIESTAS* UNDER AUGUSTUS

In the later part of the Republic, Augustus took it upon himself to enlarge the scope of *maiestas* once again. At the time Augustus was growing increasingly intolerant of the verbal abuse that his critics repeatedly hurled at him and his family. So, in response, he sought to expand *maiestas* to account for personal damages in addition to the more traditional damages to the State.[20] In doing so he enacted the *lex Julia de maiestate*, which criminalized any slander of the princeps and other prominent men and women, whether they were alive or dead. The law extended to any uttering, writing or publication in verse or in prose, whether it was spoken or written under one's own name, anonymous name or pseudonym.[21] This was the State's first encounter with the concept of protecting the "deified princep" by means of criminal prosecution. Not only that, but it was the first instance in which persons of distinction could use their official position offensively to turn an ordinary slander into *maiestas*.

In a single sentence, Tacitus relates without detail that the first target of Augustus' new crime was Cassius Severus, who wrote several insulting satires that had apparently defamed a number of prominent members of the community.[22] The prosecution was successful, though Tacitus fails to share this fact, and Severus was exiled in 8 A.D. A precedential case, which brought to life Augustus' amendment, finally had been laid down. It was no longer simply *faux pas* to criticize the work of a current or former emperor, or the conduct of a prominent figure in the community, for the risk of prosecution, and death, was much too great.

In approximately 19 or 18 B.C., with his critics in check, Augustus took the additional, more significant step of transferring jurisdiction of the *maiestas* proceedings from the individual courts (*quaestiones*) to the senatorial court.[23] This transfer created a unique strain among the senatorial ranks. For one, senators' votes as to the guilt of the accused were no longer secret, and the senators were compelled to make speeches as to the penalties to be imposed.[24] Consequently, since a senator's views would become known either to Augustus or to his appointed leaders, the senators were obliged to demonstrate their

---

[20] Michele Lowrie, *Slander and Horse Law in Horace, Sermones 2.1*, 17 LAW & LITERATURE 405, 420 (2005) (explaining that Augustus extended the crime of maiestas to regulate defamatory songs and books, which thereafter limited free speech in Rome).

[21] Barbara Levick, *Tiberius the Politician* [hereinafter, "Levick"] (New York: Routledge, 1976), 191.

[22] Ann. I., 69-73.

[23] Levick, 184 (describing the transfer of jurisdiction to the senatorial court as "momentous").

[24] *Id.*, 184-85.

loyalty to the emperor in the hopes that such fawning would bolster their reputations. This of course created a forum comprised of puffery and self-aggrandizing. It was political profiteering of the highest order. What is more, senators were now prosecuting members of their own order for *maiestas* crimes that prosecutors usually handled in the lower courts. This is not to say that senators never prosecuted each other previously, but now there was an element of compulsion, since it was the senators' duty to look after the princeps' interests.[25]

By the time *maiestas* fell into Tiberius' hands, the precedents above had affixed themselves to the roots of the crime itself. Tiberius knew that Rome's prior emperors enforced these laws vigorously, as criminal procedure in addition to *maiestas* was a respected legacy of the Republic.[26] For years the senate revised and amended these laws, sometimes keeping the prior laws intact and sometimes abolishing various parts altogether. Faced with such a dated and complex set of laws, it is unlikely that Tiberius could predict that their subsequent use would get out of control, if indeed it ever did.

Tiberius, at the outset, sought to revitalize an active and functional set of laws that preserved the majesty of the State. Surely these laws were criticized, but there was never any intention on the part of the Senate or the populace to abolish even a trace of *maiestas* once Tiberius assumed power. For the people, *maiestas* proceedings were nothing new, and it was no secret that the *crimen maiestatis* had a scandalous reputation long before the start of the Principate, much less when Tiberius assumed control of the State. According to Tacitus, the revival of the *lex maiestatis* came in the form of a simple statement – to enforce the laws – and it very well could have been accompanied by a wave of the emperor's hand in a manner indicating that he had much more important matters with which to deal. This was indeed an order for his praetor to observe the spirit of the *lex maiestatis*, not necessarily an order to observe its letter, without exception.[27] For Tiberius, it was more important to have his authorities enforce the laws in the present, with the understanding that he could limit those laws at the appropriate time in the future, which, eventually, he did.

---

25 Imperial Inquisitions, 21-22.

26 Mommsen, 144.

27 D.C. Shotter, "The Trial of Clutorius Priscus [hereinafter "Priscus Trial"]," *Greece & Rome* 16 (1969): 14.

II. EARLY MAIESTAS CASES: CIVIL LIBERTIES FROM AN UNLIKELY SOURCE

During the early part of his reign, as Romans praised Germanicus as the father of the country, Tiberius sought to advertise his political platform as one built of patriotism and loyalty to Rome. To do so, he needed something unique. He needed a process by which Romans from all social levels could assert their loyalty to the State and, in turn, reap a life-changing reward. Despite its criticisms, the *lex maiestatis* offered the perfect solution. Moreover, since the *lex maiestatis* was already in place, as we discuss above, all that was required of Tiberius was to revive it. And so he did.

Tiberius' plan was to reinstitute *maiestas* proceedings with several exceptions. Tiberius' primary purpose, as it was in the past, was to allow citizen-accusers the opportunity to prosecute other individuals who committed in their eyes a betrayal to Rome, such as defecting soldiers or spiteful citizens. But Tacitus characterizes Tiberius' intention as something more,[28] as he fails to highlight in his hasty accounts the several limitations that Tiberius placed on the *maiestas* proceedings early on. The emperor was surely aware of the potential for these trials to spin out of control if they remained unchecked. As a former prosecutor, the emperor prided himself on his knowledge of Roman law, and, having found himself on the other side of the aisle several times before, he was conscious of the dangers that traitors faced and realized the inherent risks that accompanied their convictions. In this light, Tiberius was committed to strengthening any protections that he could possibly offer. Several examples make this obvious.

A. WORDS CAN BE SPOKEN

Tiberius' first act was to soften one of the blows left over from Augustus. Initially, what differed under Tiberius' plan was that complaints based on mere words were not actionable. As Tacitus put it, "Deeds only were liable to accusation; words went unpunished."[29] For example, in one instance an accuser alleged that Appuleia Varilia, Augustus' grand-niece, committed treason as a result of her ridiculing a slew of untouchables. As alleged, Varilia gave several disparaging speeches about her uncle Augustus, the emperor Tiberius and, even worse, Tiberius' mother.[30] Then, adding insult to injury, the senators tacked on an additional charge of adultery. Tiberius' reaction was startling. He first

---

28 Tacitus, Annals II. 45-50.

29 Ann. I. 69-73

30 Tacitus, Annals II. 50-54.

insisted that the treason charge be severed from any other charges against Varilia, who would then submit to two separate trials. This small act was crucial. Tiberius knew that senators on occasion would tack-on to the indictment an additional *maiestas* charge, sometimes without any grounds to do so, in an attempt to conflate the unrelated claim with the treason charge and to garner more concern and attention in the senate. Thus, by separating the *maiestas* charge from the adultery charge in Varilia's case, Tiberius ensured that each crime stood on its own, which inevitably highlighted the weakness of the *maiestas* charge.

Taking it a step further, Tiberius explained that for the senate to rule against Varilia on the treason charge, they would have to find only that she spoke out against Augustus.[31] In other words, he would not allow the senators to inquire about any statements as to himself. The consuls were stunned, which prompted them to ask whether they should consider Varilia's statements about Tiberius' mother. Tiberius chose not to address their question, at least not immediately.[32] The next day Tiberius returned to the senate and "begged in his mother's name" that they not consider any statements made against her. After his pleas, he simply acquitted Varilia of treason and ended the affair before the trial began.[33]

This case illustrates that Tiberius was willing to stretch the law in favor of the defendant when the opportunity arose. From here on, treason charges would not issue upon mere words critical of himself or his family. This was more than a limitation; it was a recognition that, because of Tiberius' position, citizens would likely speak out against his conduct, even on a personal level, and that in certain circumstances they should be allowed to do so. Under Tiberius, *maiestas* trials were not meant to become an unwavering cap placed on the individual liberties that his constituents enjoyed. Free speech, without consequences, was available to the people once again. Varilia's acquittal clarifies this point.

Even after Varilia's trial, however, a handful of senators believed that citizens should not be allowed to write insulting satires about the emperor and then argue, to avoid prosecution, that the writing contained mere words. This indeed would leave untouched a swarm of anonymous writers that commented often

31 *Id.* ("As to the charge of treason, the emperor insisted that it be taken separately, and that she should be condemned if she had spoken irreverently of Augustus. Her insinuations against himself he did not wish to be the subject of judicial inquiry.").

32 *Id.* ("When asked by the consul what he thought of the unfavourable speeches she was accused of having uttered against his mother, he said nothing.").

33 *Id.*

on Tiberius' cruelty and arrogance. The act of writing was a physical one – one that could potentially incite public resentment – and thus for these senators it constituted a "deed" for purposes of the *lex maiestatis*. Tiberius disagreed. Eventually, though absent from the trial, his efforts to reform the use of *maiestas* proceedings against libel and slander reached their peak in the trial of Caius Lutorius Priscus.

In 21 A.D. an informer charged Priscus with treason for having authored a disparaging poem about Tiberius' would-be successor, Drusus, who was currently ill.[34] Priscus in his vanity read the poem aloud to Publius Petronius' mother-in-law, Vitellia, and several other high-ranking women present at Petronius' house. In this way, Priscus committed both a libel and a slander in one simple act. Making matters worse, Priscus previously authored a similar poem just after the death of Germanicus. The first poem became wildly popular and Priscus received a hefty profit from its subsequent publication. The fear in this case was that if Drusus died, and Priscus published his most recent poem, he would yet again reap a profit at the expense of an individual who was next in line to take the throne.[35] For his accusers, this was unacceptable. And, from the brief description that Tacitus provides, we see that the *delatores* grew desperate in their efforts to obtain a conviction.

Glaring from the trial is that Priscus' *maiestas* charge was based on conflicting testimony. Vitellia swore before the senate that she had not heard a word of Priscus' poem. And Tacitus tells us that the remaining witnesses were "frightened into giving evidence."[36] Despite this discrepancy, the senators swiftly convicted Priscus of treason and sentenced him to death.[37] Tiberius, meanwhile, took no interest in either the accusations or the trial. It was Marcus Lepidus that took Tiberius' place. Tacitus narrates in splendid detail Lepidus' speech in favor of commuting Priscus' sentence, which was a service that Tiberius often provided the accused when he disagreed with the senate's would-be sentence.[38] The senators remained adamant. Just after Lepidus completed his speech, the senators ordered that Priscus be "dragged off to prison and instantly put to death." Indeed, the senators carried out the post-trial proceedings with such haste it was as though they feared that had Tiberius

[34] Tacitus, Annals III. 44-49 (recounting the charges).

[36] Tacitus, Annals III. 49-54

[37] *Id.* ("But those who criminated him fatally were rather believed, and on the motion of Haterius Agrippa, the consul-elect, the last penalty was invoked on the accused.").

[38] *Id.* Often have I heard the emperor complain when any one has anticipated his mercy by a self-inflicted death.").

entered the senate house prior to the order, he surely would have foiled their plans. When Tiberius finally appeared, he could only clean up their mess.

Tacitus tells us that Tiberius complained of the senators' "hasty punishment of mere words," while he praised Lepidus for his attempt to secure a lesser sentence. On his motion, the senate passed a resolution that required authorities to wait nine days until they carried out the senate's decrees. This not only gave the condemned individual additional time to plead his or her case, but it gave the senators additional time to mull over their callous sentences. In response, Tacitus wryly observed that "the Senate had not liberty to alter their purpose, and lapse of time never softened Tiberius."[39] But there is nothing to corroborate such a pessimistic outlook. Tiberius often found himself on the back end of the senate's harsh resolutions, left only with a few supporters and little time either to commute a sentence or to remind the senators of their neutral roles. This was yet another example of Tiberius' intent to limit the *maiestas* proceedings, though one for which he arrived too late.

B. SUBVERTING THE DEIFIED PRINCEP

Tiberius' next move was to deemphasize the sacred ideal that surrounded the position of emperor. Recall that under Augustus' *lex Julia*, charges could issue in the event an individual disparaged him or his predecessors in a variety of ways.[40] Underlying this construct was Augustus' belief that the position of emperor carried with it the sanctity of the gods. This new concept made Tiberius uncomfortable, since he preferred that the emperor's role represent something more reachable and humanistic.[41] He refused to be called *pater patriae* ("father of the country"), a title that Augustus readily accepted, because of its sacral overtones.[42] Instead he wished to be called, quite simply, "Tiberius Caesar Augustus," dropping the traditional qualifier, "Imperator," likewise because of its pompous implications.

---

39 Tacitus, Annals III. 49-54.

40 *See generally* Cummings, *supra* note 5, at 544 (explaining that counterfeiting, which was considered treasonous, was considered a significant crime "because it was considered to be the desecration of the image of the sovereign (the divine emperor) by making a fraudulent likeness on bogus coins."). Cummings goes on to assert that counterfeiting was not just an economic crime, but an affront to the sovereign himself. *Id.* He says, "[s]uch an attack merited a severe punishment, and Roman counterfeiters were frequently burned." *Id.*

41 Mommsen, 131 (noting that "[w]hat is more remarkable is that Tiberius sought to shape the principate in as practical a manner as possible and to play down its ideal aspect.").

42 *Id.*

In vitiating from his reign the concept of the deified princep, Tiberius allowed treason charges to issue against Falanius and Rubrius, whose trials Tacitus called "the first experiments of [*maiestas*] accusations,"[43] which of course is a mistake, as the characterization fails to heed the wealth of *maiestas* trials that took place in the decades before. To support the charge against Falanius, his accuser alleged that Falanius sold a statue of Augustus in conjunction with the sale of his gardens. As to Rubrius, his accuser alleged that he violated the divinity of Augustus by committing perjury. Tiberius responded with a single letter to the consuls. It was not at all what the senate expected. In sharp contrast to how Augustus would have responded, Tiberius explained in terse language that it was not a crime for an individual to sell an emperor's image along with his gardens or homes. He reasoned that it was quite common for an individual to sell a deity's image along with his gardens, so why not an emperor's image? For Rubrius, Tiberius likened his perjury to a deception of Jupiter – the patron deity of the Roman Principate – and thus it was of no concern to the State. He said, according to Tacitus: "Wrongs done to the gods were the gods' concern."[44] With that, Falanius and Rubrius went free. Arguably, Tiberius saved Falanius' and Rubrius' lives, although we can only assume this outcome because Tacitus either refused to comment on the trials' results or simply gave up on the accounts altogether. Either way, these preliminary trials do not corroborate Tacitus' view that Tiberius instituted a wealth of corrupt proceedings in reviving the *lex maiestatis*.

In another case, an unknown accuser charged Lucius Ennius, a Roman Knight, with *maiestas* upon information that Ennius melted down a statue of Tiberius and had it formed into a silver plate.[45] Tiberius, as expected, quashed the *maiestas* charge and expressed once again that the alteration of a mere figure of Caesar was not a violation of the majesty of the State.[46] But despite this ruling, and in a likely attempt to gain the emperor's favor, Ateius Capito insisted that the charges go forward. He stated, according to Tacitus: "Granted that the emperor might be indifferent to a personal grievance, still he should not be generous in the case of wrongs to the commonwealth."[47] Tiberius was unmoved. Tacitus relates that Tiberius "interpreted the remark according to its drift rather than its expression" and thus he confirmed the veto of Ennius' trial.

---

[43] *Id.* (explaining first that Tiberius sought to revive and enforce prosecutions for treason, and that it would "not be uninteresting if [Tacitus] relate in the cases of Falanius and Rubrius, Roman knights of moderate fortune, the first experiments of such accusations. . . .").

[44] Ann. I, 73-77 ("As to the oath, the thing ought to be considered as if the man had deceived Jupiter.").

[45] Ann. III, 66-70.

[46] *Id.* ("but the emperor forbade his being put upon his trial.").

[47] *Id.*, 70-74.

Sadly, though, Capito had disgraced himself. Tacitus remarks that the senator was well-versed in the law, but after this display, "he had now dishonoured a brilliant public career as well as a virtuous private life."[48] Tiberius' pronouncements as to the rights of the accused were unyielding to say the least.

At this point, *maiestas* trials were rather bland events through which Tiberius limited the broad and arbitrary charges that the prior precedent supported. In other words, these early trials gave Tiberius the opportunity he desired to instill in the populace a sense of patriotism, while at the same time offering them the civil rights that Augustus previously took away. Tacitus' failure to convey these limitations exemplifies a rhetorical pattern that calls into question the historian's narrative with respect to these trials.[49] And, it is one that continues throughout the Annals.

III. THE DRUSUS AFFAIR: A LACK OF MALICIOUS MOTIVES

By 16 A.D. *maiestas* proceedings had evolved and, according to Tacitus, *delatores* turned out in record numbers. They were relentless. In one instance Roman authorities charged Libo Drusus with treason after he consulted with astrologers about his pedigree.[50] Tacitus explained that the Drusus affair marked the first occasion in which accusers conjured up magnificent stories to obtain a conviction. But whether the event actually contributed to the "practices which for so many years [ate] into the heart of the State,"[51] as Tacitus asserts, is a question left unanswered. What we see, perhaps, is an emperor having second thoughts as to his ability to control the proper uses of the *lex maiestatis*. Tiberius was rather languid throughout the Drusus affair, and, to a point, he seemed disinterested. For this, Tacitus depicts Tiberius as heartless and cruel, but the evidence tells a different story.

Libo's trial, according to Tacitus, was a sham. The account is one in which the evidence against Libo consisted of flimsy accusers and a bundle of equally-

---

48 *Id.*

49 *But see* Judith Ginsburg, "Speech and Allusion in Tacitus, Annals 3.49-51 and 14.48-49," *The American Journal of Philolgy* 107 (1986): 527 (explaining that Tacitus portrayal is not unreliable; he simply uses various literary techniques such as allusion, which make the narration seem unreliable).

50 Tacitus, Annals II. 27-32.

51 *Id.* ("I will explain, somewhat minutely the beginning process, and end of the affair, since then first were originated those practices which for so many years have eaten into the heart of the State.").

flimsy documents.[52] But before Tacitus introduced the evidence, he chose first to induce sympathy for the accused. His first point was to show that Libo did not enter a conspiratorial situation on his own, but rather that he was enticed into the situation by others.[53] To make the story more powerful, Tacitus notes that it was Catus, "an intimate friend," who encouraged the slow-witted Libo to seek out an astrologer and to entangle himself in "extravagance and debt."[54] It was a setup from the beginning. Once Libo acted on his childlike temptations, Tacitus explained that Catus concocted a crime and took the story directly to Tiberius.

From there, Tacitus takes the reader to a brief dinner scene in which Tiberius invited Libo to his table and watched him suspiciously while concealing his own resentment.[55] In this, Tacitus would have us believe that Tiberius took astrology so seriously that he was intensely wary of others that did so as well. Perhaps this was true, but something was missing. As Tacitus recounted this frightening scene, he blatantly excluded one crucial fact – Libo not only consulted with astrologers, but he also possessed a disturbing list of emperor's and senators' names with threatening marks written beside them.[56] As it turned out, Libo was not so innocent. Tiberius certainly had a valid interest in observing citizens that possessed threatening papers regarding the State and its leaders. So, with this in mind, Tacitus concealed the sinister list until he recounted Libo's trial, thus offering a misleading representation of poor, brainless Libo while at the same time impeaching Tiberius' character.

At the trial Tiberius remained impartial, for it is likely that after observing Libo up close he considered Libo's behavior misguided rather than malicious.[57] Tacitus notes that at the start of Libo's trial Tiberius read the charges "with such calmness as not to seem to soften or aggravate the accusations."[58] This is

---

[52] *Id.* (writing that Libo's accusers "produced an extravagantly absurd accusation," as they proclaimed that Libo asked the astrologer a number of questions that were "senseless and idle" and even "pitiable."

[53] Shotter, D.C. *The Trial of M. Scribonius Libo Drusus* [hereinafter *The Trial of Libo Drusus*]. Historia: Zeitschrift fur Alte Geschichte, Vol. 21, No. 1 (1st Qtr., 1972), pp. 88-89.

[54] Tacitus, Annals II. 27-32 ("Firmius Catus, a senator, and intimate friend of Libo's, prompted the young man, who was thoughtless and an easy

[55] *Id.* ("Meanwhile he conferred the praetorship on Libo and often invited him to his table, showing no unfriendliness in his looks or anger in his words (so thoroughly had he concealed his resentment")).

[56] *Id.* ("But there was one paper in Libo's handwriting, so the prosecutor alleged, with the names of Caesars and of senators, to which marks were affixed of dreadful or mysterious significance.").

[57] *The Trial of Libo Drusus* at 89.

[58] Tacitus, Annals II. 27-32.

in stark contrast to Libo, who Tacitus described as "jaded with fear and mental anguish" and hardly able to stand at his own trial.[59] By focusing on Libo's despair, Tacitus portrays Tiberius as a cold, bloodthirsty tyrant. But this is entirely unproven.

Tiberius, as we see later on, believed in correct judicial procedure, and there is simply nothing to show that Tiberius' behavior masked a vengeful or evil motive. Before the affair ended, Libo took his own life. Afterward Tiberius issued a sworn statement, asserting that had Libo not committed suicide, he would have pleaded with the senators to let him live, "guilty though he was."[60] And, after the Drusus affair calmed down Tiberius allowed days of public thanksgiving, during which citizens made several offerings to Roman deities on Libo's behalf. As a more permanent honor, Tiberius accepted the senate's proposal that September 13, the day of Libo's suicide, be observed from then on as a day of festival. Tacitus shares these acts only in passing and mentions them, so he says, to expose an "evil in the State."[61]

IV. REFORM OF THE *LEX MAIESTATIS*

As the number of *maiestas* trials increased, Rome's hatred of *delatores* increased along with them.[62] The popular sentiment was that this class of men was comprised of ruthless opportunists who acquired standing and wealth at the expense of others. Upper-crust citizens viewed them as neither statesmen nor officials. Instead they were part of a negative social category[63] that the higher ranks perceived as low-born and ill-equipped to wield such power. Aligning himself with popular opinion, Tacitus described Caepio Crispinus, a well-known *delator*, as "needy, obscure, and restless."[64] He went on to explain that

---

59 *Id.* ("On the day the Senate met, jaded with fear and mental anguish, or, as some have related, feigning illness, he was carried in a litter to the doors of the Senate House, and leaning on his brother he raised his hands and voice in supplication to Tiberius, who received him with unmoved countenance.").

60 *Id.* ("Yet the prosecution was continued in the Senate with the same persistency, and Tiberius declared on oath that he would have interceded for his life, guilty though he was, but for his hasty suicide.").

61 Ann., II. 32-35 ("Days of public thanksgiving were appointed on the suggestion of Pomponius Flaccus. Offerings were given to Jupiter, Mars, and Concord, and the 13th day of September, on which Libo had killed himself, was to be observed as a festival, on the motion of Gallus Asinius, Papius Mutilus, and Lucius Apronius. I have mentioned the proposals and sycophancy of these men, in order to bring to light this old-standing evil in the State.").

62 Levick, 189 (noting that "Delators were hated under the Principate").

63 Imperial Inquisitions, 11.

64 Ann., I. 73-77.

after Crispinus accused the proconsul of Bithynia of *maiestas*, his life became driven by "stealthy informations . . . following which beggars became wealthy, the insignificant, formidable, and brought ruin first on others, [and] finally on themselves."[65] Crispinus' accusation against his superior was likely offensive, but it was nothing unique. We can infer, then, that Tacitus introduces Crispinus merely as an example of how the position of *delator* was particularly vexatious in the eyes of the larger community.[66]

More importantly, Tacitus' description of Crispinus highlights two essential motivations for a typical *delator*. The first is a strong want of profit, while the second is a desire for political and social advancement. These incentives, according to Tacitus, became engrained in the hearts of every *delator*. The expectation of power and profits was so potent, in fact, that *delatores* on many occasions attempted to secure prosecutions using hearsay testimony, false evidence or coerced witnesses. It was no secret that *delatores* who found themselves in financial trouble would use any means of advancement. In turn, false accusations flourished. And the risk of future false accusations grew even greater at the end of the State's economic expansion. Tiberius, meanwhile, was aware of this. He understood that the use of unfounded *maiestas* claims and questionable evidence required a response; thus, he accepted various proposals from his closest advisors.

A. *CALUMNIA*

The most popular suggestion was to abolish the *praemia accusatorial*, though Tiberius, to the dismay of his advisors, refused to do so. Upon reflection, he realized that such a proposal was not a solution at all.[67] Abolition of the *praemia accusatoria* would only vitiate the incentive for financial gain. It would not, however, reduce the incentive for political advancement. Indeed, even without the *praemia*, enterprising *delatores* still had an incentive to come forth with groundless *maiestas* claims in the hopes of working their way up the senatorial ranks. So, with this in mind, Tiberius wanted a solution that was all-encompassing. He needed a harsh penalty, one that would make the presentation of false *maiestas* charges a criminal act, thus serving not only as a

---

[65] *Id.* (noting also that Crispinus "wormed himself by stealthy informations into the confidence of a vindictive prince, and soon imperiled all the most distinguished citizens").
[66] Imperial Inquisitions, 206-07 (discussing the *delator* Caepio Crispinus).
[67] Levick, 190 (noting that in defending the *praemia* Tiberius was "defending a system which could not be replaced.").

deterrent, but as a punishment.[68] As it turned out *calumnia*, or malicious prosecution, was a likely consequence.[69]

By 21 A.D., with the death of Germanicus behind him, Tiberius' role as a mediator had become a chore. He kept a close watch on the *delatores* that he empowered and took a keen interest in those trials that offered an opportunity for reform. Two incidents that arose earlier that year were particularly promising.[70] In the first, Tacitus relates that two Roman knights of equestrian descent, Coelius Cursor and Considius Aequus, brought *maiestas* charges against a popular praetor, Magius Caecilianus.[71] But the trial fell apart in its early stages because the two knights failed entirely to present any concrete evidence in support of their case. After review of the evidence, or lack thereof, the senators determined that the charges were false.

Tiberius was enraged. He insisted that Cursor and Aequus be punished for *calumnia*,[72] though Tacitus fails to explain the precise punishment that the two men endured. At this point, the punishment is inconsequential. We know that the senate was free to impose sentences for *calumnia* that ranged from loss of senatorial rank to exile from Rome. But for our purposes, the case serves as one of the leading examples of how Tiberius introduced a helpful precedent for cases in which *delatores* offered phony charges against the accused.

In another case, Catus Firmius, a well-known senator, charged his own sister with *maiestas*. Recall that Catus was one of the masterminds behind Libo Drusas' trial,[73] the outcome of which Tiberius was yet to forget. The charges that Catus brought turned out to be false and, accordingly, the senate, on Tiberius' motion, convicted Catus of *calumnia* and sentenced him to exile.

---

68 *Id.*, 190 ("The proposal for abolition apparently dealt only with maiestas, but the *lex Maiestatis* was not the only statute that offered rewards; . . . ; what was required was a harsher penalty for *calumnia*, malicious prosecution.").

69 Jablon, *supra* note 5, at 252. Jablon comments that the system of rewards for forfeiture proceedings and prosecutions may have been too successful, "as evidenced by the fact that some delicts provided that the defendant would be paid a penalty should the prosecution bring a false case." *Id.* Jablon also notes the "similarity of the modern charge of malicious prosecution." *Id.* at n. 25 (citing J.A. Crook, *Law and Life of Rome* 276-77 (1994)).

70 *Id.*, 198 (noting that if the Princeps knew the facts of Cursor's and Aequus' trial, he should be lauded for having "discouraged irresponsible delation of *maiestas*.").

71 Ann., III. 34-39

72 *Id.*

73 Ann. IV, 30-34 ("Catus, as I have related, had drawn Libo into a snare and then destroyed him by an information.").

Tiberius intervened, however, and surprisingly he vetoed the sentence of exile and sought merely to have Catus expelled from the senate.

In response, Tacitus claims that Tiberius reduced Catus' sentence because of the senator's service in convicting Libo.[74] But the more likely reason for the reduction was Tiberius' awareness that Catus' detestable conduct in charging his own sister with *maiestas* would exacerbate the community's hostility towards him.[75] The senators would detest him, and upper-class citizens would loathe him. From then on Catus would be a social outcast, which, in ancient Rome, was just as severe as one's physical expulsion from the State. For Tiberius, such a punishment was sufficiently harsh.

B. A NEUTRAL ENVIRONMENT

Looking beyond his control of the *delatores*, Tiberius also sought to control the senators. In doing so he would transform the procedures through which the senators considered the evidence in support of *maiestas*. It is important that Tiberius' objective did not involve a change to the criminal code or to Rome's written statutes; rather, the emperor set his sights on the senators' abilities to reflect on the evidence. Using various trials Tiberius would impose on the senators a certain vigilance with respect to the charges and the evidence before them. They would learn under Tiberius to be not only mindful, but in many ways skeptical of the accuser and of his intentions in bringing the charges to the senate. In this way, Tiberius would intervene in the senate's judicial affairs, offsetting penalties, giving grace periods[76] or vetoing sentences,[77] while at the same time he expressed an ongoing fear that perhaps the senate was neglecting its duty to remain neutral under the circumstances.[78] He admonished the senate verbally or set an example through his own actions. Whichever method he chose, it was a means to maintain strict judicial impartiality.

For instance, in a case we mention above, Tacitus reports that Caepio Crispinus brought *maiestas* charges against his superior Granius Marcellus, the governor of

[74] *Id.* ("Tiberius remembering this service, while he alleged other reasons, deprecated a sentence of exile, but did not oppose his expulsion from the Senate.").
[75] Levick, 197.
[76] Rutledge, 78 (relating that in one instance Tiberius intervened in a case, giving a grace period to all debtors and creditors to settle their accounts after delatores began prosecuting at an alarming rate those individuals, including senators, that made loans at an excessive rate of interest).
[77] Ann. IV, 30-34 (deprecating Catus' sentence from exile to expulsion from the senate).
[78] Levick, 197 (explaining that Tiberius' became more involved in the judicial process because "the relentless pressure of the succession struggle brought several friends to their death.").

Bithynia, for making disparaging remarks about Tiberius. And, although Tacitus offers little detail as to the remarks that Marcellus supposedly made, the historian asserts that the charge of *maiestas* was unavoidable because the accusations involved the "worst features of the emperor's character."[79] Notwithstanding this presumption, the charges against Marcellus only got worse. The senate eventually turned over the case to Romanus Hispo, who acted as *subscriptor* and appended to the original charge an additional accusation that Marcellus had altered the statues in his garden.[80] According to Tacitus, Marcellus "struck off" the head of Augustus from one statue and placed the bust of Tiberius on the headless sculpture that remained.[81] On top of that, Marcellus then placed his own statue in a position higher than those reserved for the emperors. Even still, the charges never got off the ground.

In Tacitus' report, as soon as Hispo read the charges to the senate, Tiberius' "wrath blazed forth, and, breaking through his habitual silence," he warned the senators that he would openly vote in the case and that the senators would be obliged to vote the same way.[82] Markedly, however, Tacitus does not tell the reader which way Tiberius would actually vote. Instead, without saying it, Tacitus forces the reader to draw the inference that Tiberius' "wrath" was spawned by Marcellus' defamatory statements; thus, of course Tiberius would vote to condemn him. This position, however, is entirely uncorroborated. Tacitus' portrayal fails to consider that Marcellus' case came at a time when extortionate proceedings in the provinces, such as Bithynia, roused Tiberius tremendously.[83] What is more, as explained previously, by this point Tiberius had declared that the senators could not consider *maiestas* charges based on personal attacks to his character. Tiberius likely asked himself, "Did these senators not remember my ruling in Falanius' and Rubrius' trials?" or, perhaps, "Why are we wasting time listening to these trivial charges?" The senators' brazen ignorance of Tiberius' earlier pronouncements must have stirred the emperor dearly. This realization cannot be taken lightly, as it further dispels Tacitus' position with respect to Tiberius' next reaction.

---

79 Rutledge, 90 (noting that *maiestas* was inescapable because "in this instance, it was based (according to Tacitus) on the princeps' vices.").
80 Ann. I, 73-77.
81 *Id.*
82 Ann. I, 73-77 ("[Tiberius] exclaimed that in such a case he would himself too give his vote openly on oath, that the rest might be under the same obligation. There lingered even then a few signs of expiring freedom.").
83 John Charles Tarver, *Tiberius, the Tyrant* [hereinafter "Tarver"] (Archibald Constable and Co., 1902), 307-08.

Following Tiberius' outburst, Cneius Piso asked the emperor, "In what order will you vote, Caesar? If first, I shall know what to follow; if last, I fear that I may differ from you unwillingly." In light of this question, Tiberius regretted his earlier remark.[84] He realized that had he voted in Marcellus' case, with the expectation that the senators follow his lead, the senate's neutral stance in judicial affairs would be lost. For Tiberius, this was an unworkable consequence. And though we can agree with Tactius that Tiberius' initial outburst was thoughtless, it was only a momentary lapse in reasoning. Once he listened to Piso's inquiry, Tiberius showed that he was not unyielding. Tacitus acknowledged that Tiberius was "deeply moved" by Piso's question and even somewhat penitent of his statements. In the end, he allowed the senators to vote on the case independently and restored their ability to decide *maiestas* cases from a neutral, unbiased position.[85] Without Tiberius' input, the senators acquitted Marcellus of treason.

Moving forward, Tacitus relates the trial of Caius Silanus,[86] which is noteworthy, as it is one of the first cases in which Tiberius put limits on the emperor's involvement in making provincial appointments. The record, according to Tacitus, is as follows. Mamercus Scaurus, an ex-consul, accused Silanus of *repetundae*, a form of extortion through which the accuser seeks restitution for injuries to the State. To boot, seizing the opportunity,[87] Junius Otho, a praetor, and Brutidius Niger, an aedile, submitted an additional charge of *maiestas*.[88] With the charges in place, the trio immediately put together an unassailable case. First, they conjured up numerous, high-profile witnesses to testify during the trial. Next, they had Silanus' slaves tortured and forced them to testify on behalf of the prosecution. Finally, they spoke with Silanus' character witnesses and warned them not to help him. It a ruthless performance, one that Tacitus describes as a combination "perilous even to an innocent man."[89] Even still, during the trial Silanus faced a host of adverse senators, all of whom were trained orators and prosecutors.[90] And, if this were

84 Rutledge, 91.

85 Ann. I, 72-73 ("Tiberius was deeply moved, and repenting of the outburst, all the more because of its thoughtlessness, he quietly allowed the accused to be acquitted of the charges of treason.").

86 Ann. III., 61-66.

87 Richard Bauman, *Human Rights in Ancient Rome* (Routledge, 2000), 63 (indicating that over time the crimes of *repetundae* and *maiestas* were partially fused).

88 Ann. III., 61-66 (explaining that Otho and Niger "simultaneously fastened on him and charged him with sacrilege to the divinity of Augustus, and contempt of the majesty of Tiberius. . . .").

89 Ann. III, 66-70 (Gellius Publicola and Marcus Paconius, . . ., swelled the number of the accusers" so that "[n]o doubt was felt as to the defendant's conviction").

90 *Id.*

not enough, Tiberius himself insisted on cross-examining the defendant, without the benefit of rebuttal testimony.[91] According to Tacitus, it was all too much for Silanus to handle, thus he abandoned his own defense. But when it came time for the senate to fashion an appropriate sentence, Tiberius took it upon himself to go beyond what was asked of him and affirm an important "constitutional sentiment."[92]

As punishment, the senate banished Silanus to Gyarus and divvied up his property accordingly. Then, to deflect blame for the appointment of Silanus, Cornelius Dolabella pointed out the difficulties in choosing provincial leaders and suggested that no one from a "disgraceful life and notorious infamy" be eligible to lead a province. Thus, he moved the senate to allow the emperor to intervene more often in the senate's provincial appointments, which, in essence, was an amendment to the existing laws. Tiberius refused and stopped the senators before the motion was carried. He warned them that they ought not decide their appointments through the use of hearsay, referring of course to his own knowledge of the reports with respect to Silanus.[93] He explained that the emperor does not know everything, and that he should not be exposed to the "ambitious scheming of others."[94] More importantly, he affirmed that the "laws are ordained to meet facts" and that the senate should "not revolutionise a wisely devised and ever approved system." To conclude, he said, "[r]ights are invariably abridged, as despotism increases; nor ought we fall back on imperial authority, when we can have recourse to the laws."[95]

Tiberius' speech is rather influential, though Tacitus merely describes it as a rare sentiment for the emperor. What Tacitus fails to acknowledge, however, is that Tiberius gave extraordinary weight to the rules of law, which provided that the senate, by itself, make provincial appointments. There was no reason, then, for the senate to make these appointments with Tiberius at the helm. The prior laws were in place for a reason. Tiberius therefore stepped back and reminded the senators that imperial authority could not solve their problems. Indeed, Tiberius stressed that his involvement in the process should be limited, and when the senators doubted a decision, they should rely on legal authority, not

91 *Id.* ("Tiberius did not refrain from pressing him with angry voice and look, himself putting incessant questions, without allowing him to rebut or evade them, and he had often even to make admissions, that the questions might have been asked in vain.").
92 *Id.* (noting that "such constitutional sentiments were so rare with Tiberius, that they were welcomed with all the heartier joy.").
93 *Id.*
94 *Id.*
95 *Id.*

an executive decision. This case, we see, is a commendable example of executive restraint.

In another account, Calpurnius Piso, the governor of Syria, was accused of corrupting his soldiers and of poisoning Germanicus, Tiberius' adopted son and a popular commander in the Eastern provinces. Germanicus' companions detested Piso and, according to Tacitus, they would spare nothing in their attempt to obtain a conviction.[96] In fact, with so many of them insisting that they serve as deponents and witnesses in the trial, it was difficult for Tiberius to name a prosecutor. Piso's accusers therefore requested that Tiberius lead the inquiry, although such an arrangement carried with it an enormous conflict, given Tiberius' relation to Germanicus. Surprisingly, Piso did not fret. He understood, in light of the "bias of the people and of the Senate" against him, that Tiberius was perhaps the only person that would not waver to partiality, notwithstanding that Piso was on trial for the death of Tiberius' adopted son.[97] This reaction is rather telling.

One could argue that Tiberius' neutral, if not detached attitude toward Germanicus' death, which Piso recognized, supports an inference that Tiberius was somehow involved in the incident. But drawing such an inference, with nothing more, would be unreasonable. It is more likely that Tiberius' approach to Piso's trial confirmed his commitment to cautious, equitable trial procedure. Tiberius of course recognized the severity of the charges against Piso. But more importantly, he understood given Germanicus' popularity that it would be difficult to facilitate a fair trial.[98] Under the circumstances, he would have to balance two competing forces. On the one hand were Germanicus' supporters, who spilled out into the streets, seething with resentment and encompassing Rome's most influential class. On the other were the rights of the accused, which the emperor could not abandon, for such a choice would illuminate the wickedness for which he was so often criticized. Tiberius was left, then, with

[96] Ann. III, 7-12 (noting that it was difficult to name a prosecutor because Germanicus' companions insisted that "they themselves meant to report their instructions from Germanicus, not as accusers, but as deponents and witnesses to facts.").
[97] *Id.* ("This even the accused did not refuse, fearing, as he did, the bias of the people and of the Senate; while Tiberius, he knew, was resolute enough to despise report, and was also entangled in his mother's complicity. Truth too would be more easily distinguished from perverse misrepresentation by a single judge, where a number would be swayed by hatred or ill-will.").
[98] See *Id.* (explaining that Piso retained counsel to represent him after some difficulty and that his counsel agreed to represent him "amid the excitement of the whole country, which wondered how much fidelity would be shown by friends of Germanicus, on what the accused rested his hopes, and how far Tiberius would repress and hide his feelings.").

the middle of the two, which was an objective position that required him to oversee a trial in which he had a keen personal interest.

Piso, the man accused of killing one of Rome's most popular figures, felt that Tiberius was fit to do so. He indeed knew that Tiberius was "resolute enough" to see beyond the immaterial evidence that his accusers would inevitably present.[99] In Piso's eyes, Tiberius would not leave unbalanced a scale that weighed his rights with those of his accusers. And if this were not enough to convince those who sat in the "silence of suspicion" outside the senate house,[100] Tiberius' own statements offered further support.

After listening "to the threatening speeches of the prosecutors and to the pleadings of the accused," Tiberius wiped his hands of responsibility and turned over the case to the full senate.[101] The next day Tiberius entered the senate house and delivered a moving speech. Tacitus described it as one "of studied moderation." There, Tiberius recounted Piso's accusations and implored the senators to deliberate the charges "with minds unbiased." [102] He urged them to be wary of any falsehoods and exaggerations that Piso's accusers would present, as he himself would be outraged if he faced an overzealous attempt to convict an innocent man.[103] As to his personal angst, Tiberius pled with the senators to refrain from taking the alleged charges as true simply because the case was so "intimately bound up with [his] affliction."[104] On this point, according to Tacitus, Tiberius explained that "[f]or my part, I sorrow for my son and shall always sorrow for him; still I would not hinder the accused from producing all the evidence which can relieve his innocence or convict Germanicus of any unfairness, if such there was."[105] Tiberius concluded by observing that Piso's case should be tried and judged like all others, without heed to his sorrow.[106]

---

99 *Id.*

100 *Id.* ("Never were people more keenly interested; never did they indulge themselves more freely in secret whispers against the emperor or in the silence of suspicion.").

101 *Id.*

102 *Id.* ("Whether he there had provoked the young prince by willful opposition and rivalry, and had rejoiced at his death or wickedly destroyed him, is for you to determine with minds unbiased.").

103 Tacitus, Annals III. 12-15 ("As for [false accusers], I am justly angry with their intemperate zeal. For to what purpose did they strip the corpse and expose it to the pollution of the vulgar gaze, and circulate a story among foreigners that he was destroyed by poison, if all this is still doubtful and requires investigation?").

104 *Id.* ("And I implore you not to take as proven charges alleged, merely because the case is intimately bound up with my affliction.").

105 *Id.*

106 *Id.*

Specifically he said: "In all else let the case be tried as simply as others. Let no one heed the tears of Drusus or my own sorrow, or any stories invented in our credit." Unfortunately, the next day an unknown assailant murdered Piso before the deliberations ended, which left the senators unable to test the effectiveness of Tiberius' pleas.

Tiberius was not a man that questioned the rights of those who faced the rule of law. From the start of Piso's trial, Tiberius was concerned not only with the presentation of the evidence, but with the deliberations that would take place upon its admission. It was clear from Tacitus' account that the trial's fairness outweighed Tiberius' personal feelings. He showed an almost fanatical ability to disconnect himself emotionally from the accusations, while preserving, once again, the sanctity of just trial procedure. This conduct certainly belies the hearsay rumors that Tacitus disclosed, out of nowhere, at the end of the proceedings.[107] With this in mind, it is consistent that, "assuming an air of sadness," Tiberius acquitted Piso of the treason charge.

CONCLUSION

In the Annals, Tacitus introduces the reader to a world in which Romans hesitated to speak their opinions aloud. On his account, the law of treason was gaining strength, as the risk of accusation, whether false or not, diffused throughout the empire and sprouted like weeds in the wealthy homesteads of Rome's aristocracy. Tacitus would have us believe that the *maiestas* proceedings exemplified Rome's civil decline and that it was Tiberius who let them get out of control. In short, it was Tiberius' means to an end. But while the proceedings may have encouraged surreptitious conduct by poor and wealthy citizens alike, the reinstitution of the *lex maiestatis* by Tiberius was not an evil decision. It was political, and it was one for which Tiberius would exercise extreme caution in reviving. That being the case, the *maiestas* proceedings we encounter in Books I through IV of the Annals show that Tiberius had no intention of allowing citizens to run wild against their would-be victims. In this way, Tiberius put in place a number of restrictions and defenses in favor of the accused. From these accounts, while Tacitus failed to acknowledge the benefits

[107] Tacitus, Annals III. 15-18 (asserting rumors, which he "heard old men say," with respect to Tiberius' involvement in Germanicus' death. Tacitus admits, however, that he could not affirm any of the alleged statements he supposedly overheard).

of Tiberius' progressive stance, it is one for which Tiberius should be praised, not criticized.[108]

108 Donald R. Dudley, *The World of Tacitus* (London: Secker & Warburg, 1968) (acknowledging that Tacitus creates false impressions through unfavorable topic sentences and that Tiberius' interventions in various trials should have been in his favor).

ON THE FORMATION OF THE AMERICAN CORPORATE STATE: THE FULLER SUPREME COURT, 1888-1910

GEORGE SKOURAS

1) INTRODUCTION

With the collapse of the American financial system in 2008, and its widespread consequences for the American people and indeed the global economic impact of the collapse, it became apparent that certain corporations became "too big to fail." It aroused widespread interest among the public as to how these corporations ever achieved such a status. This article hopes to return to a historical point in time, the Gilded Age and Progressive era, in order to attempt to locate the seeds of today's "too big to fail" corporations. By focusing on the Fuller Supreme Court, 1888-1910, we can locate the origin of the American corporate state.[1]

The legal support of laissez-faire capitalism set in motion the foundation of current corporate institutions. Although there is not much dispute of the excessive use of laissez-faire doctrine during the Fuller Court, there has emerged in the past couple of decades a group of revisionist scholars willing to explain the Court's actions free from the Progressive school of history. Three major scholars representing three types of schools of thought were selected: Bruce Ackerman, neo-federalist dualist democracy school, James Ely, Jr., neo-liberal conservative school, and Howard Gillman, neo-institutionalist school.

I will attempt to first lay out the use of laissez-faire capitalist doctrine by the Fuller Court, and then I will turn to the revisionist interpretation of the Court. This work will seek to answer two questions: 1) Was the Fuller Supreme Court

[1] The use of the phrase "corporate state" will be taken to mean of a general power over government and society broadly speaking, the corporatization of America, as a matter of default. That is to say, if we can say that the state function of America during the Gilded Age and Progressive era was fragmented (deliberately so by the nature of the Constitution), then we should be able to observe how such a vacuum of political power can be claimed as a matter of default by emerging corporate power. As the nature of rural America changed due to industrialism, it continued to operate under "limited government" principles even though industrialism required direct government intervention in the private sector if it was to control the power of the corporation. That is, the corporate state will refer to the default power as a result constitutional fragmentation and the Founder's creation of a weak Federal government.

justified interpreting and using the Due Process Clause of the Fourteenth Amendment to support laissez-faire capitalism and lay the legal foundation for the modern corporate state? 2) And are modern revisionists correct interpreting the Fuller Court decisions as a product of the Gilded Age and Progressive era?

2) THE FULLER SUPREME COURT

The Fuller Court tilted in favor of the emergent corporate state at the expense of labor. Although this statement is controversial especially without qualifications, given the totality of the body of cases decided by the Fuller Court over the span of twenty-two years, it nevertheless can be justified if we limit the domain of the Court's case considerations to four key groupings: 1) taxation, 2) monopoly/antitrust, 3) labor, and 4) American expansionism cases. The Court set in motion a body of law and a philosophy of corporatism. How did this happen? It happened because in America the Supreme Court functions more as a political body rather than as a legal body. By viewing the Supreme Court as a political body, we are better able to see the fragmentation of the American system of government.[2]

The Corporate State won the battle as to the future of the cultural, economic, and political system of the United States during the Gilded Age and Progressive Era.[3] And the Fuller Supreme Court helped usher it in. The political, economic, and legal battles that were waged over the structure and role of the corporation in America,[4] roughly between 1880-1910, resulted in a corporate victory over the people. The "partnership" form of business[5] prevalent prior to the Civil War was eclipsed by the corporate structure.

---

2 Max Lerner, *The Supreme Court and American Capitalism*, *in* ESSAYS IN CONSTITUTIONAL LAW 107-144 (Robert G. McCloskey, ed., Vintage Books 1957) (1933) (a view of the Court as a political body).

3 THE GILDED AGE (H.Wayne Morgan, ed., revised & enlarged edition, 1970); ALAN TACHTENBERG, THE INCORPORATION OF AMERICA: CULTURE AND SOCIETY IN THE GILDED AGE (25th anniversary ed., Hill and Wang, 2007); ARTHUR S. LINK & RICHARD L. MCCORMICK, PROGRESSIVISM (1983); JOHN WHITECLAY CHAMBERS II, THE TYRANNY OF CHANGE: AMERICA IN THE PROGRESSIVE ERA, 1890-1920 (2nd ed. 1992); ROBERT H. WIEBE, THE SEARCH FOR ORDER 1877-1920 (1967); GRANT MCCONNELL, PRIVATE POWER AND AMERICAN DEMOCRACY (1966); OLIVER ZUNZ, MAKING AMERICA CORPORATE 1870-1920 (1990); JACK BEATTY, THE AGE OF BETRAYAL: THE TRIUMPH OF MONEY IN AMERICA 1865-1900 (2007).

4 ARTHUR SELWYN MILLER, THE SUPREME COURT AND AMERICAN CAPITALISM (1968).

5 Although corporations existed prior to the Civil War in the United States, the nature, number, purpose, function, and size of these entities were transformed after the Civil War. *See,* Oscar

Today, we confront the "too big to fail"[6] corporation. The Fuller Court set the corporation free from the historical and traditional state sponsored moorings that anchored it to the political community.[7] The issues of corporate size[8] and free competition --- "bigness"[9] leading to the American empire[10] ---were major issues that confronted the Fuller Court during the Middle Republic.[11] War and industrialism[12] greased the wheels of the modern American corporate state.

The Fuller Court took the Due Process Clause of the Fourteenth Amendment[13] and transformed it into a "bulwark for laissez-faire capitalism."[14] How did it

---

Handlin, *The Development of the Corporation*, *in* THE CORPORATION: A THEOLOGICAL INQUIRY (Michael Novak & John W. Cooper, eds. 1981).

[6] The "too big to fail" corporation has its origins in the Progressive era and their efforts to bust up monopolies and trusts. WALTER ADAMS AND JAMES W. BROCK, THE BIGNESS COMPLEX: INDUSTRY, LABOR, AND GOVERNMENT IN THE AMERICAN ECONOMY 26-27 (1986).

[7] CARL N. DEGLER, OUT OF OUR PAST: THE FORCES THAT SHAPED MODERN AMERICA 271 (3rd ed. 1984).

[8] ADAMS & BROCK, supra note 6, at 26; *See also*, THOMAS C. COCHRAN & WILLIAM MILLER, THE AGE OF ENTERPRISE: A SOCIAL HISTORY OF INDUSTRIAL AMERICA 181-210 (rev. ed. 1961) (*See, e.g.,* Chapter Nine, "The Rise of Finance Capitalism," the gist of it being consolidation and bigness is good for profits; competition and small business size is bad for profits.)

[9] ADAMS & BROCK, supra note 6. *See also*, WILLIAM APPLEMAN WILLIAMS, THE TRAGEDY OF AMERICAN DIPLOMACY 44 (New Ed. 1988) (The Bigness complex led to pressure for overseas markets, which led to a policy of imperialism. According to Williams, "The McKinley Administration knew that an important and growing segment of the business community wanted prompt and effective action in Cuba and Asia.")

[10] *Hawaii v. Mankichi*, 190 U.S. 197 (1903) (the rights of grand jury indictment did not apply to the territories); *Dorr v. United States*, 195 U.S. 138 (1904) (Philippines case of trial without jury; the right to jury trial not applicable to the territories, a euphemism for colonies.); *Balzac v. People of Porto Rico*, 258 U.S. 298 (1922) (Since Puerto Rico was not incorporated into the United States, the petitioner was not entitled to sixth amendment protection); (additional cases involving the territories decided by the Fuller Court, generally known as the *Insular Cases* are *Kepner v. United States*, 195 U.S. 100 (1904); *Fourteen Diamond Rings v. United States*, 183 U.S. 176 (1901); *Dooley v. United States*, 183 U.S. 151 (1901); *Huus v. New York & Porto Rico S.S. Co.,* 182 U.S. 392 (1901); *Downes v. Bidwell*, 182 U.S. 244 (1901); *Armstrong v. United States*, 182 U.S. 243 (1901); *Goetze v. United States*, 182 U.S. 221 (1901); *DeLima v. Bidwell*, 182 U.S. 1 (1901)). *See generally*, JACKSON LEAR, REBIRTH OF A NATION: THE MAKING OF MODERN AMERICA 1877-1920 (2009) and GABRIEL KOLKO, MAIN CURRENTS IN MODERN AMERICAN HISTORY (1984).

[11] I will use terms such as the Middle Republic to refer to the period in American history roughly from post-Civil War (1866) to Great Depression (1929-1940). I will also use term such as the "Lochner-era" to refer to a subset of this broader Middle Republic period. The Fuller Court is yet another subset of this period.

[12] NORMAN WARE, THE INDUSTRIAL WORKER 1840-1860: THE REACTION OF AMERICAN INDUSTRIAL SOCIETY TO THE ADVANCE OF THE INDUSTRIAL REVOLUTION (1964).

[13] The Fouteenth Amendment forbids the states of depriving any person of life, liberty, or property without due process of law. A similar provision is found in the Fifth Amendment with

accomplish this? It gave it a substantive economic interpretation.[15] It relied on the treatises of Cooley and Tiedeman[16] to help fortify the protection of property. Also, Justice Stephen Field[17] served as one of the key players on the Court defending property rights.

The Reconstruction Amendments opened the door for the Court to use the Due Process Clause as a policy instrument for an emerging Industrial America. The Court redirected the Fourteenth Amendment from helping the former slaves[18] to helping build the corporate state.[19] And, it became a given by the

---

restrictions that apply to the federal government. The Due Process Clause traces its origin to the Magna Carta. For additional research on the Fourteenth Amendment, *See*, CHESTER ANTIEAU, THE ORIGINAL UNDERSTANDING OF THE FOURTEENTH AMENDMENT (1981); MICHAEL K. CURTIS, NO STATE SHALL ABRIDGE: THE FOURTEENTH AMENDMENT AND THE BILL OF RIGHTS (1986); WILLIAM E. NELSON, THE FOURTEENTH AMENDMENT: FROM POLITICAL PRINCIPLE TO JUDICIAL DOCTRINE (1988).

14 MICHAEL KAMMEN, A MACHINE THAT WOULD GO OF ITSELF: THE CONSTITUTION IN AMERICAN CULTURE 7 (1987); *See generally*, SANFORD LEVINSON, OUR UNDEMOCRATIC CONSTITUTION: WHERE THE CONSTITUTION GOES WRONG (2006) (a broader critique on the undemocratic nature of the Constitution).

15 WILLIAM M. WIECEK, LIBERTY UNDER LAW: THE SUPREME COURT IN AMERICAN LIFE 116 (1988) ("Bradley's dissent in *Slaughterhouse* was more far-reaching. In a brief passage, he conjured up the doctrine of substantive due process out of the natural rights tradition…the transformation of the concept of property from tangible objects (e.g., land, wagons, horses) to intangible rights and expectations, such as the abstract right to sell one's labor or the expectation of profit. [P]rocedural due process enabled courts to oversee the rules by which trials were conducted. Substantive due process, on the other hand, protected property rights from legislative impairment.")

16 JAMES W. ELY, THE CHIEF JUSTICESHIP OF MELVILLE W. FULLER 1888-1910, at 63-64 (1995); *See also,* CHRISTOPHER G. TIEDEMAN, A TREATISE ON THE LIMITATIONS OF POLICE POWER IN THE UNITED STATES CONSIDERED FROM BOTH A CIVIL AND CRIMINAL STANDPOINT (Union, N.J.: Law Exchange 2001) (1886); THOMAS M. COOLEY, TREATISE ON THE CONSTITUTIONAL LIMITATIONS WHICH REST UPON THE LEGISLATIVE POWER OF THE STATES (Union, N.J.: Lawbook Exchange 1998) (1868); James W. Ely, Jr., *Economic Due Process Revisited*, 44 VAND. L. REV. 213 (1991); Louise A. Halper, *Christopher G. Tiedeman, 'Laissez-Faire Constitutionalism' and the Dilemmas of Small-Scale Property in the Gilded Age*, 51 OHIO ST. L. J. 1249 (1990); *See generally*, GEORGE SKOURAS, TAKING LAW AND THE SUPREME COURT: JUDICIAL OVERSIGHT OF THE STATE'S ACQUISITION, USE, AND CONTROL OF PRIVATE PROPERTY (1998) (on the history of the police power and regulatory takings law).

17 CARL BRENT SWISHER, STEPHEN J. FIELD: CRAFTSMAN OF THE LAW (1930); Charles W. McCurdy, *Justice Field and the Jurisprudence of Government-Business Relations: Some Parameters of Laissez-Faire Constitutionalism, 1863-1897*, 61 JOURNAL OF AMERICAN HISTORY 970 (1975); HOWARD FURER, THE FULLER COURT 1888-1910 (1986). PAUL KENS, JUSTICE STEPHEN FIELD: SHAPING AMERICAN LIBERTY FROM THE GOLD RUSH TO THE GILDED AGE (1997).

18 *Civil Rights Cases*, 109 U.S. 3 (1883) (Civil rights for blacks were ignored and economic rights for the emerging corporation were privileged); *See also, Plessy v. Ferguson*, 163 U.S. 537 (1896) (The Fourteenth Amendment does not prohibit private citizens from discriminating against blacks, with regard to hotel, theater, or railroad accommodations. The Court promulgated the

close of the Waite Court that corporations are "persons."[20] Corporations gained the same protections as persons under the Fourteenth Amendment, while African-Americans became less than a person.[21]

Further, the Fuller Court gutted the Wilson-Gorman Tariff Act of 1894 containing the income tax provision.[22] The history of the United States is a history of hostility towards taxation and suspicious of labor. It is a liberal ideology that privileges property owners at the expense of the poor and working class.[23] Property power and economic expansion served American *Manifest Destiny*---a doctrine of colonialism, conquest of Western territories first and later global territories.[24] The failure to sustain the income tax resulted in a very serious loss to public supervision of the emerging corporate state because the public agencies and structures that needed to be built to monitor and supervise the corporation were lacking. Since the government coffers were empty, the corporation was left free of government supervision and only the most perfunctory oversight could be supported given the general philosophy of

doctrine of "separate but equal" in the segregation of black America). For a comprehensive view of the Reconstruction period, *See generally*: ERIC FONER, RECONSTRUCTION: AMERICA'S UNFINISHED REVOLUTION 1863-1877 (1988).

19 BERNARD H. SIEGAN, PROPERTY RIGHTS: FROM THE MAGNA CARTA TO THE FOURTEENTH AMENDMENT (2001) (Siegan provides a historical background for the origins of modern property rights leading to the Fourteenth Amendment from a conservative perspective); *See also*, G. EDWARD WHITE, THE AMERICAN JUDICIAL TRADITION: PROFILES OF LEADING AMERICAN JUDGES 86 (1976) ("[T]he Fourteenth Amendment gradually came to be used by the Court to bar state regulation of industrial enterprises. Implicit in this…were two collateral themes: a disinclination on the part of the Court to protect civil rights of blacks as it became more inclined to safeguard the property rights of entrepreneur[s].")

20 *Santa Clara County v. Southern Pac. R. Co.*, 118 U.S. 394 (1886), declare corporations are persons.

21 WILLIAM M. WIECEK, LIBERTY UNDER LAW: THE SUPREME COURT IN AMERICAN LIFE 99 (1988) ("A narrow construction, such as was suggested by Miller in *Slaughterhouse,* would constrict the ability of the national government to protect blacks' rights, leaving the freedmen's future in the control of the Democratic, racist, ex-secessionist, ex-Confederate Redeemers who were then taking control of the southern state"); *See also*, *Slaughter-House Cases*, 83 U.S. 36 (1873).

22 *Pollock v. Farmers' Loan and Trust Co.,* 158 U.S. 601 (1895) (Court held income tax to be unconstitutional).

23 *Loewe v. Lawlor*, *(The Danbury Hatters' Case),* 208 U.S. 274 (1903)(Court decided that a labor boycott of D. E. Loewe & Company by the Hatters' Union was deemed a conspiracy in restraint of trade that violated the Sherman Antitrust Act and awarded threefold damages to the company.)

24 H. W. BRANDS, THE RECKLESS DECADE: AMERICA IN THE 1890S (1995).

"limited" government. The federal and state efforts to control the corporation were inadequate.[25]

A fragmented state,[26] federalism and separation of powers, allowed the Fuller Court to combat so-called "class legislation" using the Due Process Clause. And to further consolidate property power it embedded the Due Process Clause in a philosophy of natural rights even though natural rights were not supposed to be the preferred method of legal analysis. According to Horwitz,[27] instrumental law eclipsed natural law prior to the Civil War, but it was nevertheless not discarded as a means of underpinning substantive economic due process. That is, the doctrine of natural law was not discarded during the Middle Republic, and it was used to bludgeon labor, taxation policy, and big government in the name of individualism.

The Fuller Court used the Due Process Clause to maintain "limited government" but not limited corporate power. It kept looking for answers in a fading rural America rather than a Corporate-Industrial America. What is clear

---

25 Statutory efforts served as a threat but not much more with the passing of the Sherman Antitrust Act and Clayton Act. Some early success at regulatory control, *Munn v. Illinois*, (*The Granger Cases*), 94 U.S. 113 (1877), *Budd v. New York*, 143 U.S. 517 (1892), *Standard Oil Co. of New Jersey v. United States*, 221 U.S. 502 (1910), *Swift and Co. v. United States*, 196 U.S. 375 (1905), and *United States v. American Tobacco Co.*, 221 U.S. 106 (1911) (state regulatory and federal monopoly cases showed the government meant business by actively using police power and the Sherman Antitrust Act). But eventually as the Due Process Clause gained economic substance, it became harder and harder to control corporations); *See generally*, VINCENT P. DE SANTIS, THE SHAPING OF MODERN AMERICA 1877-1920, at 12 (3rd ed. Harlan Davidson, Inc., 2000) (Chapter 1, "The Rise of Industrial America"---the role of the holding company in evading antitrust); *See also*, *supra* note 21 at 134-135 (Wiecek says, "Congress in the Clayton Act of 1913 had vaguely attempted to exempt organized labor from antitrust prosecutions by providing that labor was "not a commodity or article of commerce," and had flatly prohibited labor injunctions unless necessary "to prevent irreparable injury to property." The Court nullified these provisions in a series of cases that upheld use of the labor injunction to stop secondary boycotts (*Duplex Printing Press v. Deering*, 1921) and to halt picketing in a printing boycott (*American Steel Foundries v. Tri-City Central Trades Council*, 1921). For good measure, the Court also voided a state statute that prohibited injunctions against peaceful picketing (*Traux v. Corrigan*, 1921").

26 STEPHEN SKOWRONEK, BUILDING A NEW AMERICAN STATE: THE EXPANSION OF NATIONAL ADMINISTRATIVE CAPACITIES 1877-1920, at 27 (1982) ("Most notable in this regard was the way nineteenth century courts filled a governmental vacuum left by abortive experiments in the administrative promotion of economic development"); *See also*, Theda Skocpol, *Bringing the State Back In: Strategies of Analysis in Current Research*, *in* AMERICAN SOCIETY AND POLITICS: INSTITUTIONAL, HISTORICAL, AND THEORETICAL PERSPECTIVES 90-111(Theda Skocpol & John L. Campbell, eds. 1995).

27 MORTON J. HORWITZ, THE TRANSFORMATION OF AMERICAN LAW 1780-1860 (1977).

is that the perpetuation of the idea of "limited government" serves and served the corporate interests perfectly. The less government, the more corporation.[28]

The Fuller Court bears an important responsibility for those deleterious conditions that were the result of industrialization. How so? The Justices believed that the private market and individual freedom would come together to rectify the excesses of industrialization. Consequently, the Court adopted laissez-faire approach that left America at the mercy of the emergent corporate state without any checks or controls as to its size, function, aims, and residues of its existence. Even the Court of the Franklin Delano Roosevelt era, the Hughes Court, was not able to break free of the large corporate structure that was set in motion during the Gilded Age and Progressive Era---giantism with regard to corporations.[29] The industrial corporation continued as before[30] and could not be dislodged as the key institution of modern society even under worst Depression conditions America had ever seen---that is how strongly the corporate structure embedded itself in American society during the Middle Republic.

The America of the small farmer and small shop owner came to an end after the Civil War. The Fuller Court was able to lay the groundwork during this gap in time, after the Civil War and the completion of the industrial transformation, to shape the law according to a form of economic liberalism that has marked

[28] MORTON MINTZ & JERRY S. COHEN, AMERICA, INC.: WHO OWNS AND OPERATES THE UNITED STATES 21 (1971). ("Calvin Coolidge once told us that "the business of America is business." The fashion has been to judge this notion quaint. But the President is owed something better than condescension. He should be thanked for laying down an Orwellian stepping-stone to a perception of our true condition: Big Business *is* government.")

[29] CASS R. SUNSTEIN, THE SECOND BILL OF RIGHTS: FDR'S UNFINISHED REVOLUTION AND WHY WE NEED IT MORE THAN EVER 67 (2004) ("For Berle, corporate power was a serious threat to both democracy and economic growth. He believed that corporations had increasingly obtained the status of monopolies and did violence to the old idea of free and open competition"). *See also*, J. LEONARD BATES, THE UNITED STATES 1898-1928: PROGRESSIVISM AND A SOCIETY IN TRANSITION (1976). *See generally*, JACKSON LEARS, REBIRTH OF A NATION: THE MAKING OF MODERN AMERICA, 1877-1920 (2009) (Giantism also leads to imperialism as a regular feature of American foreign policy since the close of the 19th century). *See generally*, RICHARD SENNETT, THE CULTURE OF THE NEW CAPITALISM (2006); STEVEN J. DINER, A VERY DIFFERENT AGE: AMERICANS OF THE PROGRESSIVE ERA (1998) (Diner presents a cogent social history of the period).

[30] PAUL A. BARAN & PAUL M. SWEEZY, MONOPOLY CAPITAL: AN ESSAY ON THE AMERICAN ECONOMIC AND SOCIAL ORDER (1968); *See also*, JOHN KENNETH GALBRAITH, THE NEW INDUSTRIAL STATE (3rd ed., Houghton Mifflin Comp., 1978); IRA KATZNELSON & MARK KESSELMAN, THE POLITICS OF POWER: A CRITICAL INTRODUCTION TO AMERICAN GOVERNMENT 111 (1975) ("[A]nother advantage to investors was that the corporations could be used to reduce the risks of competition.")

the United States ever since. The Fuller Court was not ignorant of the fact that Jeffersonian and Jacksonian America was coming to an end. The question became, as various competitors emerged to supplant small town America---corporations and unions---as to which should serve as the proper inheritor of the Jeffersonian ideal. The Court deemed the working class, with only their labor power for sale, and their unions as neither comporting nor resembling the Jeffersonian model, and they found that the corporate model had a better fit to the Lockean and Marshall Court constitutional interpretation of property rights in America. In other words, the Court favored capital over labor because labor was a dangerous phenomenon. It was dangerous in the Justice's estimation because they could read about labor struggles in daily newspapers and also see a link between labor and socialism in Europe. Given the mental disposition of the Justices (all having been born pre-Civil War) and with their hands on the political power of judicial review, it should not take any stretch of the imagination (or leaps of faith) to infer that they would kill any legislation that had the remotest possibility of being dangerous to American values of freedom and liberty.

Although later Courts, such as the New Deal Court and Warren Court attempted to undo some of the laissez-faire doctrines supported by the Fuller Court, they have only partially succeeded. However, revisionists see the Fuller Court as a passing phase of American history with much of its agenda clipped by the New Deal and Warren Courts. And the revisionists believe the Court can maintain a separation between law and politics. The revisionists miss the fact that the Fuller Court was acting as a political body in the clothing of a legal body. Let us turn to the revisionists now.

3) REVIOSIONISTS OF THE FULLER COURT

Immediately after World War II, there emerged a group of scholars that wanted to revisit the Gilded Age and Progressive era. They came to be called consensus historians, Hartz, Hofstadter , and Boorstin[31] because they believed America was 'born liberal'[32] and free of the class conflict that crippled European

[31] LOUIS HARTZ, THE LIBERAL TRADITION IN AMERICA (1955); RICHARD HOFSTADTER, THE AGE OF REFORM: FROM BRYAN TO F.D.R. (1960), ANTI-INTELLECTUALISM IN AMERICAN LIFE (1962), SOCIAL DARWINISM IN AMERICAN THOUGHT (1955), THE AMERICAN POLITICAL TRADITION AND THE MEN WHO MADE IT (Vintage Books, 1989) (1948) and THE PROGRESSIVE HISTORIANS: TURNER, BEARD, PARRINGTON (1968); DANIEL BOORSTIN, THE GENIUS OF AMERICAN POLITICS (1953).

[32]*See generally*, L.T. HOBHOUSE, LIBERALISM (Oxford University Press, 1964) (a general analysis of the philosophy of liberalism); JOHN GRAY, LIBERALISM: ESSAYS IN POLITICAL PHILOSOPHY (1991); JOHN STUART MILL, ON LIBERTY AND OTHER WRITINGS (Cambridge University Press,

societies. Since America lacked a feudal past they argued, it lacked the class structure prevalent in Europe. These consensus historians attempted to recast the American past by stripping away slavery, violence, class conflict, imperialism, and native liquidations in order to present a clean history of American development. [33] The consensus historians were reacting to an earlier generation of Progressive historians---Beard, Parrington, Schlesinger, and Turner.[34] They believe these Progressive historians painted a picture of America with too many conflict scenes. And the Progressive movement [35] in general was mostly a middle class movement that wanted to ameliorate the impact of large industry on society.[36] The Progressives[37] did not want to dismantle corporations but rather to bring them under the control of government via regulation.[38] And because Beard[39] emphasized economic and class analysis, he became a favorite target of the consensus historians. Although these Progressives historians left gaps unexplained in the documentary

---

1989); ISAIAH BERLIN, FOUR ESSAYS ON LIBERTY (1969); LIBERALISM AND ITS CRITICS (Michael Sandel, ed. 1984); DAVID JOHNSTON, THE IDEA OF A LIBERAL THEORY: A CRITIQUE AND RECONSTRUCTION (1994) (for a modern defense of liberalism) and DAVID HARVEY, A BRIEF HISTORY OF NEOLIBERALISM (2005).

33 These historians believe in American exceptionalism. However, by emphasizing a "clean" history, they overlooked the animal side of the human being. Figures such as Darwin, Marx, and Freud had the insight that animality is at the core of our species. The primal drives that move the human animal are not "conscious" or "rational" forces but instinctual drives and the unconscious. *See,* DAVID RIESMAN, INDIVIDUALISM RECONSIDERED 206-245 (1954) (in particular see the chapter on: "Authority and Liberty in the Structure of Freud's Thought"); *See generally,* SIGMUND FREUD, CIVILIZATION AND ITS DISCONTENTS (W.W. Norton & Comp., 1989) (1930).

34 CHARLES A. BEARD, AN ECONOMIC INTERPRETATION OF THE CONSTITUTION OF THE UNITED STATES (The Free Press, 1986) (1913). V. L. PARRINGTON, MAIN CURRENTS OF AMERICAN THOUGHT (University of Oklahoma Press, 1987) (1927). FREDERICK JACKSON TURNER, THE FRONTIER IN AMERICAN HISTORY (The University of Michigan Press, 2006) (1893). ARTHUR M. SCHLESINGER, SR., THE NEW VIEWPOINTS IN AMERICAN HISTORY (1922).

35 In general Progressive activists and intellectuals were from a middle class background and were interested in reform rather than revolution.

36 One of the early Progressives Herbert Croly accused the Fuller Court of usurping the policy-making role of the legislature through their interpretation of the Due Process Clause; *See,* HERBERT CROLY, PROGRESSIVE DEMOCRACY (Oxford University Press, 1961) (1915).

37 SIDNEY FINE, LAISSEZ FAIRE AND THE GENERAL WELFARE: A STUDY OF CONFLICT IN AMERICAN THOUGHT 1865-1901 (1964) (in particular, his chapter on "Laissez Faire Becomes the Law of the Land," at 126-164); *See generally,* CLARENCE B. CARSON, THE GROWTH OF AMERICA 1878-1928 (1985) (for a more conservative/libertarian reading of the Gilded Age and Progressive Era period).

38 GABRIEL KOLKO, TRIUMPH OF CONSERVATISM (1977).

39 CHARLES A. BEARD, AN ECONOMIC INTERPRETATION OF THE CONSTITUTION OF THE UNITED STATES; *see also,* RAYMOND SEIDELMAN, DISENCHANTED REALISTS: POLITICAL SCIENCE AND THE AMERICAN CRISIS 1884-1984, at 60-100 (1985) (Chapter Three, "Science as Muckraking: The Cult of Realism in the Progressive Era").

evidence[40] or were later found to have been mistaken on one point or another, nevertheless, they attempted to note the role of economics in the establishment of political structures.

Since many people of the 1950s were uncomfortable with the use of class[41] analysis, it was helpful for these consensus historians to find in American society evidence of non-class based institutions. It was important to find institutions that reflected American freedom rather than economic exploitation, slavery, and other less democratic features of American history. By looking at the reportage of the muckrakers,[42] during the industrialization of America, one can see a tooth and claw economic doctrine in action--- that left millions of American exposed to waste, filth, dangerous working conditions, low pay, violence, segregation, etc. The consensus historians took note of this unfortunate state of affairs during critical points in American history, but they felt it should not color the whole of American history. They were sure that there existed pockets of history that illustrate the positive aspects of American freedom.

The liberal vision of America as presented by the 1950s consensus historians started to be questioned in 1960s and 1970s by an emerging ideological school

---

40 ROBERT E. BROWN, CHARLES BEARD AND THE CONSTITUTION: A CRITICAL ANALYSIS OF "AN ECONOMIC INTERPRETATION OF THE CONSTITUTION" (1956). FORREST MCDONALD, WE THE PEOPLE: THE ECONOMIC ORIGINS OF THE CONSTITUTION (1958). MERRILL JENSEN, THE NEW NATION: A HISTORY OF THE UNITED STATES DURING THE CONFEDERATION 1781-1789 (1950) (attempted to preserve the Progressive understanding of the Revolutionary era when its premises were being attacked).

41 SAMUEL P. HAYS, THE RESPONSE TO INDUSTRIALISM 1885-1914, at 37 (1957) ("The stark reality of social conflict deeply stunned Americans who had cherished the view that class divisions did not exist in their country"); *See also*, NORMAN POLLACK, THE POPULIST RESPONSE TO INDUSTRIAL AMERICA (1966); John WHITECLAY CHAMBERS II, THE TYRANNY OF CHANGE: AMERICA IN THE PROGRESSIVE ERA 1890-1920 (1992); *See also*, JACK BEATTY, THE TRIUMPH OF MONEY IN AMERICA 1865-1900, at 200 (Beatty says: "In "The Owners of the United States," a writer in the *Forum*, extrapolating from the 1880 census, figured that 25,000 people owned half the wealth and 250,000, 75 to 80 percent of it. "Who owns the United States?" he asked. "The USA is practically owned by less than 250,000 persons." Using the 1890 census, a contributor to POLITICAL SCIENCE QUARTERLY calculating "The Concentration of Wealth" found that "4,047 families possess as much as do 11,593,887 families." "This result," he wrote, "seems almost incredible"").

42 Here are some of the Muckrakers of the period: LINCOLN STEFFANS, THE SHAME OF THE CITIES (1904). UPTON SINCLAIR, THE JUNGLE (Penguin Classics, 1985). JACOB RIIS, HOW THE OTHER HALF LIVES: STUDIES AMONG THE TENEMENTS OF NEW YORK (1906). IDA TARBELL, THE HISTORY OF THE STANDARD OIL COMPANY (Dover Publications, 2003).

of historians (Bailyn, Wood, and Pocock).[43] This school believes Hartz over-emphasizes liberalism. The ideological historians believe liberal consensus historians neglect the "republican"[44] aspect of American development. And they saw the New Deal case law[45] serving as a corrective to excessive economic liberty.

The 1990s generation of revisionists, Bruce Ackerman, James W. Ely, Jr., and Howard Gillman, is making another attempt to free the Fuller Court from the grip of Progressivism. During the 1990s these three prominent scholars sought to revise the Progressive interpretation of the Fuller Court. They represent three schools of thought: 1) Neo-Federalism (liberal republicanism, dualist) School---Ackerman, 2) Classic-liberal conservative School---Ely, and 3) Neo-Institutionalist School---Gillman. They object to the Legal Realist[46] and Progressive interpretation of the Court and post hoc attacks on its formalist jurisprudence. They feel that the formalist jurisprudence used by the Fuller Court was fully consistent with the spirit of the age. Be it electoral primacy (Ackerman), natural rights (Ely), or institutional constraints (Gillman), I hope to show that these revisionists are mistaken in treating the Court as a legal body rather than a political body. They want to re-contextualize the Fuller Court as being in the flow and spirit of the age. However, looking at the matter from a Critical Legal Studies School perspective, the Court was not interpreting law but making law. The Critical School of thought, borrows an important element from the Realists,[47] which suggests that law is politics by other means.

---

[43] GORDON WOOD, THE CREATION OF THE AMERICAN REPUBLIC 1776-1797 (1969); BERNARD BAILYN, THE IDEOLOGICAL ORIGINS OF THE AMERICAN REVOLUTION (1967); J.G.A. POCOCK, THE MACHIAVELLIAN MOMENT: THE FLORENTINE POLITICAL THOUGHT AND THE ATLANTIC REPUBLICAN TRADITION (1975).

[44] Republicanism as in small "r" Jeffersonian or Machiavellian variation of republicanism, not the modern Republican Party sense.

[45] Cases that helped curtail the Gilded Age and Progressive era Court's rulings: *Home Building & Loan Association v. Blaisdell*, 280 U.S. 398 (1934); *Nebbia v. New York*, 291 U.S. 502 (1934); *West Coast Company v. Parrish*, 300 U.S. 379 (1937); *National Labor Relations Board v. Jones & Laughlin Steel Corp.*, 301 U.S. 1 (1937); *United States v. F. W. Darby Lumber Company*, 312 U.S. 100 (1941); *Wickard v. Filburn*, 317 U.S. 111 (1942).

[46] In short, Legal Realism is a legal philosophy that challenges the view that law is an autonomous and independent practice free from the personal views of judges. It challenges the view that judges can be objective and free from personal, political, social, economic, and cultural beliefs and can objectively judge laws and rules free from these human influences.

[47] *E.g.,* Realisms was not a unified philosophy and involved many variations. Here are some of the Legal Realists: Oliver Wendell Holmes, Roscoe Pound, Jerome Frank, Karl Llewellyn, Robert Hale, Felix Cohen, Louis Brandeis, Benjamin Cardozo, Felix Frankfurter, William O. Douglas, etc.

Further, the revisionists are mistaken in viewing America from the prism of liberal democracy. And although these revisionists recognize that America is not a class free country, they seem to circumscribe economic primacy as a key component of class structure. It has been taken for granted that America is an open society with fluid class structure. There are no fixed classes in America. However true this assertion seems to be, it should not be taken as unqualifiedly true. The philosophy of individualism, along with the consolidation of corporate power, has closed off the upward movement for the majority of Americans from the start of American history.

Given the Progressive interpretation of viewing the Fuller Court as pro-business and anti-labor, pro-capital power and limited government, can these revisionists explain the Court's behavior?

a) The Neo-Federalist (liberal republican, dualist) synthesis School---Bruce Ackerman

Ackerman represents a School of neo-federalism, liberal republicanism[48] that attempts to synthesize liberalism and republicanism, Locke and Machiavelli---he

48 BRUCE ACKERMAN, 1WE THE PEOPLE: FOUNDATIONS (1991) and 2WE THE PEOPLE: TRANSFORMATIONS (1998); Ackerman drawing support for his Neofederalism thesis in: THE FEDERALIST PAPERS; GORDON WOOD, THE CREATION OF THE AMERICAN REPUBLIC 1776-1797 (1969); EDMUND S. MORGAN, INVENTING THE PEOPLE: THE RISE OF POPULAR SOVEREIGNTY IN ENGLAND AND AMERICA (1988); HANNAH ARENDT, ON REVOLUTION (1963); BERNARD BAILYN, THE IDEOLOGICAL ORIGINS OF THE AMERICAN REVOLUTION (1967); J.G.A. POCOCK, THE MACHIAVELLIAN MOMENT: THE FLORENTINE POLITICAL THOUGHT AND THE ATLANTIC REPUBLICAN TRADITION (1975); Frank Michelman, *Law's Republic*, 97 YALE L.J 1493 (1988); Cass Sunstein, *Beyond the Republican Revival*, 97 YALE L.J 1539 (1988) and THE PARTIAL CONSTITUTION (1993); Suzanna Sherry, *Responsible Republicanism: Educating for Citizenship*, 62 U. CHI. L. REV. 131 (1995); critics of Ackerman work include: Michael Les Benedict, *History and Constitutional Theory: Reflections on Ackerman, Reconstruction, and the Transformation of the American Constitution*, 108 YALE L.J 2011 (1999) and *Laissez-faire and Liberty: A Reevaluation of the Meaning and Origin of Laissez-Faire Constitutionalism*, 3 LAW & HISTORY REV. 243-331 (1985); Miriam Galston and William A. Galston. *Reason, Consent, and the U.S. Constitution: Bruce Ackerman's "We the People"*, 104 ETHICS 446 (1994); Thomas Landry, *Ackermania!: Who Are We the People?*, 47 U. MIAMI L. REV. 267 (1992); William Fisher, *The Defects of Dualism*, U. CHI. L. REV. 955 (1992); Michael Klarman, *Constitutional Fact/Constitutional Fiction: A Critique of Bruce Ackerman's Theory of Constitutional Moments*, 44 STAN. L. REV. 759 (1992); Eben Moglen, *The Incomplete Burkean: Bruce Ackerman's Foundation for Constitutional History*, 5 YALE J.L. & HUMAN. 531 (1993); Randy E. Barnett, *Constitutional Legitimacy*, 103 COLUM. L. REV. 111 (2003); David E. Bernstein, *Lochner Era Revisionism, Revised: Lochner and the Origins of Fundamental Rights Constitutionalism*, 82 GEO. MASON L. REV. 1 (2003); other scholars questioning the neo-federalist approach: Ahkil Reed Amar, *A Few Thoughts on Constitutionalism, Textualism, and Populism*, 65 FORDHAM L. REV. 1657 (1997), *The Bill of Rights as a Constitution*, 100 YALE L.J.

attempts in his revisionism to synthesize the liberal and republican schools of thought to produce a neo-federalism (dualist democracy). He views the Fuller Court as following the election returns. According to him, the repudiation of laissez-faire doctrine was not prevalent until the New Deal.[49] So it is not fair to blame the Fuller Court for endorsing laissez-faire policies.

Clearly, Ackerman, wedded to the rule of law, misses asking the broader question: whose law? Working within the system leads Ackerman to be captivated and captured by the period he seeks to analyze. Ackerman explains the period thus:

> To the contrary: the Justices had just lived through the failed Populist effort to mobilize the American people against the evils of laissez-faire capitalism---a movement that climaxed with the nomination of William Jennings Bryan as the Democratic candidate for the Presidency in 1896. Rather than leading to a Rooseveltian transformation, Bryan's nomination served only to catalyze a decisive popular counterreaction on behalf of William McKinley and the Republican Party.[50]

What he is trying to say is this: the role of property in American society was settled by the 1896 election. The People elected a President that favored business and property over the Populist and Progressive agenda of farmers and workers. So there was nothing unusual about the Court's treatment of labor in general and the Lochner[51] decision in particular. It simply affirmed the right to

1131 (1991) and THE BILL OF RIGHTS: CREATION AND RECONSTRUCTION (2000); OWEN FISS, TROUBLED BEGINNING OF THE MODERN STATE 1888-1910 (1993); SANFORD LEVINSON, OUR UNDEMOCRATIC CONSTITUTION: WHERE THE CONSTITUTION GOES WRONG (AND HOW WE THE PEOPLE CAN CORRECT IT (2006); other scholars using critical and realist analysis challenging the revisionists:WILLIAM EDWARD LEUCHTENBURG, THE SUPREME COURT REBORN: THE CONSTITUTIONAL REVOLUTION IN THE AGE OF ROOSEVELT (1996); LAURA KALMAN, THE STRANGE CAREER OF LEGAL LIBERALISM (1996); MORTON J. HOROWITZ, THE TRANSFORMATION OF AMERICAN LAW (1979); CHRISTOPHER TOMLINS, LAW, LABOR, AND IDEOLOGY IN THE EARLY AMERICAN REPUBLIC (1993).

[49] Ackerman, WE THE PEOPLE: FOUNDATIONS at 100: ("If, then, something was fundamentally wrong with *Lochner*, it has to do with the particular way middle republican courts conceptualized the nature of fundamental rights. It is here, however, where anachronism distorts modern vision in condemning the middle republic's emphasis on private property and freedom of contract. Given the popular repudiation of laissez-faire during the New Deal, it is no longer right for modern courts to interpret constitutional liberty in free market terms. But before the 1930's, things looked very different. Even during the early republic, the courts had marked out contract as a domain of freedom peculiarly appropriate for national protection.")

[50] Ackerman, WE THE PEOPLE: FOUNDATIONS at 101.

[51] *Lochner v. New York*, 198 U.S. 45 (1905) (The Court upheld the freedom of contract doctrine, that the State had no business interfering in privately agreed to contracts); *See also*, PAUL KENS,

contract without government intervention. So those later generations of intellectuals that want to condemn the Lochner-era are mistaken because the People spoke, and they decisively chose McKinley over Bryan.

What is missing here is the critical element that leaves a number of questions and gaps in the literature as to why the Supreme Court was justified in reading the Fourteenth Amendment as pro-business and anti-labor provision based on election returns. Who is 'We the People' that Ackerman has in mind?[52] Does it matter even if 'we are people' capable of empowering such a system? Could patronage interfere with the goals of 'we the people'? Does it matter whether giant corporation are able to displacing these laws if these laws do not suit their interests? Does the existence of a Spoils System[53] matter as far as elections and the electorate is concerned? Ackerman seems to set these questions aside in favor of the big question: was an election held and who was the victor in that election?

The Fuller Court according to Ackerman's dualist constitutional model must reconcile two different historical periods. It must reconcile the Founder's Constitution with a post-Civil War Constitution. However, this view is not plausible because the Fuller Court used the Due Process Clause, not to reconcile the Founding and Reconstruction, but to privilege the Justice's values, preferences, and politics. What the People wanted was beside the point. Rather than embody the values of the American people based on election results, the Fuller Court used the Due Process Clause to privilege those values that were embedded in the Lockean philosophy of property. Ackerman simply accepts the idea that election returns reflect the will of the American people. The Critical Legal Studies School[54] and Legal Realism question whether the

---

LOCHNER V. NEW YORK: ECONOMIC REGULATION ON TRIAL (1998); *See also,* G. EDWARD WHITE, *Revisiting Substantive Due Process and Holmes's Lochner Dissent*, 63 BROOK. L. REV. 87 (1997); *See generally*, MICHAEL E. TIGAR & MADELEINE R. LEVY, LAW & THE RISE OF CAPITALISM (1977).

52 Robert D. Marcus, *The Business of Politics: National Party Structure in the Gilded Age*, *in* READINGS IN AMERICAN POLITICAL HISTORY 260-276 (Frank Otto Gatell, Paul Goodman, & Allen Weinstein, eds. 1972) (politicians of both parties did all they could to align themselves with the new elite industrialists.)

53 ALLAN NEVINS, THE EMERGENCE OF MODERN AMERICA 1865-1878, at 178-202 (1927) (see his descriptions of the spoils system and corruption in Chapter VII, "The Moral Collapse in Government and Business").

54 THE POLITICS OF LAW (David Kairys, ed., 3rd ed. 1998); *See, in* THE POLITICS OF LAW the following works: Elizabeth Mensch, "The History of Mainstream Legal Thought"; Joseph William Singer, "Property"; Morton J. Horwitz, "The Rise and Early Progressive Critique of Objective Causation" ;William H. Simon, "Contract versus Politics in Corporation Doctrine"; Karl Klare, "Critical Theory and Labor Relations Law," and Robert Gordon, "Some Critical

type of synthesis (between voters and law) Ackerman seeks to deploy, and it might be seen as more of a strategy to split the electorate or divide the electorate than serve to reflect the common interests of the electorate in challenging the corporation. Critical legal realism sees problems of indeterminacy, objectivity, and fairness baked into the existing liberal-democratic model in representing the common interests of workers and the general electorate. Elections in America are more geared to divide and conquer the electorate rather than reflect its common interests. The Corporate state likes to use a philosophy of individualism as a smoke screen to hide corporate interests in a divided and fragmented American political structure.

The problem with Ackerman's neo-federalism school is that the separation of powers, power of judicial review, and federalism are not consistent with democracy. Ackerman wants to square the Constitution with democratic values. And he knows that the Founders put provisions into the Constitution as deterrence to democracy. As to the political power of judicial review, this power is nowhere to be found in the Constitution and was simply claimed by the Supreme Court. But even if such a power should be placed in the Constitution, should nine individuals be able to determine policy for 300 million Americans? Unfortunately, Ackerman does not see it that way. For him, the Fuller Court took the Due Process Clause of the Fourteenth Amendment and applied it on behalf of property interests because the Court was acting consistently with the electoral results of the 1896 elections. Ackerman is a democrat first and a rights foundationalist second.

Further, Ackerman also downplays the role of Legal Realism in the American legal system. He wants to synthesize the realists approach with his own constructivist approach to reach post-realist interpretivism. Ackerman has little to say about higher lawmaking or natural law as a source of constitutional rights or values. Nor does natural law play a role in American's history, according to Ackerman, because it does not fit his model of dualist constitutionalism.

The protection of democracy was not an issue with these Courts. Democracy was mostly despised by the Founders and the term did not gain good currency

---

Theories of Law and their Critics"; *See also*, Mark Tushnet, *Critical Legal Studies: An Introduction to Its Origin and Underpinnings*, 36 J. LEGAL EDUC. 505 (1983); Robert Gordon, *Critical Legal Histories*, 36 Stan. L. Rev. 57 (1984); MORTON J. HORWITZ, THE TRANSFORMATION OF AMERICAN LAW 1780-1860 (1977). Duncan Kennedy, *The Structure of Blackstone's Commentaries*, 28 BUFF. L. REV. 205 (1979); ROBERTO MANGABEIRA UNGER, THE CRITICAL LEGAL STUDIES MOVEMENT (1986); MARK KELMAN, A GUIDE TO CRITICAL LEGAL STUDIES (1987).

until fairly late in the nineteenth century. Consequently modern theorists such as Ackerman, who defend the actions of these Courts, on democratic principles are in fact defending a mythology of democracy.

b) The Classical-Liberal Conservative School---James W. Ely, Jr.

Ely, and other members of the Lockean school,[55] find that laissez-faire[56] capitalism was an accepted philosophy of the Gilded Age. And natural law served as a foundational doctrine for the capitalist market. By anchoring the Due Process Clause in natural law, the justices were able to remove it from democratic demands.

Ely represents a school of classic-liberal conservatism. He points out that the Fuller Court provided continuity and stability to the nation. By appealing to natural law, the justices could remove property from the threat of legislative confiscation.[57] Ely puts it this way: "Evidently influenced by natural law

---

55 JAMES W. ELY, JR., THE GUARDIAN OF EVERY OTHER RIGHT: A CONSTITUTIONAL HISTORY OF PROPERTY RIGHTS (1992), THE CHIEF JUSTICESHIP OF MELVILLE W. FULLER 1888-1910 (1995), *Property Rights and Democracy in the American Constitutional Order, in* THE JUDICIAL BRANCH (Kermit L. Hall & Kevin T. McGuire, eds. 2005) and *Economic Due Process Revisited*, VAND. L. REV. 213 (1991); FORREST MCDONALD, WE THE PEOPLE: THE ECONOMIC ORIGINS OF THE CONSTITUTION (1958); Randy E, Barnett, *Constitutional Legitimacy*, 103 COLUM. L. REV. 111 (2003); BERNARD H. SIEGAN, PROPERTY RIGHTS: FROM THE MAGNA CARTA TO THE FOURTEENTH AMENDMENT (2001); Miriam Galston and William Galson, Reason, *Consent, and the U.S. Constitution: Bruce Ackerman's "We the People"*, 104 ETHICS 446 (1994) (Galston's are rights foundationalists first); Charles W. McCurdy, *Justice Field and the Jurisprudence of Government-Business Relations: Some Parameters of Laissez-Faire Constitutionalism 1863-1897*, 61 JOURNAL OF AMERICAN HISTORY 970 (1975) and *American Law and the Marketing Structure of the Large Corporation 1875-1890*, 38 JOURNAL OF ECONOMIC HISTORY 631 (1978); Paul Murphy, *Time to Reclaim: The Current Challenge of American Constitutional History*, 69 AM. HIST. REV. 64-79 (October 1963); Alan Jones, *Thomas M. Cooley and the Interstate Commerce Commission: Continuity and Change in the Doctrine of Equal Rights*, 8 POLITICAL SCIENCE QUARTERLY 602-627 (1966) and *Thomas M. Cooley and 'Laissez-Faire Constitutionalism': A Reconsideration,* JOURNAL OF AMERICAN HISTORY 752-771 (1967); RICHARD A. EPSTEIN, TAKINGS: PRIVATE PROPERTY AND THE LAW OF EMINENT DOMAIN (1985) and BARGAINING WITH THE STATE (1993); RAOUL BERGER, THE FOURTEENTH AMENDMENT AND THE BILL OF RIGHTS (1989) and GOVERNMENT BY JUDICIARY: THE TRANSFORMATION OF THE FOURTEENTH AMENDMENT (2nd ed., 1997).

56 Ely, GUARDIAN OF EVERY OTHER RIGHT at 88 ("Because judges are influenced by social forces and intellectual currents in general society, the principles of laissez-faire constitutionalism gained currency among Supreme Court justices in the 1880s.")

57 EDWARD CORWIN, THE "HIGHER LAW" BACKGROUND TO AMERICAN CONSTITUTIONAL LAW (Cornell University Press, 1928) (First printed as Harvard Law Review Article, Edward S. Corwin, *The "HigherLaw"* Background of American Constitutional Law, 62 HARV. L. REV. 149 (1928)) ; see also, the liberal defense of property on natural law grounds, JOHN LOCKE, TWO TREATISES ON GOVERNMENT (Peter Laslett ed., 3rd ed., Cambridge University Press, 1988) and

theory, Fuller concluded that private property existed before the creation of political authority and that a principal purpose of government was to protect property rights. He identified property ownership with the preservation of individual liberty."[58] Ely also points out the Court's hostility towards labor.[59] However, the use of natural law and personal antipathy by the Justices towards labor shows the complex dynamic between finding the law and making it. The Fuller Court feared labor and acted accordingly. The association of labor with socialism, given its European context, frightened the Justices into crippling pro-labor legislation. Also Debs and other labor activists were doubly disadvantaged: not only did they confront hostile corporate interests but a judiciary stacked up against them.

Of course the workers and farmers did not go quietly and without struggle. The transformation of America from a society based on rural living to a society of city dwellers and the transformation of farmers into manufacture laborers were not the conditions conducive to a peaceful transformation. Attempts to cloth the new system with old language---the language of democracy, of individualism, of freedom of contract, of work ethics, etc.---ceased to exist under the emergence of the Industrial Revolution. Old beliefs were being applied to changed structural conditions. The Supreme Court was not ignorant of the intellectual, political, and economic debates taking place in businesses, parlors, homes, and streets.[60]

The American response to Industrialism appears to have been the most conservative as compared with the response of the Europeans. One reason as

---

WILLIAM BLACKSTONE, COMMENTARIES ON THE LAWS OF ENGLAND (Boston: Beacon Press, 1962).

58 Ely, THE CHIEF JUSTICESHIP OF MELVILLE W. FULLER, p. 32; *see also*, WILLARD L. KING, MELVILLE W. FULLER: CHIEF JUSTICE OF THE UNITED STATES, 1888-1910 (1950) and HOWARD FURER, THE FULLER COURT, 1888-1910 (1986).

59 Ely, THE JUSTICESHIP OF MELVILLE W. FULLER at 102 ("Liberty of contract was invoked in *Adair* to invalidate legislation supportive of labor organizations. Since this was one of a handful of cases in which the Fuller Court applied the liberty of contract principle, it is hard to escape the conclusion that Fuller and his colleagues were uneasy with a growing labor movement. This judicial skepticism readily matched the reluctance of society at large to accept labor unions. It is revealing that Justice Harlan, who had previously been deferential to legislative judgment, wrote the majority opinion. As Loren P. Beth has observed, "Harlan was…a child of his times in many ways; for example, he shared to some degree the rest of the Court's marked antipathy to the rise of organized labor." The *Adair* ruling provoked outrage among supporters of unions and contributed to the anti-labor image of the Fuller Court"); *see also*, *Adair v. United States*, 208 U.S. 161 (1908).

60 RAY GINGER, AGE OF EXCESS: THE UNITED STATES FROM 1877-1914 (2nd ed. 1975) (Ginger presents a broad picture and social history of the period).

to why this was the case--- given that Europe had more embedded conservative institutions than the New World--- might be this: the fragmentation of American society via racial, ethnic, religion, language, unbounded immigration, and flood of entering immigrants from Eastern and Southern European countries that were mostly of peasant stock, uneducated, poverty stricken, etc. served as a hedge to unifying labor and defusing the need to establish an American Labor Party that could effectively challenge the Bigness of the new Corporation at the dawn of the Industrial Era. "In Europe industrialization uprooted the peasants from the land and brought them to the cities, where they became revolutionary workers. But the uprooted European peasants who settled in American cities remained conservative. In America the farmers who stayed on the land played the role of European workers as a major force challenging industrial capitalism."[61] That is, the continuous flow of immigrants at the dawn of industrialization was able to fragment labor and prevent or blunt the radicalization of the worker. The corporations were able to take advantage of the situation, in further dividing and fragmenting the American populace; so that Labor lacked common interest and ability to coordinate and react to the consolidation of corporate power.

Ely's revisionist defense seems to be that if society at large could not stomach labor unions, could the Court do no other? Like Ackerman, Ely accepts the proposition that the Court was a part of a culture that valued property above all else and could do no other. However, unlike Ackerman, Ely seems to recognize that the Court did start to feel some unease with its property over labor principles.

What are the limitations of Ely's approach and the Lockean School of thought? This School is wedded to the idea that because the Fuller Court viewed property as a precondition to liberty, it was justified in making that equation. That is, Ely and others of the classical liberal school assume Fuller's taming of the Due Process Clause to comport with Lockean philosophy was justified. They share a philosophy of limited government, individualism, free markets, and strong protection of property. Natural law may have served a function in pre-Copernicun times or in Medieval theology, but its continued use could only serve establishment and property interests. The Fuller Court was not unaware that the use of natural law was no longer free of controversy. And the Progressives aptly pegged the Fuller Court for what it was---a stalwart of business and an impediment to labor.

---

61 MICHAEL PAUL ROGIN, THE INTELLECTUALS AND MCCARTHY at 187.

c) **The Neo-Institutionalist School---Howard Gillman**

Gillman, and others of the neo-institutionalist school,[62] points out that the Fuller court was not hostile to property regulation per se but to invalid "class" legislation.[63] Gillman attempts to show the Fuller Court jurisprudence as a continuation of rational and consistent doctrine. The Justices were justified to protect property because they worked within the parameters of the Supreme Court's traditions. It is not the case according to Gillman that the Justices had some personal aim to hurt labor and help business. In other words, the Justices were not voting their preferences or policies, but were institutionally constrained by legal tradition and Supreme Court rules.

And Gillman believes that the Realist interpretation does not take full account of the institutional constraints confronting the Justices. Gillman tells us that his method of analysis is:

> In what might be considered a return to what is sometimes derisively referred to as a "traditional" or "prerealist" analysis of judicial politics---more generously referred to as "postbehavioralist" analysis---this study rests primarily on an interpretation of legal texts and related materials in order to demonstrate how federal and state judges shared a common method of evaluating exercises of police powers, and how their decisions were supported by arguments that represented something more than rationalizations of idiosyncratic policy preferences and something different from an ideological commitment to laissez-faire economics or social Darwinism.[64]

In other words, politics, policy, and the personal preferences of the Justices are inadequate to explain court behavior.

---

[62] HOWARD GILLMAN, The Constitution Besieged: The Rise and Demise of Lochner Era Police Powers Jurisprudence (1993) and THE SUPREME COURT IN AMERICAN POLITICS: NEW INSTITUTIONALIST INTERPRETATIONS (Howard Gillman & Cornell Clayton, eds. 1999); SUPREME COURT DECISION-MAKING: NEW INSTITUTIONALIST APPROACH (Cornell W. Clayton & Howard Gillman, eds. 1999); *See also*, Mark Graber, *The Passive-Aggressive Virtues: Cohens v. Virginia and the Problematic Establishment of Judicial Power*, 12 CONST. COMMENT 67 (1995); [for older generation of Institutionalists, *See*, Edward S. Corwin, *The Constitution as Instrument and Symbol*, 30 AM. POL. SCI. REV. 1071 (1936); CHARLES GROVES HAINES, THE ROLE OF THE SUPREME COURT IN AMERICAN GOVERNMENT AND POLITICS, 1789-1853 (1944); ROBERT MCCLOSKEY, THE AMERICAN SUPREME COURT (1960)].

[63] Gillman, THE CONSTITUTION BESIEGED at 10; *see also*, *Lochner v. New York*, 198 U.S. 45 (1908).

[64] Gillman, THE CONSTITUTION BESIEGED at 12.

Gillman presents a cogent understanding of post-Civil War America and the transformation that was taking place.[65] Yet he believes the Court was not carving out property for special protection from the onslaught of labor, socialists, progressives, populists, and other disgruntled agitators hammering on the walls of liberalism. Gillman tells us the Court was constitutionally obligated to protect property, as it would any other right. The Justices were not amenable to legislation that provided special favors to labor. They saw any special privilege of labor as sign of class legislation and the fear of class warfare.

The limitations of the Gillman's approach, and the neo-institutionalist school, is that it attempts to negate the Legal Realist approach, under the belief that institutional constraints prevent judges from writing their political and policy preferences into the law. The Legal Realists acknowledge the role institutional constraints play in judicial decision-making. But realists carve out a role for politics, personal preferences, and legal innovation that justices and judges utilize in making their decisions. Court rules, norms, and precedent are only partly controlling in judicial decision making. This work acknowledges the role of institutions providing boundaries, but those boundaries are porous and not fixed. Institutional boundaries can constrain personal action, but cannot negate it. Boundaries, institutional constraints, restriction of judicial preferences by group dynamics, norms, etc. are biased toward establishment values. Just because they reflect establishment norms, does not mean that these boundaries are rightly drawn. Also as noted earlier, Critical Legal Studies, taking up some of the doctrines of the Legal Realists, does not separate law from politics.

4) <u>**CONCLUSIONS**</u>

The Fuller Court set the nation on a path toward the corporatization of the American society. It was using political power disguised as legal power to do this. It used a metaphysic of natural law and the Fourteenth Amendment to accomplish this transformation of the legal system. It was partial toward

65 Gillman, THE CONSTITUTION BESIEGED at 63. ("The unprecedented frequency of depressions dried up the source of wages for millions of people and made commercial competition more cutthroat. By the 1880s the protracted postwar deflationary crisis had resulted in a record rate of business failures and a further consolidation of large-scale enterprise. In all, the last quarter of the nineteenth century witnessed changes that crushed the Lockean state of nature that had inspired many of America's founders and replaced it with a Darwinian social order in which dependence rather than independence was becoming the more common social experience, manifesting most pointedly in a "chronic conflict between employers over the costs of production;" that is, in widespread and violent class conflict.")

corporate power and averse to labor power. The Court supervision of labor curtailed labor leadership from operating freely in organizing workers and used antitrust tools and the Reconstruction's Fourteenth Amendment to block labor. The use of the labor injunction became one of an arsenal of weapons used to block or curtail labor union activity.

The use of laissez-faire doctrine supported a minimalist state and the maximization of the corporate state. The fragmentation of government during this period led to the easy consolidation of power away from government and agencies and into the hands of the private sector. The Court gave its blessing to this new emergent structure called the corporation. It used its political power to insert its view of taxation at the expense of the legislative and executive branches. It further used its power to protect and support the corporation by attempting to minimize any damage the Sherman Act might do in the consolidation of capital. As the American frontier started to come to a close and the United States sought empire status, comparable to the other European powers, the Court followed the flag in the opening of foreign markets to United States trade.

Those closest to the ground, the Progressives and Populists attempted to describe the Fuller Court as a bastion for pro-business protections. However, later generations of theorists and scholars disputed the objectivity and fairness of the Progressive characterization of the Fuller Court. Ackerman, Ely, and Gillman sought to contextualize the decisions of the Fuller Court in accord with the spirit of the times and correct the Progressive class conflict or suggestion that the Court acted out of turn towards the most vulnerable people in American society. These scholars operating within the traditional liberal-democratic paradigm assume a frame of reference for the Court's decisions based on electoral returns, natural law principles, and institutional constraints.

As we can see in the aftermath of the Great Crash of 2008, we can turn our gaze back to the Gilded Age and Progressive era in searching for the legal tools used by the Fuller Supreme Court in building the Corporate state in America. This has lead to an asymmetrical power between the Corporation and the formal political structure. This asymmetry in power has worked beautifully for a small portion of the population, but it has left the vast majority of Americans hanging on the myth of judicial neutrality.

The answers to the questions posed are clearly that the Fuller Court was not justified in using the Fourteenth Amendment to build and defend laissez-faire capitalism and legitimize the corporate structure. The revisionist scholars were too hasty in their analysis of the Fuller Court. The Progressives were correct in pegging the Fuller Court as deleterious to labor, tax averse, pro-capital consolidation, and accommodation of overseas adventures as a matter of politics rather than law. The Fuller Court helped to legitimize the corporation by unhinging it from its state sponsored origins and set it free, and mostly unaccountable, onto the American public.

HOW JUDGES DON'T THINK: THE INADVERTENT MISUSE OF PRECEDENT IN THE STRANGE CAREER OF THE ILLINOIS DOCTRINE OF ANTAGONISTIC DEFENSES, 1876-1985

by Scott Hamilton Dewey, Ph.D., J.D., UCLA School of Law*

Abstract: This article reviews the theory of precedent, including various traditional arguments for or against a common law system based on precedent and stare decisis. *The article then closely follows the gradual creation of precedent in the 200 cases that comprise the entire history, from 1876 to 1985, of the development of Illinois' rule requiring severance of jointly indicted codefendants with antagonistic defenses. During that period, the Illinois rule was assumed into existence through a process of lawyers taking words out of context, courts injecting those words into case law in the course of rejecting the lawyers' arguments, later courts erroneously assuming those words to have a meaning earlier courts never gave them, other courts dutifully repeating those assumptions, and the words thus coalescing into rules, then splitting into different versions of the rule that lost any trace of their questionable origins—all through an apparently unintentional process as busy courts did their best to rely upon precedent to efficiently resolve what was a minor issue in most cases. The article concludes that along with the various other more established arguments against reliance on precedent, such as findings of conscious or unconscious but intentional manipulation of precedent to reach case outcomes that fit judges' personal or political preferences, America's lawyer-driven adversarial common law system operates as an engine of linguistic instability that leads courts to lose track of the meaning of earlier court opinions and bend and twist precedent unintentionally, even as they try to observe precedent in good faith. The inherent and seemingly inevitable linguistic indeterminacy of the process of creating precedent, and the unmoored nature of the product that results, raises further doubts whether we can properly claim that our judicial process is truly based on precedent and* stare decisis.

* Assistant Director, Research Assistance and Scholarly Support, UCLA School of Law. J.D., UCLA, 2003. Ph.D., History, Rice University, 1997. E-mail: scott.dewey@gmail.com. This article is dedicated to Judge Richard A. Posner and Professor Frederick Schauer, who among all the scholars I reviewed have, in my opinion, written most illuminatingly and captivatingly about precedent. Thanks are due to the editorial staff of *The Journal Jurisprudence* for their patience and persistence. I should also note Lynda Carr O'Conner, who helped move this project forward, if indirectly and inadvertently.

INTRODUCTION: THE MEANING (IF ANY) OF PRECEDENT

In law school, students are, effectively, beaten over the head with precedent.

Virtually every casebook in every class piles on more precedent. Students are reminded that precedent, and the doctrine of *stare decisis* that reveres that precedent, are the foundation of our whole legal system of judge-made common law. They are drilled in the use of precedent and are forced to memorize various checklists regarding the hierarchy of precedent. Thus, whether or not precedent is ever clearly defined, or merely assumed,[1] law students breathe it in for three long years and learn to take it for granted, with a general, mostly unstated assumption that precedent is necessary, inevitable, and the intellectual lifeblood of the legal profession, and that the system for creating and modifying precedent is presumably adequate, appropriate, and sufficiently well-understood.[2]

This apparent professional certainty regarding precedent may make it surprising for a current or former law student to discover that legal scholars have long acknowledged that the meaning and operation of precedent within our legal system are actually dimly understood and under-studied.[3] Because precedent and

---

1 Stefanie A. Lindquist & Frank B. Cross, *Empirically Testing Dworkin's Chain Novel Theory: Studying the Path of Precedent*, 80 NYU L. REV. 1156, 1157 (2005) ("All those who have studied the law have at least an intuitive notion of precedent or stare decisis.").

2 Granted, students at some point will have been exposed briefly to the ideas of the legal realists and possibly the Critical Legal Studies movement, but usually not enough to get in the way of the overall professional adulation of precedent.

3 *See, e.g.*, Lindquist & Cross, *supra* note 1, at 1157 ("Perhaps the most important, yet understudied, area of legal research involves precedent. . . . [T]here has been only limited theorizing about, and relatively little empirical investigation of, the operation of precedent."); Emerson H. Tiller & Frank B. Cross, *What Is Legal Doctrine?* 100 NW. U. L. REV. 517, 517, 518 (2006) ("[T]he nature and effect of [precedent] has been woefully understudied"; "Legal researchers have extensively dealt with doctrine as a normative matter but have given little attention to the manner in which it actually functions."); Larry Alexander, *Constrained by Precedent*, 63 S. CAL. L. REV. 1, 3 (1989) ("[O]ur theoretical understanding of the practice [of using precedent] is still at a very primitive stage."); Frederick Schauer, *Is the Common Law Law?* 77 CAL. L. REV. 455, 455 (1989) ("For all its ubiquity, the common law remains uncommonly puzzling."); Frank H. Easterbrook, *Stability and Reliability in Judicial Decisions*, 73 CORNELL L. REV. 422, 422 (1988) (no United States Supreme Court justice has offered a consistent theory of precedent); Frederick Schauer, *Precedent*, 39 STAN. L. REV. 571 (1987); William M. Landes & Richard A. Posner, *Legal Precedent: A Theoretical and Empirical Analysis*, 19 J. L. & ECON. 249, 250 (1976) ("The use of precedents to create rules of legal obligation has . . . received little theoretical or empirical analysis."); Anton-Hermann Chroust, *Law: Reason, Legalism, and the Judicial Process*, 74 ETHICS 1, 3 (1963) ("[L]egal rules and principles are never fully known and never fully clear, except perhaps to some particularly benighted first-year law student"; "Legal reasoning . . . is in fact 'reasoning' from concrete case to concrete case within a loosely defined and probably undefinable concatenation of half-intuitive and half-discursive mental operations that are often expressed in such vague terms as 'precedent,' *stare decisis*, and 'legal authority'"). *See also*

its use are (at least theoretically) at the core of the judicial process in our common law system, uncertainty about the doctrine of precedent necessarily raises questions about the legitimacy of the judicial process itself.

To the extent that legal scholars have discussed judicial use of precedent, this discourse typically resolves into a debate between those who claim that judicial decisionmaking based on precedent is appropriately grounded and reasonably objective and those who claim the process is not—as with the early twentieth-century debate between traditional legal formalists and legal realists, later revisited during the heyday of the Critical Legal Studies movement.[4] More recently, the debate has tended to pit social scientists—chiefly political scientists, economists, and legal scholars marching under the same banner of quantitative data analysis—against judges and traditional non-quantitative, doctrine-oriented legal scholars, with the social scientists self-confidently touting their quantitative analytical techniques as powerful new tools to examine and perhaps debunk the legal profession's traditional rationalizations of judicial decisionmaking,[5] while traditionalists, particularly judges, have returned fire with the observations that judging is a process too complex and subtle to be readily comprehended by the political scientists' data-coding and number-crunching, and that, moreover, people who have never worked as a judge or in a court do not and cannot really know all that goes into the process of judicial decisionmaking.[6]

Madeline Fleisher, *Judicial Decision Making under the Microscope: Moving Beyond Politics versus Precedent*, 60 RUTGERS L. REV. 919 (2008) ("It is clear to most scholars that modern accounts of the [judicial] decision-making process are incomplete[.]"); Sarah A. Maguire, *Precedent and Procedural Due Process: Policymaking in the Federal Courts*, 84 U. DETROIT MERCY L. REV. 99, 99 (2007) ("[Precedent] is a foundational and familiar piece of U.S. law, but at the same time, it remains somewhat mystical.").

[4] *See, e.g.*, Frank B. Cross, *Political Science and the New Legal Realism: A Case of Unfortunate Interdisciplinary Ignorance*, 92 NW. U. L. REV. 251, 255-59 (1997).

[5] *See, e.g.*, Tiller & Cross, *What Is Legal Doctrine?*, *supra* note 3, at 522 ("Quantitative analysis . . . provides scientific rigor to studies of law[.]"); Cross, *Political Science and the New Legal Realism*, *supra* note 4, at 264, 313 ("[P]olitical scientists have referred to the [traditional] legal model as a 'mythology . . . [or] meaningless' or 'silly'"; "[P]olitical scientists, as *true* legal researchers . . . " [emphasis added]).

[6] *See, e.g.*, Harry T. Edwards, *The Effects of Collegiality on Judicial Decision Making*, 151 U. PA. L. REV. 1639, 1656 (2003); Patricia M. Wald, *A Response to Tiller and Cross*, 99 COLUM. L. REV. 235, 235 (1999) ("Judging is a complex, case-specific, and subtle task that defies single-factor analysis"); Harry T. Edwards, *Collegiality and Decision Making on the D.C. Circuit*, 84 VA. L. REV. 1335, 1338-39 (1998) ("[S]erious scholars seeking to analyze the work of the courts cannot simply ignore the internal experiences of judges as irrelevant or disingenuously expressed. . . . I think that the . . . studies are flawed in their quantitative and qualitative analyses, and also in their interpretation of data. . . . Finally, both pieces seem terribly naïve in their understanding of the judges on the D.C. Circuit and how we perform our work."); Jack Knight, *Are Empiricists Asking the Right Questions about Judicial Decisionmaking?* 58 DUKE L.J. 1531, 1532 (2009) (noting skepticism of more traditionalist colleagues on the Duke Law School faculty regarding "whether empirical studies of

The recent debate has particularly focused on political scientists' claims—often called the "attitudinal model"—that quantitative analysis reveals that judges' political ideology or party affiliation impact or determine appellate outcomes, regardless of precedent.[7] Critics have countered that studies finding ideologically-driven decisions have tended to focus on the United States Supreme Court, an inherently unusual and political court, and on the most politically charged decisions among the relatively small number of federal cases that ever reach that court, such that the studies are not particularly applicable to more ordinary decisions from more ordinary courts—among other arguments.[8]

---

the courts accurately capture the main concerns and primary activities of judges"). Frank Cross, a leading quantitative analyst of judicial process, acknowledged that most political scientists' lack of legal training was problematic. *See* Cross, *Political Science and the New Legal Realism*, *supra* note 4, at 285. For a trenchant early critique of applying social-scientific quantitative analysis to the law, see Wallace Mendelson, *The Neo-Behavioral Approach to the Judicial Process: A Critique*, 57 AMER. POL. SCI. REV. 593 (1963). See also RICHARD A. POSNER, HOW JUDGES THINK 2 (2008) (noting judges' sense of difference from other lawyers).

7 Such claims have by now a lengthy lineage, a substantial part of it revolving around political scientist Harold Spaeth. *See, e.g.,* Harold J. Spaeth, *Judicial Power as a Variable Motivating Supreme Court Behavior*, 6 MIDWEST J. POL. SCI. 54, 55, 82 (1962); Harold J. Spaeth, *An Analysis of Judicial Attitudes in the Labor Relations Decisions of the Warren Court*, 25 J. POL. 290, 310 (1963); JEFFREY A. SEGAL & HAROLD J. SPAETH, THE SUPREME COURT AND THE ATTITUDINAL MODEL 31, 354 (1993); HAROLD J. SPAETH & JEFFREY A. SEGAL, MAJORITY RULE OR MINORITY WILL: ADHERENCE TO PRECEDENT ON THE U.S. SUPREME COURT 287 (1999); JEFFREY A. SEGAL & HAROLD J. SPAETH, THE SUPREME COURT AND THE ATTITUDINAL MODEL REVISITED 430-35 (2002); Richard L. Revesz, *Environmental Regulation, Ideology, and the D.C. Circuit*, 83 VA. L. REV. 1717, 1719, 1759-60 (1997); Frank B. Cross & Emerson H. Tiller, *Judicial Partisanship and Obedience to Legal Doctrine: Whistleblowing on the Federal Courts of Appeals*, 107 YALE L.J. 2155, 2175-76 (1998); Gregory C. Sisk et al., *Charting the Influences on the Judicial Mind: An Empirical Study of Judicial Reasoning*, 73 NYU L. REV. 1377 (1998); Emerson H. Tiller & Frank B. Cross, *A Modest Proposal for Improving American Justice*, 99 COLUM. L. REV. 215 (1999); Daniel R. Pinello, *Linking Party to Judicial Ideology in American Courts: A Meta-Analysis*, 20 JUST. SYS. J. 219, 229-30, 234 (1999) (synthesizing empirical studies to find statistical confirmation that "party is a dependable measure of ideology in modern American courts").

8 *See, e.g.,* Gregory C. Sisk & Michael Heise, *Judges and Ideology: Public and Academic Debates about Statistical Measures*, 99 NW. U. L. REV. 743, 772 (2005) (finding overall impact of ideology in federal courts "more moderate than large"); DONALD R. SONGER ET AL., CONTINUITY AND CHANGE ON THE UNITED STATES COURTS OF APPEALS 115-16 (2000) (finding modest difference between Democrat- and Republican-appointed judges in voting on various categories of cases); Michael J. Gerhardt, *Attitudes about Attitudes*, 101 MICH. L. REV. 1733 (2003) (generally questioning the attitudinal model); POSNER, HOW JUDGES THINK, *supra* note 6, at 27-28, 269-75 (explaining that the Supreme Court is an inherently political court that hears a tiny subset of difficult federal cases not easily resolved at a lower judicial level); Wald, *supra* note 6, at 237 (noting that lower court judges have too many cases to process to have strong feelings about most of them and that many cases, especially administrative law cases, "have no apparent ideology to support or reject at all"). The understanding that the Supreme Court is less bound by precedent in the context of constitutional cases has a long pedigree: Justice Brandeis observed in 1932 that the Court "has often overruled its earlier decisions" involving constitutional questions and recognized the need to

In recent years, the two sides of the debate seem to have moved gradually toward (though not yet arrived at) a new synthesis that reduces the theoretical polarization between the two sides, with the political scientists discovering that legal doctrine does matter after all, at least to some degree, the traditionalists accepting that extra-legal factors such as ideology and personal background are inextricably woven into the fabric of judging, and the remaining debate being now more about the degree to which, not whether, judicial decisions are influenced by both legal and non-legal factors.[9] Some scholars have recognized that the judicial reasoning process might structure how judges go about deciding cases, and so shape the decisions, even if it does not (entirely) determine the outcomes.[10] The realization that Supreme Court cases necessarily constitute a very small and non-random sample of federal cases has also led legal scholars increasingly to turn their attention to lower federal courts, where most federal doctrinal law is made

correct and improve the law by trial and error. Burnet v. Coronado Oil & Gas Co., 285 U.S. 393, 406-07 (1932) (Brandeis, J., dissenting). Justice Douglas noted in 1946 that "throughout the history of the Court stare decisis has had only a limited application in the field of constitutional law[,]" unlike areas of law where correction readily could be had through legislation. New York v. United States, 326 U.S. 572, 590 (1946) (Douglas, J., dissenting). Chief Justice Rehnquist in 1991 declared that *stare decisis* is a "principle of policy," not "an inexorable command" or "a mechanical formula of adherence to the latest decision," and that it is most favored where reliance interests are involved, as with property or contract rights, not as much in cases involving procedural or evidentiary rules. Payne v. Tennessee, 501 U.S. 808, 828 (1991). For an argument that *stare decisis* should be abandoned altogether in the context of constitutional adjudication, see James C. Rehnquist, *The Power That Shall Be Vested in a Precedent: Stare Decisis, the Constitution and the Supreme Court*, 66 B.U. L. REV. 345 (1986).

[9] *See, e.g.*, POSNER, HOW JUDGES THINK, *supra* note 6, at 10, 42-49; Frank B. Cross, *Decisionmaking in the U.S. Circuit Courts of Appeals*, 91 CAL. L. REV. 1457, 1459, 1514 (2003) (finding that "legal and political factors are statistically significant determinants of decisions, with legal factors having the greatest impact"); Tiller & Cross, *What Is Legal Doctrine?*, *supra* note 3, at 525-27; Knight, *supra* note 6, generally; LEE EPSTEIN & JACK KNIGHT, THE CHOICES JUSTICES MAKE 184, 186 (1998); Ethan Bueno de Mesquita & Matthew Stephenson, *Informative Precedent and Intrajudicial Communication*, 96 Am. Pol. Sci. Rev. 755 (2002); Lindquist & Cross, *supra* note 1, at 1173-1177, 1205-06; Maguire, *supra* note 3, at 100-01, 106, 133-34; Fleisher, *supra* note 3, at 920, 925, 964-67; DAVID E. KLEIN, MAKING LAW IN THE UNITED STATES COURTS OF APPEALS 15-16 (2002); Sisk et al., *supra* note 7, at 1498-1500; Jon O. Newman, *Between Legal Realism and Neutral Principles: The Legitimacy of Institutional Values*, 72 CAL. L. REV. 200, 204 (1984).

[10] *See, e.g.,* Mark J. Richards & Herbert M. Kritzer, *Jurisprudential Regimes in Supreme Court Decision Making*, 96 AM. POL. SCI. REV. 305, 305-06 (June 2002); Fleisher, *supra* note 3, at 960-61, 966 ("[C]onceptions of judicial decision making as an outcome-oriented process ignore one of the basic ideas underlying our system of written judicial opinions: how a judge reaches a result is as important as the result itself. In the legal market, judges sell their reasoning as much as their particular substantive opinions."). For one who has worked within a court, the latter correct observations might seem somewhat obvious, making it perhaps regrettable that attitudinalist scholars' overall lack of such experience so long delayed that key insight.

regarding much larger batches of more average cases.[11] As is so often the case in the legal profession, though, most busy practicing attorneys and judges probably have largely ignored this academic debate altogether and assume that decisions are based on precedent (while feeling intuitively that the outcome of a case may vary depending on to which judge it is assigned).[12]

If most scholars who obsess over precedent have concluded that it at least means *something* to judicial decisionmaking, and if most other scholars and virtually all practicing lawyers and judges assume that it means almost *everything*, then it's probably worth taking a moment to explain the traditional doctrine of precedent, what it is, and how it works—in theory.

"In ordinary language, a precedent is something done in the past that is appealed to as a reason for doing the same thing again."[13] Such an everyday definition of precedent approximates the legal concept of persuasive authority, not necessarily binding authority. The doctrine of precedent, however, is of course closely related

---

[11] *See, e.g.*, Evan H. Caminker, *Precedent and Prediction: The Forward-Looking Aspects of Inferior Court Decisionmaking*, 73 TEX. L. REV. 1, 3-4 (1994) ("Inferior federal courts, as a matter of empirical fact, play a far more important role in the actual lives of citizens than does the Supreme Court. The behavior of the roughly 100 circuit judges and 500 district judges is, for most citizens most of the time, far more likely to count as 'the law' than the pronouncements of the nine denizens of the Supreme Court."); Maguire, *supra* note 3, at 99 (noting that under doctrine of precedent, each case disposition adds to and becomes part of legal doctrine, so "the district and circuit courts play a profoundly important role" and have "far-reaching" influence given the "sheer number of cases those courts hear"); Lindquist & Cross, *supra* note 1, at pp. 1156, 1158 (studying more than seven hundred opinions interpreting 42 U.S.C. § 1983 from five federal circuit courts over a thirty-year period after 1961); KLEIN, *supra* note 9, at 17-18 (studying federal circuit judges, as the title implies); Cross, *Decisionmaking in the U.S. Circuit Courts of Appeals*, *supra* note 9, at 1459-60.

[12] On the persistence of the traditional legalist school of thought on precedent and judicial decisionmaking, *see, e.g.,* Cross, *Political Science and the New Legal Realism*, *supra* note 4, at 260 (noting that although "Classic unabashed formalism is no longer widely embraced," Supreme Court justices continue to espouse respect for precedent and to justify their opinions with it, and "legal scholars have implicitly accepted the use of precedent at face value"); Tiller & Cross, *What Is Legal Doctrine?*, *supra* note 3, at 518 ("Legal academics, unsurprisingly, have focused on the traditional legal model of decisionmaking based on 'reasoned response to reasoned argument'" through which (theoretically) "one obtains 'legal reasoning that can generate outcomes in controversial disputes independent of the political or economic ideology of the judge'"); SPAETH & SEGAL, *supra* note 7, at 314 ("*Stare decisis* is the lifeblood of the legal model, and the legal model is still the lifeblood of most legal scholars' thinking about law."). Regarding the well-established folk wisdom in the legal community that yes, it matters who the judge is, Posner observes, "If changing judges changes law, it is not even clear what law is." POSNER, HOW JUDGES THINK, *supra* note 6, at 1.

[13] Landes & Posner, *supra* note 3, at 250.

to the doctrine of *stare decisis*, or leaving things previously decided as they stand.[14] It is *stare decisis* that gives precedent its (supposed) power to bind later courts, particularly lower courts, within any particular jurisdiction. Legal scholar Edward Levi, in his classic discussion of legal reasoning, identified a three-step process in the creation of precedent through reasoning from one concrete case to another: first, a "compelling" or "relevant" similarity between the facts of a pending case and an earlier case is identified; second, the legal rule controlling the similar facts, inherent in the earlier case, is extracted and proclaimed by the court deciding the later case; third, that legal rule is declared to be applicable and followed (or declared inapplicable and distinguished) by the later court.[15]

Although Levi's three-step process may seem obvious to lawyers, a point perhaps deserving emphasis is that the power and significance of any precedent is mostly determined by the later court, not the former, in that an incipient legal rule, or proto-precedent, initially has no power to control anything beyond the outcome of its own case—that is, it remains merely a holding—until a later court declares it to have that power. Like movie star wannabes in Hollywood, legal rules must wait to be "discovered" before they can become binding precedents, and the later court typically defines the meaning and extent of the precedent, what situations it will bind and how far it will reach.[16] Or, as legal realist Jerome Frank observed, "For precedential purposes, a case, then, means only what a judge in any later case says it means."[17] Because the proto-precedential holding only determines its own case, in theory it should tend to be narrow in scope, so that normally a whole string of later judicial decisions building upon the original holding will be required to expand it into a more powerful and broadly applicable legal rule.[18] This, in turn, is supposed to build into the evolution of precedent a certain deliberate gradualism, which has been called the special genius of the common law.[19]

---

[14] BLACK'S LAW DICTIONARY (9th ed. 2009) translates the Latin phrase as "to stand by things decided" and notably identifies the doctrine of *stare decisis* and that of precedent as one and the same thing.

[15] EDWARD H. LEVI, AN INTRODUCTION TO LEGAL REASONING 1-2 (1949); Chroust, *supra* note 3, at 3-4.

[16] Chroust, *supra* note 3, at 3; Landes & Posner, *supra* note 3, at 249-50.

[17] JEROME FRANK, COURTS ON TRIAL: MYTH AND REALITY IN AMERICAN JUSTICE 279 (1949).

[18] Landes & Posner, *supra* note 3, at 250.

[19] Judge Posner characterizes legal reasoning by analogy, in essence, as "a method of cautious, incremental judicial legislating" involving "a certain caution in departing from existing rules." Richard A. Posner, *Reasoning by Analogy*, 91 CORNELL L. REV. 761, 773, 774 (2006). Justice Scalia has explained, "Of course, in a system in which prior decisions are authoritative, no opinion can leave *total* discretion to later judges. It is all a matter of degree. At least the very facts of the particular case are covered for the future. But sticking close to those facts, not relying upon overarching generalizations, and thereby leaving considerable room for future judges is thought to be the genius of the common law system. The law grows and develops, the theory goes, not

The doctrine of precedent mostly looks backward, seeking guidance in the past. Yet another point deserving emphasis is what Frederick Schauer has called "The Forward-Looking Aspect of Precedent."[20] For even if precedent is ultimately shaped primarily by the later court that discovers it, the original court can attempt to force the hand of future courts to some extent by how aggressively or conservatively, broadly or narrowly it structures a proto-precedential holding, by how it lays out and characterizes the facts of the case decided, and by which facts are included or left out, emphasized or minimized.[21] Thus, "A judge finding it necessary to make law for *this* case must nevertheless decide how wide a range of future cases to [try to] control."[22]

Moreover, contrary to the theory of common law gradualism, American courts often are not bashful about engaging in judicial lawmaking: "With great frequency, judges make more law than is necessary to decide the case at hand, and then, in subsequent cases, treat this judge-made law as constraining."[23] As Schauer notes, in words that apply to both an originating court and a later, discovering court:

Dealing with the use of past precedents thus requires dealing with the presence of the previous decisionmaker's *words*. These words may themselves have authoritative force, . . . and thus we often find it difficult to disentangle the effect of a past *decision* from the effect caused by its accompanying words. More pervasively, even a previous decisionmaker's noncanonical descriptions channel the way in which the present views those past decisions. So long as the words of the past tell us how to view the deeds of the past, it remains difficult to isolate how much of the effect of a past decision is attributable to what a past court has *done* rather than what it has *said*.[24]

through the pronouncement of general principles, but case-by-case, deliberately, incrementally, one-step-at-a-time." Antonin Scalia, *The Rule of Law as a Law of Rules*, 56 U. CHI. L. REV. 1175, 1177 (1989). After thus explaining how the common-law approach is supposed to work in theory, however, Justice Scalia expresses doubts about this approach as the true "course of judicial restraint, 'making' as little law as possible in order to decide the case at hand" and questions whether "both writing and reading the 'holding' of a decision narrowly, thereby leaving greater discretion to future courts" really works in practice. *Id.* at 1178, 1179.

[20] Schauer, *Precedent*, *supra* note 3, at 572.

[21] *See* Lindquist & Cross, *supra* note 1, at 1163.

[22] Schauer, *Is the Common Law Law?*, *supra* note 3, at 458. Judge Posner notes that appellate judges tend to "report the facts in their opinion[s] in such a way as to make them fit the legal conclusion smoothly or shape the precedent that the decision will create." POSNER, HOW JUDGES THINK, *supra* note 6, at 69.

[23] Schauer, *Is the Common Law Law?*, *supra* note 3, at 457.

[24] Schauer, *Precedent*, *supra* note 3, at 573.

Schauer's observation should give comfort to anyone who has ever experienced frustration at trying to extract the "rule" from a case, whether as a law student, clerk, attorney, or judge. For the creation of precedent involves a potentially complex dance between the original court and the later discovering court in their descriptions and characterizations of factual situations and legal principles. For purposes of the present article, it is important to remember that other courts must rely on both the original court and the discovering court to do their respective jobs "right," and responsibly, in creating precedent, even though there is no clear definition or delimitation of what either court may or must do.[25] Furthermore, just as in history, where we are only able to see the past "through a glass darkly,"[26] Schauer notes,

The passage of time compounds the difficulty of disentangling a precedent from its specific linguistic account, because the process of characterizing a decision does not end with its first formulation. We necessarily and continuously reinterpret the past as we proceed into the future. People other than the initial decisionmakers use and talk about, and in the process, recharacterize, the decisions of yesterday. The story of a decision changes as it passes from generation to generation, just as words whispered from child to child do in a game of 'telephone.' Past decisions thus come to the present encrusted with society's subsequent characterizations of and commentary on those decisions.[27]

For all these reasons, precedent can be problematic. Yet theoretically it offers clear benefits for decisionmaking that outweigh the costs. These include (with some conceptual overlap): fairness/equality/similar treatment of similarly situated parties; certainty/predictability/reliance; impartiality/non-arbitrariness/heightened appearance of justice; coherence; stability; heightened credibility, strength, and prestige of the decisionmaking institution; standardization; and efficiency.[28] Another arguable strength of precedent in practice, though one partly at cross-purposes to these other supposed virtues and the whole theory of the doctrine, is its flexibility. Although precedent may be strictly and rigidly binding in theory, in actuality, because of courts' discretion to define the cases before them as well as to interpret earlier decisions, courts can frequently avoid being bound by precedent, whether by distinguishing cases on their facts or by declaring part of

[25] *See, e.g.,* Chroust, *supra* note 3, at 4; Lindquist & Cross, *supra* note 1, at 1163.

[26] 1 *Corinthians* 13:12.

[27] Schauer, *Precedent*, *supra* note 3, at 574.

[28] *Id.* at 595-602; Earl Maltz, *The Nature of Precedent*, 66 N.C. L. REV. 367, 368-72 (1988); Lindquist & Cross, *supra* note 1, at 1159-61. Justice Scalia, discussing judging generally and not precedent specifically, similarly emphasizes the importance of equal treatment, the appearance of fairness, and predictability. Scalia, *supra* note 19, at 1178-79.

the language of an earlier holding to be dictum and so not part of the resulting legal rule.[29]

Similarly, although a truly strict application of the doctrine of *stare decisis* might preclude the pruning of any duly created precedent from the common law, in practice such pruning is allowed and needed, and the accumulation of various precedents in an area of law can help indicate in which direction that area of law is evolving and which precedents are outliers or mistakes to be ignored, avoided, or discarded.[30] "It is the readiness of the common law judges to discard that which does not serve the public that has contributed to the survival and adoption of common law, wholly or partly, in so many lands."[31] Legal authorities, from chief justices of American states soon after the U.S. Constitution's ratification to the Lord High Chancellor of the United Kingdom in 1960, have long assumed that precedent can and must be pruned, *stare decisis* notwithstanding.[32] Schauer notes that flexibility and prunability, however, call into question to what degree courts are really constrained by precedent as the doctrine of *stare decisis* demands,[33] and Justice Cardozo, while accepting the need for change and correction, warned against judges disrespecting or discarding precedent too freely.[34]

Notwithstanding the common law's theoretical ability to cleanse and purify itself of problematic precedents, it clearly sometimes can have difficulty doing so. Charles Alan Wright recounted how a bad decision in the federal Third Circuit misinterpreted a federal rule of civil procedure so as to make summary judgment effectively unavailable in that jurisdiction, and after seeing a fellow district judge slapped down for challenging the erroneous decision, other district judges meekly followed the bad precedent, precluding its coming up to the circuit again for

---

[29] Lindquist & Cross, *supra* note 1, at 1163-64; Maltz, *supra* note 28, at 384.

[30] Maltz, *supra* note 28, at 383.

[31] HENRY J. ABRAHAM, THE JUDICIAL PROCESS 10 (7th ed. 1998).

[32] *Id.* at 361; Caleb Nelson, *Stare Decisis and Demonstrably Erroneous Precedents*, 87 VA. L. REV. 1, 29-31 (2001).

[33] Schauer, *Is the Common Law Law?*, *supra* note 3, at 456.

[34] ABRAHAM, *supra* note 31, at 10. Cardozo justified replacement of outmoded precedent in language that hearkens back to a time (before the horrors of the Third Reich) when most sophisticated western intellectuals accepted the basic tenets of eugenics: "Few rules in our time are so well established that they may not be called upon any day to justify their existence as means adapted to an end. If they do not function they are diseased. If they are diseased, they must not propagate their kind. Sometimes they are cut out and extirpated altogether. Sometimes they are left with the shadow of continued life, but sterilized, truncated, impotent for harm." BENJAMIN N. CARDOZO, THE NATURE OF THE JUDICIAL PROCESS 98-99 (New Haven: Yale University Press, 1921; reprinted in CARDOZO ON THE LAW (Birmingham, AL: Legal Classics Library, 1982)).

review.[35] Wright cited this as a "classic example of what has been termed 'a Gresham's Law of Procedural Precedents'—the tendency, 'accentuated by the reporting of the striking or technical procedural decisions more extensively than of the merely permissive rulings,' of bad procedural precedents to drive out the good."[36]

In addition to the features that supposedly make precedent and *stare decisis* good for the law and the public, scholars have drawn on rational self-interest theory from economics or public choice theory from political science to suggest features that make the doctrines good for judges as well. These include, among others, helping each judge lock in the precedential impact of her opinions by mutually agreeing, tacitly, to respect each others' opinions; building and maintaining the judiciary's prestige; helping to establish consistency in the law; helping to provide benchmarks for setting and meeting the professional standards of the judicial community; the "'intrinsic pleasure' of writing and exercising analytical prowess," and maximizing judges' leisure time.[37] The latter reason is closely related to the court efficiency justification, and these two intertwined features of precedent are particularly important for purposes of this article. Another noteworthy judicial goal—perhaps more a negative goal than the positive goals listed above—is safety, and something for the judge or the judicial profession to hide behind if a case attracts the glare of public scrutiny or higher court review.[38] As such, even if precedent and precedent-based reasoning are, consciously or unconsciously, only a fig leaf covering other motivations, it's good for both judges and the law to have better-constructed and more reliable fig leaves. Judge Posner has observed, "Most judges, like most serious artists, are trying to do a 'good job,' with what is 'good' being defined by the standards of the 'art' in question."[39] From both within and without the legal profession, the quality of judicial artistry is defined by careful, reasonable doctrinal analysis.

---

[35] *See generally* Charles Alan Wright, *Rule 56(e): A Case Study on the Need for Amending the Federal Rules*, 69 HARV. L. REV. 839 (1956).

[36] *Id.* at 849-50, 849 n.41 (quoting from Clark, *'Clarifying' Amendments to the Federal Rules?* 14 OHIO ST. L.J. 241, 245 (1953).

[37] Erin O'Hara, *Social Constraint or Implicit Collusion?: Toward a Game Theoretic Analysis of Stare Decisis*, 24 SETON HALL L. REV. 736, 748-53 (1993); Richard A. Posner, *What Do Judges and Justices Maximize? (The Same Thing Everybody Else Does)*, 3 SUP. CT. ECON. REV. 1, 19 (1993); Lindquist & Cross, *supra* note 1, at 1165-66; KLEIN, *supra* note 9, at 16-18; Sisk et al., *supra* note 7, at 1499 (noting that despite finding evidence that judicial decisions are influenced by personal and political preferences, "it was impossible not to be captivated by the excitement, the devotion to legal analysis, the depth and rigor of constitutional analysis, and yes, the true pleasure revealed by the judges in their engagement with a meaningful legal problem.").

[38] *See* POSNER, HOW JUDGES THINK, *supra* note 6, at 70-72.

[39] *Id.* at 12.

Yet "precedent, as an inherently constraining form of argument, is more suited to some forms of decisions than to others."[40] Law students and practitioners are generally familiar with the longstanding distinction between more rigid legal rules and more flexible legal standards.[41] Rules constrain judicial discretion more, so are by definition more in keeping with a strict application of *stare decisis*; standards inherently allow greater judicial discretion and so fit with a weaker model of precedent. Louis Kaplow has cogently explained, "The central factor influencing the desirability of rules and standards is the frequency with which a law will govern conduct[,]" such that "when frequency is low, a standard tends to be preferable[,]" while rules are more efficient and useful in situations that recur frequently.[42] Frederick Schauer has pointed out that in some decisionmaking situations, "it is precisely the *thisness* of the case that is most vital[,]" such that past similar situations may not be similar enough to provide meaningful guidance.[43] For instance, sometimes the need " 'to get it just right'" will trump the "virtues of stability" that precedent offers.[44] The need to get it just right helps explain the traditionally relaxed application of *stare decisis* in Supreme Court constitutional decisions.[45] Whether or not there is a need to get a decision just right, any situation that is either rare or intensely fact-specific, or both, should be one where predictability matters less if at all, thus favoring a standard/weak precedential approach over a rule/strong precedential approach. Chief Justice Rehnquist appears to have followed similar reasoning in pointing to property or contract rights cases involving reliance interests as deserving stricter application of *stare decisis* (providing greater predictability), while the need for *stare decisis* is diminished where procedural or evidentiary rules are involved (allowing greater attention to "thisness").[46]

In an effort to describe how the use and evolution of precedent works in practice, both constraining judges and allowing them discretion, legal philosopher Ronald Dworkin has suggested the model of a chain novel, with various different authors serially adding to a single narrative with the goal, continually sought even if not perfectly attained, of creating a seamless, coherent, and internally consistent narrative that looks as though it might have been produced by a single author.[47]

---

[40] Schauer, *Precedent*, *supra* note 3, at 604-05.
[41] Tiller & Cross, *What Is Legal Doctrine?*, *supra* note 3, at 517.
[42] Louis Kaplow, *Rules versus Standards: An Economic Analysis*, 42 DUKE L.J. 557, 563, 621 (1992).
[43] Schauer, *Precedent*, *supra* note 3, at 601.
[44] *Id.*
[45] *See* discussion in note 8, *supra*.
[46] Payne v. Tennessee, 501 U.S. 808, 828 (1991).
[47] RONALD DWORKIN, LAW'S EMPIRE 228-39 (1986); see also Lindquist & Cross, *supra* note 1, at 1167-69.

Because the plot choices and added details from earlier coauthors in the chain should gradually fill in the canvas with main characters, background, and story line, the process will tend to constrain the freedom and fancy of later coauthors, who are obliged to make additions to the chain that reasonably fit with the rest and to develop coherent, workable interpretations of the whole novel that allow their additions to fit.[48] Under the theory of the chain novel, a responsible coauthor thus is not at liberty to bring in entirely new storylines and characters from left field that have no conceivable relationship to the existing story.

Stefanie Lindquist and Frank Cross point out that Dworkin's chain novel theory is an example of "the more general theory that precedent is path-dependent."[49] In other words, the actions of earlier judges should progressively circumscribe and limit the universe of options available to later judges in considering similar issues.[50] Oona Hathaway has identified three different varities of path dependence that may illuminate the operation of judicial precedent: economic, or "increasing returns," path dependence, where a step in one direction makes it progressively easier and less costly to take further steps in the same direction;[51] the punctuated equilibrium theory of biological evolution, holding that evolution occurs in a stair-step or plateau fashion, with long periods of stasis interrupted by short bouts of rapid change, which in the law might correspond to sweeping new statutory enactments, constitutional amendments, or overruling of long-established precedents;[52] and sequencing path dependence, a mathematical model showing how the order in which initially available alternatives are considered sometimes can determine the outcomes of decisions.[53]

Lindquist and Cross note that for general decisionmaking theory, path dependence offers the benefit of stability, but also the risk of locking in an inferior alternative because it happened to come first.[54] They also observe that for Dworkin's chain novel theory of precedent to have the path-dependent properties

---

[48] *See* both sources cited in note 47. My description admittedly oversimplifies Dworkin's lengthy discussion of the process he envisions.

[49] Lindquist & Cross, *supra* note 1, at 1169.

[50] *Id.*; *see also, generally*, Oona A. Hathaway, *Path Dependence in the Law: The Course and Pattern of Legal Change in a Common Law System*, 86 IOWA L. REV. 601 (2001).

[51] Hathway, *supra* note 50, at 608-13, 627-35.

[52] *Id.* at 613-17, 635-45; Lindquist & Cross, *supra* note 1, at 1170-71.

[53] Hathaway, *supra* note 50, at 617-22, 645-50; Lindquist & Cross, *supra* note 1, at 1171.

[54] Lindquist & Cross, *supra* note 1, at 1171-72. Jared Diamond notes the continued dominance of the QWERTY typewriter keyboard at the expense of other, more efficient designs as an example of path dependence locking in an inferior option. *See* DIAMOND, GUNS, GERMS AND STEEL 248, 418 (1997); *see also* Hathaway, *supra* note 50, at 605, 611-12. Apple Mac aficionados would similarly point to the dominance of the IBM PC and Microsoft's DOS-based Windows operating system.

the theory entails, precedent must actually constrain judicial decisionmaking, and more so as the chain lengthens.[55] From their extensive quantitative analysis of § 1983 holdings from various federal circuits over a thirty-year period, Lindquist and Cross found that contrary to the chain novel hypothesis, precedent seemed to show a diminishing rather than increasing effect over time, suggesting that the proliferation of precedents gives judges greater freedom to express their personal and political predilections, as legal realists traditionally contended.[56] They note that "Many commentators have accepted [Dworkin's] theory as a description of how precedent *should* work in the conventional understanding of law but have questioned whether it does so function in practice."

In sum, despite legal practitioners' generally unquestioning acceptance of these doctrines, the theory of precedent, *stare decisis*, and the common law in general remain in many ways complex, problematic, and unsettled. Further study is warranted.

Here I will temporarily drop the mask of the objective voice from nowhere so typical of academic writing and instead speak in the first person, in keeping with Benjamin Franklin's sound suggestion that one of the keys to civil discourse is, rather than to proclaim that something is so, to say, "I conceive or apprehend" that something is so—recognizing that one's statements and impressions are not necessarily either universal, objective, or correct, and inviting, not demanding, that the audience consider them.[57] For I would like to share some subjective personal impressions regarding precedent and the judicial process. I also would like to make an apology.

In an earlier article, I made various pronouncements about what I perceive to be typical characteristics of judges as well as recurring problems with precedent.[58] My observations were based on personal experience, and were implicitly subject to the Franklin qualification—but on re-reading that article for the first time in several years, I find that I should have made that qualification explicit. Also, although I still stand behind the content of the comments I made as being generally correct reflections at least of my own experience, I find that the tone should have been gentler and more respectful, both to better demonstrate my deep and sincere

---

[55] Lindquist & Cross, *supra* note 1, at 1173, 1187-88.

[56] *Id.* at 1200.

[57] BENJAMIN FRANKLIN, THE AUTOBIOGRAPHY OF BENJAMIN FRANKLIN 17 (Peter Conn ed., 2005) (1771). The law of defamation also respects this distinction.

[58] Scott Hamilton Dewey, *The Case of the Missing Holding: The Misreading of* Zafiro v. United States*, the Misreplication of Precedent, and the Misfiring of Judicial Process in Federal Jurisprudence on the Doctrine of Mutually Exclusive Defenses*, 41 VALPARAISO L. REV. 149, 254-66 (2006).

respect for judges and to make it clearer to readers that in my opinion, problems that I identified with the use and transmission of precedent were not the fault of individual judges, or even of the judicial profession, but rather result from shortcomings of the American common law system as presently structured. Although few federal judges have the time to slog through a 120-page law review article on a relatively minor subject, if any did and found my tone to be disrespectful, I must apologize.

I should also confess that having worked for years as a judicial attorney for a state appellate court—thus as a sort of under-assistant adjunct quasi-judge, required to research and draft a good many appellate opinions—I fell into many of the same traps that I described in the earlier article and will describe in this one. So, far from feeling superior to or dismissive of the judges who have faced similar problems, I entirely sympathize. Moreover, I feel that I personally share many of the tendencies and characteristics that I have seen in judges, so I sympathize on that basis, too.

Let me emphasize: I respect judges as a group more than other participants in our legal system, including attorneys and law professors. More than most of the others, judges exemplify public service, sacrificing personal gain, leisure time, and (usually) celebrity while working just as hard or harder than their non-judicial counterparts. Judges, in my view, are the primary source of any actual justice that comes out of our adversarial legal system, for while attorneys' goal may be to win regardless of where truth, fairness, or abstract justice may lie, judges seek to attain all those higher goals while also carefully respecting the rules of our adversarial legal process.[59] It's a demanding job that most laypeople and even many attorneys and law professors do not really understand,[60] and to me, judges are the usually unsung, often underappreciated heroes of our justice system.

Over the course of several years, I worked for three (or four) different judges, one of them a federal district judge, two of them state appellate judges (the fourth a proto-judge—a law professor who was married to a judge, was angling for a judgeship, and received a state judicial appointment soon after I worked for him). Although I cannot claim any deep insight into the judicial mind, I certainly have seen that mind, and the judicial community, at work. From that observation, I have drawn some (hopefully valid) generalizations.

---

[59] Also, even though judges have much more actual power and responsibility than law professors, the average judge is less self-important than the average law professor.

[60] As Judge Posner observes, "I am struck by how unrealistic are the conceptions of the judge held by most people, including practicing lawyers and eminent law professors, who have never been judges—and even by some judges." *See* POSNER, HOW JUDGES THINK, *supra* note 6, at 2.

All of "my" judges are intensely intelligent, conscientious, and hard-working. Although I might have been somewhat fortunate, my experiences with other chambers lead me to believe that these attributes are significantly more common among judges than among the general public or, frankly, the general run of lawyers. Judges tend to be high-achievers, not perhaps in a flashy way, but more likely in a persistent, determined way. In my experience, judges worry, sincerely, about little as well as big cases, trying hard to get them "right." Given these attributes, unsurprisingly, judges tend toward perfectionism, and like other perfectionists who always make extra efforts to do things just right, they may feel the sting of criticism, or being told they were wrong, more sharply than the ordinary person. This helps account for reversal anxiety. Although some commentators may tend to minimize the significance of reversal anxiety among judges, I would not. I have seen it in operation and believe it is very real, at least with some cases.[61]

I believe this is partly because, notwithstanding a century of discourse on how judges necessarily *make* the law, or Justice Jackson's institutionally self-deprecating (but correct) observation that the Supreme Court is only infallible because it is final,[62] I suspect that most judges—unconsciously if not consciously—still believe that if only they try hard enough and have enough time, there is a pre-existing, objective "right" answer out there to be found, as under the traditional, nineteenth-century formalist view of the law. It is my impression that this attitude is held more like a religious belief than an intellectual understanding, and so occupies a different part of the judge's psyche than mere facts. Just as individuals, depending on their religious traditions and how fervently they embrace them, could "know" as a fact that abortion is legal and widespread but still be morally appalled by the thought of it, or know that pork is at some level a food like any other but still be unable to eat it, or know that there may be billions of stars and galaxies out there but still believe there is a God who takes a special interest in our

---

[61] In an earlier article, I referred to judges' "terror" of reversal. By a straightforward dictionary definition, this term is hyperbolic and inappropriate, given that judges face possible reversal with every decision they make, and they continue to do their jobs. But by a different definition, the term does apply. The "terror" judges—perhaps especially fledgling judges—feel at reversal, I believe, is more like the terror a consistently top-performing student feels at the prospect of getting a D- or F despite all her best efforts—the terror of feeling that your unblemished record and reputation will be shattered, and that it will affect your future. People who have been in that situation will remember that such "terror" can be very real. Judge Posner notes less dramatically that "judges do not like to be reversed," both for career reasons and power reasons, and so judges may consciously or unconsciously bend the facts of their opinions to fit established legal categories more snugly and so give better chances of avoiding reversal. POSNER, HOW JUDGES THINK, *supra* note 6, at 70.

[62] Brown v. Allen, 344 U.S. 443, 540 (Jackson, J., concurring) ("We are not final because we are infallible, but we are infallible only because we are final.").

planet or some of the people on it, my sense is that many/most judges "know" that judges *make* law but still believe, at the core of their beings, that they are faithfully *finding* it—at least as much as possible. They try *not* to make law. Justice Jackson notwithstanding, judges also tend to be more respectful of authority than the average person (or lawyer), which includes the hierarchical organization of courts—the judicial profession appropriately tends to select such individuals. Thus judges tend to accept the holdings of higher courts as "right" and may feel some embarrassment when their decisions were held "wrong," or frustration and resignation when they had to grapple with cases so complicated and confusing that there was little hope of getting them entirely "right."

The judicial culture and community furthers these tendencies toward perfectionism and a quasi-mystical faith in "right" answers. Judges read each others' (published) opinions[63]—indeed, they may be explicitly professionally obliged to, under a duty to keep abreast of the latest doctrinal developments within their jurisdictions. They have to follow closely which decisions are reversed or upheld, and they (and judicial attorneys or other court staff) are also well aware of which of their fellows tend to get reversed frequently. Some judges who are upheld nearly all the time may develop a certain heightened confidence bordering on smugness; judges who are reversed more than most may be the subject of hushed whispers or tongue-clucking reflecting an unstated understanding that they are to some extent losers at the judicial game, a game which most judges, I think, believe implicitly if not explicitly is not just a matter of luck, or is less a matter of luck than it may actually be. Even the "winners" at the game will remember very clearly the few times they have ever been reversed. Reversal ratios are reviewed whenever a judge is considered for elevation to a higher court, and judges are well aware of this. So reversal anxiety is closely linked to hopes for elevation, which is a powerful motivating factor for many judges. Some rare, thicker-skinned judges might go for years tempting reversal by knowingly and deliberately making decisions politically, ideologically, or procedurally out of step with the higher court. Although like-thinkers will applaud such behavior, it tends to make the wider judicial and legal community uncomfortable, sort of like apostasy to an established religion, and may tend to lead to some degree of professional marginalization (as with the federal Ninth Circuit to some extent). I also suspect such behavior is much more likely to occur among the lifetime-appointed federal judiciary than among more vulnerable elected/reconfirmed state judges.

As highly intelligent people, judges are, inevitably, both creative and curious to some extent, but at least when it comes to judging, their creativity and curiosity

[63] And thanks to the Internet revolution and online legal research, they also will frequently stumble upon and read their colleagues' unpublished opinions as well.

tend to be cabined and constrained, more like with art forms focused on careful, accurate reproductions according to an elaborate set of rules, such as performing classical music or practicing ancient Chinese calligraphy, than freer and more experimental art forms such as improvisational jazz or painting like Jackson Pollock. I find that judges, as careful perfectionists, temperamentally tend to be rule-followers and like to have rules to follow—how else can you measure your proximity to perfection? That is entirely in keeping with their role and with public expectations; most citizens would not like the idea of judges as risk-takers performing uncontrolled experiments, and where courts have engaged in some experimental behavior, such as mandating school desegregation by busing, the public has not been amused. There are some notable judicial innovators, but they are rare.[64] I believe it is fair to say that most judges conceive of themselves and their roles primarily as rule-followers, not innovators. As Judge Posner observes, "The decision-making freedom that judges have is an involuntary freedom."[65]

If judges generally are inclined toward perfectionism, to believe in right answers, to follow rules and not take chances, and are aware that their performance is monitored by their fellow judges—and if, moreover, this is precisely how the judicial profession and society at large feel judges should be—then this helps explain both precedent and the professional worship of precedent, as well as the tendency of precedent to harden into firmer rules—standards becoming rules over time, for instance. Although some legal scholars have dismissed precedent-based decisionmaking as a mere fig-leaf covering individual preferences, or as "CYA" judging, the fact remains that some fig leaves are better than others, judges know that other judges (or attorneys or law professors) may scrutinize their fig leaves, and careful, doctrine-based decisionmaking, whether for CYA purposes (including protection from reversal and from criticism by peers or others in the legal

---

[64] One example that springs to mind is the ubiquitous Judge Richard A. Posner, who gets away with it as a life-tenured federal appellate judge, one of the (if not *the*) most respected and cited living legal scholars in America, and an uncommonly effective writer. For one minor sample, see the discussion of Posner's innovative handling of the single most important antagonistic defenses case ever, *Zafiro v. United States*, 506 U.S. 534 (1993)/*United States v. Zafiro*, 945 F.2d 881 (7th Cir. 1991), in Dewey, *supra* note 58, at 160-65. Another example of a judicial innovator is one of my personal favorite judges, Judge Jack B. Weinstein of the Eastern District of New York, who frequently has experimented creatively with rules of procedure and evidence in tackling some of the biggest and most complex and difficult class-action litigations of the past half-century, including those regarding asbestos and Agent Orange. As a federal district judge, though (hence more subject to reversal than circuit judges are), Judge Weinstein's judicial innovations reportedly have led to reversal fairly often and I suspect might make many more traditional-minded judges uncomfortable. *See* Martha Minow, *Judge for the Situation: Judge Jack Weinstein, Creator of Temporary Administrative Agencies*, 97 COLUM. L. REV. 2010, 2031 (Nov. 1997) (noting frequent reversals by the Second Circuit that won Judge Weinstein the nickname " 'reversible Jack'").

[65] POSNER, HOW JUDGES THINK, *supra* note 6, at 9.

profession) or not, is exactly what our legal system expects judges to do.[66] As various scholars have pointed out, careful, precedent-based reasoning as a requirement for judicial decisionmaking—moreover, reasoning that is reviewed by other appellate panel members—necessarily helps to inject professional discipline into judicial process even where decisions may be motivated all or in part by personal or political preferences.[67] Anyone who has worked closely with judges can attest that they work much harder, and suffer over doctrinal reasoning much longer, than would be necessary just to create a minimum doctrinal fig leaf (justifying or rationalizing argument). Furthermore, as Judge Wald has rightly pointed out, the incredibly wide range of issues that can come before generalist judges helps to assure that in many or most cases, judges probably will not have a strong personal preference one way or the other.[68] As Judge Posner observes, most cases are routine.[69]

Another factor that, I believe, favors precedent involves pulling aside the black robes a little,[70] for in reality, much of the work of courts is now done by judicial adjuncts—clerks in the federal courts, clerks or judicial attorneys in state courts. Judges manage teams of subordinates, and on many opinions act as chief editor rather than chief author. That is nothing to be embarrassed about, or to try to hide from the public—it's the way the system works, and has to, unless the public wants to pay for a lot more judges or find a way to limit the volume of litigation (or criminal activity), or else accept much more summary justice.[71] Practices vary,

---

[66] Notably, the main difference between published and unpublished opinions is the elaborateness of the precedential fig leaf. Depending on the judge, the chambers, or the case, unpublished opinions are often not so different from published ones.

[67] *See, e.g.*, Fleisher, *supra* note 3, at 960-61, 966; Richards & Kritzer, *supra* note 10, at 305-06, 307-08 (June 2002); POSNER, HOW JUDGES THINK, *supra* note 6, at 12 ("Most judges, like serious artists, are trying to do a 'good job,' with what is 'good' being defined by the standards for the 'art' in question. The judicial art prominently includes the legalist factors, and so those factors figure prominently in judicial decisions—and rightly so."). Posner is forthright regarding how non-doctrinal considerations also figure into the equation of judicial decisionmaking, however. *See id.* at 10-11, 72-73 (and generally).

[68] Wald, *supra* note 6, at 237.

[69] POSNER, HOW JUDGES THINK, *supra* note 6, at 46.

[70] Judge Posner notes, frankly, that "most judges are cagey, even coy, in discussing what they do." *Id.* at 2. He also comments on judges' "professional mystification" to "overcome the laity's mistrust" by "developing a mystique that exaggerates not only the [judge's] skills but also his disinterest," *id.* at 3, and finds that they are reticent about talking frankly about judging, even to each other. *Id.* at 6; see also *id.* at 72. This being so, judges do not like to have the judicial black robes pulled aside, even a little.

[71] I sense that some judges still seem somewhat uncomfortable about discussions of the role of clerks, or perhaps even the acknowledgment of their existence, to the nonlegal community. Nevertheless, the role of judicial adjuncts is major and growing, especially in busy legal/judicial markets, and in the long run, there will be no use in judges trying to hide it from the general public

and some appellate judges still write all their own opinions with only research help from subordinates, but many if not most allow their subordinates to research and draft many or most of the cases that come into chambers, although the judges still of course keep overall responsibility for the work products and decisions that result and generally take that responsibility very seriously. The point here is that this should favor the observance of precedent. Judicial attorneys/clerks normally will be younger, less experienced, closer to law school and their training in use of precedent, and less confident to just decide unilaterally what they think the law should be and go with that, or even if they do, more likely to structure a careful, precedent-based argument to support that direction in order to justify it to the judge as well as to the wider world. Such judicial adjuncts are likely to feel the need for a fig leaf even more than judges do. Even more experienced judicial attorneys are still clearly subordinates, less confident or able to unilaterally declare what the law is than a judge, and their conclusions are less final. In one sense, the position of judicial adjuncts in relation to their judges is something like that of inexperienced new judges relative to experienced senior judges on the same court (hesitant, and with a lot to learn); in other ways, the relationship is like that of judges on a lower court relative to judges on a higher court (subject to reversal). Thus, in my experience, the use of judicial adjuncts builds a heightened regard for precedent and an additional layer of review of that precedent into the system.

Moreover, in my own experience, the legal realists' glib argument that there's precedent to cover any situation at a whim is not really true in most circumstances.[72] It may be truer of some cluttered, undisciplined old areas of the common law, like torts, but in other areas or cases, precedent often points in relatively clear directions that are hard to resist. If, for example, twenty cases point in one direction while only one or two point the other direction, one has a harder

---

or from themselves. If the growing reliance upon judicial adjuncts is truly a bad thing, then it will have to be confronted, limited, and regulated in a way it has not been in the past; if it is not a bad thing, then it will have to be accepted as the fact of legal and judicial life that it increasingly is. In my own, admittedly somewhat limited experience, I have found both federal clerks and state judicial attorneys to be generally competent, conscientious, and responsible, and certainly not a disaster for the justice system. For some perceptive commentary on the growing role of judicial adjuncts in various courts, and how this might or might not be a problem, *see, e.g.*, David J. Garrow, *Acolytes in Arms*, 9 GREEN BAG 2D 411 (Summer 2006); Rick A. Swanson & Stephen L. Wasby, *Good Stewards: Law Clerk Influence in State High Courts*, 29 JUST. SYS. J. 24 (2008); Robert S. Thompson, *Comment on Professors Karlan's and Abrams'* Structural Threats to Judicial Independence, 72 S. CAL. L. REV. 559 (1999); Sally J. Kenney, *Puppeteers or Agents? What Lazarus's* Closed Chambers *Adds to Our Understanding of Law Clerks at the U.S. Supreme Court*, 25 LAW & SOC. INQUIRY 185 (Winter 2000); JOHN B. OAKLEY & ROBERT S. THOMPSON, LAW CLERKS AND THE JUDICIAL PROCESS (1980).

[72] I agree with Judge Posner's conclusion that "the realists exaggerated the open area, sometimes implying that all cases are indeterminate." POSNER, HOW JUDGES THINK, *supra* note 6, at 112.

time constructing a careful, precedent-based argument going the other direction. Legal reasoning courses may train attorneys to find one favorable case, focus on it, and say it controls the whole decision (while softpedaling countervailing authority), but I have not found judges or judicial attorneys to operate that way. To determine what the relevant law is, they tend to look carefully at a number of neighboring cases—often even if such cases were not mentioned in the briefs—and if these are too many (or too hard) to distinguish, they usually will not follow an outlier.

Precedent also may affect the aggressiveness of decisions even when it does not determine their valence. Social science studies seemingly tend to focus on valence (the most obvious and quantifiable measurement of outcome, up or down) rather than how far-reaching the decision is. Even if ideology were determining outcomes, it might be that the thicket of countervailing precedents weakens the opinion in question over what pure ideology might have wished—exerting a braking action. This likely would be difficult to study by traditional quantitative analytical techniques and would instead require looking at each case with a sense of how constrained the language is relative to the standard of pure unconstrained ideology. At any rate, precedent may have significant but subtle impacts that are hard to measure.

For all these objective or subjective reasons, I personally agree with the camp that holds that precedent matters quite substantially to judicial decision-making.[73] From experience, I also find that there are strong practical reasons favoring precedent—reasons that only someone who has worked at length in a court might really understand.

One goal that judges and judicial adjuncts share, a goal that Judge Posner has described repeatedly and convincingly, is efficiency in the face of time and resource constraints.[74] Although no one aspect of precedent is sufficient alone to justify or explain the existence of the doctrine, in my experience, the efficiency

[73] In the interest of full disclosure, I should probably note that I am also not quite as impressed with number-crunching studies of the judiciary as some of the more avid number-crunchers are. Judge Posner, who is more favorable toward quantitative analysis, nevertheless points out how "many judicial decisions are made under conditions of uncertainty, precluding quantification of the relevant variables." POSNER, HOW JUDGES THINK, *supra* note 6, at 109, *see also id.* at 148. For some informed, insightful commentary on both the strengths and shortcomings of applying quantitative analysis to judicial opinions, see generally Deborah R. Hensler, Beyond Prosletyzing: Some Thoughts on Empirical Research on the Law (unpublished manuscript, on file with the author); Deborah R. Hensler, *Researching Civil Justice: Problems and Pitfalls*, 51 LAW & CONTEMP. PROBS. 55 (1988). *See also* Gerhardt, *supra* note 8, at 1749-52.

[74] *See, e.g.*, POSNER, HOW JUDGES THINK, *supra* note 6, at 145.

factor is a powerful practical reason that should not be underemphasized. For whatever judges are doing in theory, in actuality, they are deciding cases—lots of them.[75] Courts are relatively large bureaucracies with many workers engaged in processing an unending—and usually steadily growing—stream of cases. The time of judges and judicial adjuncts is not unlimited, and the constitutional status of courts makes them relatively difficult to expand and unable to expand themselves unilaterally. Judges facing increasingly crowded dockets have no choice but to be concerned with efficiency and expeditiousness.[76] Following precedents presumably "takes less time and effort than revisiting questions" and deciding them from the ground up whenever they reappear.[77] As Lindquist and Cross observe, "The system is structurally ideal for judges; matters on which a judge's preference intensity is relatively low may be quickly resolved in accordance with existing precedent, while matters about which the judge cares deeply can be analyzed more thoroughly and resolved by setting new precedents, to be followed by future judges."[78]

My own experience is in keeping with Lindquist and Cross' analysis. For me, as for other judicial officers and adjuncts, precedent offered a convenient way not to think about certain issues. Lest this statement sound flippant, cavalier, or irresponsible, let me explain. In the case-processing business that judges are in, it is dangerous to devote too much time and attention to any one case, or too much time to any one issue in any one case, among the many cases and issues one must process in a timely way to keep on top of the docket and have cases ready before oral arguments. As Judge Posner observes, judges, unlike legal academicians, do not have limitless time in which to consider a case and get it just right;[79] to do so would be, inevitably, to slight the many other cases on the docket that also need and deserve timely resolution. Personal preferences aside, I think I was like other judicial staff in welcoming clear authority that would let me resolve an issue relatively quickly, painlessly, and confidently, so that I could move on to consider other issues. This was especially so when the particular issue was a relatively

---

[75] Judge Posner notes that law, for judges, is "the activity of deciding cases," adding, "The duty to decide is primary." Posner, *Reasoning by Analogy*, *supra* note 19, at 770.

[76] *See, e.g.,* Wald, *supra* note 6, at 237 ("The size and complexity of our docket only rarely affords the liberty of ideological musing[.]"); Richard A. Posner, *The Role of the Judge in the Twenty-First Century*, 86 BOSTON U. L. REV. 1049, 1050 (2006) (noting strain on federal appellate courts if caseloads continue to grow, and difficulty of expanding appellate courts); KLEIN, *supra* note 9, at 17-18 (noting sharpening time constraints on federal appellate judges); Frank M. Coffin & Robert A. Katzmann, *Steps Towards Optimal Judicial Workways: Perspectives from the Federal Bench*, 59 N.Y.U. ANN. SURV. AM L. 377, 385 (2003).

[77] Lindquist and Cross, *supra* note 1, 1165-66.

[78] *Id.* at 1166.

[79] Posner, *The Role of the Judge in the Twenty-First Century*, *supra* note 66, at 1054.

peripheral one, or the subject of a relatively weak argument. There are few limits on the numbers of issues attorneys may raise in briefs, so they tend to throw in the kitchen sink, raising numerous minor issues along with major ones. Presumably to keep under their word limits, attorneys often mention the more minor issues briefly and somewhat elliptically, which can make them harder rather than easier for the court to consider, because judges and judicial attorneys, being conscientious, generally take the time to try to figure out and pay respect to each argument and subargument, even those that pretty clearly appear to be junk arguments. All too often, I found briefs to be poorly written and organized and remarkably unhelpful in general—meaning that I had to do the work the attorney was supposed to have done.[80] I personally found nothing more annoying than an apparently minor issue or side argument that took an undue amount of time and kept me from turning my attention to weightier questions that needed careful consideration and resolution. Clear precedent on an issue, where it existed, was an especially welcome friend for rejecting such nuisance arguments.

In short, to get back to the somewhat flippant, sassy title of this article, precedent gives (and is supposed to give, and it is necessary that it or something else gives) judges the opportunity *not to think* about each little issue that comes in the chambers door—or at least not think as long or as searchingly as otherwise might be required.[81] It is supposed to be a legitimate shortcut, resting on the work and wisdom of earlier courts and judges in considering and resolving the same or similar issues. It keeps courts from being in the position of Hobbes' idiot, seeing a

---

[80] According to David Klein, a good many federal appellate judges agree. *See* KLEIN, *supra* note 9, at 58 (citing judges reporting occasionally missing crucial authorities because of inadequate briefs and that "The briefs do a miserable job," "The worst thing about judging is the low quality of the lawyers," and "Briefs are very, very unreliable. The quality of appellate advocacy, I think, is declining. More and more lawyers write poorly."). See also Swanson & Wasby, *supra* note 71, at 33-34 (noting frequency with which lawyers fail to bring crucial facts or points of law to state high courts' attention). Of course, Klein's federal appellate judges likely have it easy on that score compared to state appellate judges, given that federal courts are more paper-intensive at both the trial and appellate levels, and the average level of attorney performance is generally conceded to be higher in federal than in state courts. Thus, whatever problems federal judges report regarding briefs and attorneys are likely to be significantly worse in state courts. That the attorney culture in state courts is typically more oral and less written than in federal courts also may impact the quality of state court briefs. I recall when I was an extern in federal district court, and a very well-known, successful local criminal attorney who usually practiced in state courts came to our court to plead against extradition of a client. He frankly had no legitimate arguments anyway, but his briefs were so poor that the clerks laughed at them and showed them to us externs as examples of what not to do in federal court. The attorney remained impressive orally and on his feet, though, even as his motions were denied.

[81] The title is, of course, a riff on Judge Posner's fine book on judicial process, HOW JUDGES THINK, *supra* note 6. It also derives from legal realist Max Radin's 1925 article, *The Theory of Judicial Decision, or How Judges Think*, 11 A.B.A. J. 357.

parade of similar phenomena but counting "one" each time one passes and treating it as entirely new and unique because of an inability to recognize the similarity.

But this takes us back to the issues that Schauer and others have addressed. My efficiency and confidence in rejecting or accepting an argument based upon precedent presumed, as judicial staff must, that the precedent was good, and so relied on the earlier courts that had created and transmitted the precedent to me across the years. Though most of the opinions I drafted were, like most judicial opinions, unpublished, they nevertheless helped to perpetuate and reinforce the precedent in question, particularly given that judicial staff using online legal research databases now can (and do) consult unpublished as well as published authorities for ideas about how to handle similar cases.

So, what if the precedent I relied on was unsound?

In the (many) pages that follow, I discuss an example of unsound precedent taking root and entrenching itself deeper and deeper within a jurisdiction, with new, reaffirming precedent piling itself high atop the originating and discovering decisions and covering their tracks until it became virtually impossible to detect their unsoundness—primarily through a process of judges working in good faith and reliance upon past courts as I did. Notably, the particular example is one where the precedent was applied mostly to side- or throwaway arguments that courts wished to address quickly. Although this example by no means gives the whole story of the (mis)use of precedent, I contend that it characterizes all too much of the use of precedent, and helps to build fundamental flaws into our common law system.

The testing ground for creation and transmission of precedent that is examined in this article involves the Illinois state courts' doctrine of antagonistic defenses—Illinois' version of a doctrine that exists in nearly all American state or federal jurisdictions.[82] The doctrine goes by various alternate names in different jurisdictions: irreconcilable defenses, mutually antagonistic defenses, mutually exclusive defenses. Some jurisdictions distinguish between higher forms of antagonism by labeling them mutually antagonistic or mutually exclusive as against merely antagonistic; Illinois does not. Many states and most federal circuits borrowed their versions of the doctrine from one of the three federal appellate circuits that spontaneously originated iterations of the doctrine during the 1960s and '70s, but Illinois' version is home-grown, dates back a century or more, and

---

[82] *See generally* Wade R. Habeeb, Annotation, *Antagonistic Defenses as Ground for Separate Trials of Codefendants in Criminal Cases*, 82 A.L.R. 3d 245 (2005).

was (seemingly) little influenced by decisions in other jurisdictions. The federal part of this story was discussed at excessive length elsewhere;[83] the Illinois part of this story is discussed at excessive length in the pages that follow.

In whatever version, the basic idea of the doctrine is that although defendants indicted jointly for the same criminal transaction normally will be tried jointly, the trial court must try them separately if their defenses are so antagonistic that one or more defendant would suffer prejudice from a joint trial.[84] Perhaps the classic definition of sufficient antagonism to require severance of trials in the federal system is when for the jury to believe one defendant, it must convict the other;[85] but that is not the only definition in federal courts or state courts, where various alternate definitions exist, including when defenses are irreconcilable and the conflict may lead the jury to infer that both defendants are guilty;[86] when defendants take the stand to accuse their codefendants and exculpate themselves;[87] when defendants accuse each other, regardless of whether they take the stand to do so;[88] and so on. A jurisdiction will often have more than one definition, sometimes contradicting each other. Although cases of true antagonism requiring severance should be very rare and fact-specific, as courts have observed, the claim of such antagonism has become a standard ploy that criminal defense attorneys frequently raise in cases with multiple defendants.

Another point that nearly all the different versions have in common is that, based on long and careful study of the doctrine's development in most federal and state jurisdictions, it is my considered opinion that the doctrine of antagonistic defenses is, in essence, a "junk" doctrine in nearly every, if not every, jurisdiction. That is, in most jurisdictions, it entered the case law, spontaneously or by importation, without a proper holding or even proper consideration of what the supposed rule meant, but then took on a life of its own and propagated numerous progeny that hide its questionable origins and lend it an undeserved air of legitimacy, inevitability, and long pedigree. Thus, the doctrine of antagonistic defenses, though not perhaps terribly interesting in itself, presents a fascinating case study of the theories and processes of precedent and *stare decisis* gone haywire and seemingly unable to correct themselves. I believe I have demonstrated that with

[83] *See* Dewey, *supra* note 58. The D.C., 5th, and 7th Circuits were the ones that developed the most influential versions of the doctrine. *Id.* at 170-71.

[84] *See id.* at 151-52. A full list of the relatively limited scholarly literature on the topic may be found in *id.* at 153 n.17. *See also* Habeeb, *supra* note 81 (covering state and federal jurisdictions).

[85] *See* Dewey, *supra* note 58, at 171, 176-80.

[86] *See id.* at 170-76.

[87] *See, e.g.*, People v. Braune, 363 Ill. 551, 2 N.E.2d 839 (1936).

[88] See, e.g., People v. Daugherty, 102 Ill.2d 533, 468 N.E.2d 969 (1984).

regard to the federal circuits, particularly by showing how some federal circuits became so entangled in their own confused versions of the doctrine that they have been unable to discard them even after the United States Supreme Court told them to do so.[89] I believe that I could demonstrate that with regard to most states, with the exception of a handful of mostly low-population states that never particularly developed a doctrine of antagonistic defenses, most notably West Virginia. And I believe that I will demonstrate that to readers regarding the state of Illinois in the pages that follow.

American legal scholarship has always been heavily slanted toward federal law, of course, and law students and professors might be inclined to think, "Who cares about state law, particularly a state I don't live in?"[90] However, just as scholars of precedent fairly recently realized that that they had to shift their focus down from the Supreme Court to lower federal courts because that's where the law really is, the same reasoning applies to state law and state courts with even greater force—for most people, that's where the doctrinal law that affects them is created and enforced, particularly with regard to criminal law and criminal procedure. Others who care about state law but live outside Illinois might be inclined to snigger at the Sucker State. They shouldn't. Generally, their own jurisdictions, federal or state, haven't done any better than Illinois did in (mis)handling the doctrine of antagonistic defenses and have experienced similar problems.

This article is definitely not intended as an attack on Illinois or its courts and judges, but rather an effort to illuminate what may be systemic and recurrent problems with judicial process in courts nationwide. To try to help avoid hurt feelings (since as a former court employee, I know how sensitive judges can be regarding criticism), I end the story in 1985, hopefully giving most if not all participants in my story time to exit the stage gracefully one way or another. And although this story specifically concerns the evolution of a legal doctrine in Illinois, it generally concerns a much wider problem that goes right to the heart of the American common law system. For if precedent cannot be created or transmitted correctly, or adjusted or discarded when it isn't, then the interwoven doctrines of precedent and *stare decisis* can have no legitimacy. The strange career

[89] *See* generally Dewey, *supra* note 58.

[90] When I was working in a federal court, a funny, good-natured law professor who visited the court reflected on the difference between practicing in state and federal court and described state courts with a Yiddish word that I don't remember but that clearly conveyed the idea of "junk," "trash," or "ghetto." Although that is doubtlessly somewhat harsh and unfair toward most lawyers, judges, and court staff who work in state courts, there is no question they rank lower in the legal profession's hierarchy, and that many law schools and professors correspondingly tend to be dismissive of state law and courts.

of the Illinois antagonistic defenses doctrine is a century-long story of precedent and *stare decisis* breaking down in at least one area of the law.

Readers also may ask, "Why Illinois?" A disclaimer: I have no particular connection with the state. After reviewing the doctrinal trajectories of many different states, I found its to be somewhat longer and more engaging than most. Its antagonistic defenses doctrine is also of interest in that it is entirely home-grown, not derived from the federal versions that I have already studied ad nauseum. Also, the Illinois doctrine got a starring role in Justice Stevens' concurring opinion in *Zafiro v. United States*,[91] the case in which the Supreme Court specifically instructed the federal circuits that there is no mandatory automatic severance rule for antagonistic/irreconcilable/ mutually exclusive defenses—and were frequently ignored.[92] Justice Stevens, in arguing for a narrowing of the holding in *Zafiro*,[93] cited *People v. Braune*,[94] a 1936 Illinois case that is one of the most striking, dramatic antagonistic defenses cases from any jurisdiction in any decade. The strange career of *Braune*—decided, ignored, forgotten, then suddenly rediscovered after 40 years—is just one more interesting piece of the strange career of the Illinois doctrine of antagonistic defenses.

The following account gives the story of the gradual assuming into existence of a rule nobody ever intended that was neither necessary nor justified.[95] It began with the sporadic appearance of the word "antagonism" or "antagonistic" in contexts clearly distinct from that of antagonistic defenses, such as joint-representation cases where the same lawyer or lawyers represented two codefendants with conflicting interests, or cases regarding the admissibility against a defendant of incriminating pretrial statements by codefendants, which Illinois courts had recognized as a problem potentially requiring severance of codefendants already by 1916, long before *Bruton v. United States*,[96] the United States Supreme Court's most powerful statement on that issue. Lawyers later took such statements regarding antagonism out of context to argue that antagonism in itself required severance of codefendants. This led later courts to mention the term in

[91] 506 U.S. 534 (1993).

[92] *See generally* Dewey, *supra* note 58.

[93] 506 U.S at 541-45 (Stevens, J., concurring).

[94] 363 Ill. 551, 2 N.E.2d 839.

[95] This explains the other part of the article title, which is a reference to C. Vann Woodward's classic study of the origins of racial segregation in America, THE STRANGE CAREER OF JIM CROW (1955), which describes how a new and unfortunate legal and cultural institution emerged and gradually took root, then later came to be viewed as natural, inevitable, and eternal. In other words, memory of segregation's actual and fairly recent historical origins was quickly lost, and the unsound new innovation was presumed to have existed from time immemorial.

[96] 391 U.S. 123 (1968).

conjunction with severance in later opinions, which in turn reinforced the nascent, if juridically unfounded, intellectual association between antagonism and severance.

With time, this relationship had become so unquestioningly assumed that courts began to state it as a rule. With more time and further summarization and paraphrasing of what earlier courts had said, the rule transformed into an exclusive rule: severance may only be had where there are antagonistic defenses. Through a process of good logic following bad, this in turn led to the recategorization of incriminating codefendant statements, an independent potential basis for severance that existed long before there was any talk of antagonistic defenses, as a subcategory of antagonistic defenses, even if the pretrial statements had no relationship to the defenses offered. Most opinions offering the antagonistic defenses rule came to be ones regarding codefendant statements where the rule was unnecessary and inappropriate, even as other courts went on deciding the same sorts of codefendant statement issues without ever mentioning antagonism (presumably because counsel did not raise the issue). A plethora of opinions stating the antagonistic defenses rule in passing before affirming the trial court quickly piled high atop the original opinions that made the ambiguous, confused, or erroneous statements giving rise to the rule, helping to hide its questionable origins and give it an air of long-established pedigree. Confusion about similar terms in different contexts also led the misbegotten antagonistic defenses rule to jump into and contaminate the otherwise separate, unrelated line of cases regarding joint representation.

Meanwhile, ironically, a 1936 case involving actual antagonistic defenses, and in which the extreme facts entirely justified severing the codefendants, was ignored for nearly forty years. That case was rediscovered and brought out of mothballs right around the same time that a court realized that no previous court had yet made an appropriate effort to define "antagonism" during the preceding fifty years that the supposed rule was taking shape. Thereafter, the long-forgotten true case of antagonistic defenses was misread and misused to help justify the antagonistic defenses rule that had grown up entirely without it. Although this story stops in 1985, the confusion persists to the present.

The data set for this century-long longitudinal study of the development of a body of precedent includes the slightly more than 200 cases that comprise what I refer to as Illinois' antagonistic defenses "lineage."[97] This lineage includes every case that refers to antagonistic defenses, plus some others that do not but were cited as authority on that point by others that do. The idea was to check for absolutely

[97] *See* Alphabetical Case Index—Illinois Antagonistic Defenses Lineage, *infra.*

certain whether there was any holding establishing a legitimate, non-erroneous, not already previously contaminated basis for the doctrine. I have satisfied myself that there wasn't. Hopefully the following lengthy discussion will satisfy the reader as well.

But, on with the story.

IN THE BEGINNING: EARLY CASES AND THE ABSENCE OF "ANTAGONISM," 1876-1925

White v. People (1876),[98] the earliest relevant case in the antagonistic defenses lineage in Illinois jurisprudence, and seemingly the first case to reverse for lack of severance, said nothing about antagonism and cited no authority. The case hinged on multiple instructional errors, plus a procedural error based on an improper date on the death-penalty form.[99] White claimed that only he and codefendant Cozens were present when the victim, Harris, was fatally shot, but White said he did not participate in the killing and only aided in the coverup afterward, including concealment of the gun used.[100] Cozens made a similar argument.[101] The trial court's jury instruction said that if the jury found that both defendants were present at the scene and had used the gun, kept and concealed the gun, and mutually concealed the fact of the crime, then the jury should find both guilty of murder—making no allowance for White's contention that he was merely an accessory after the fact.[102] The *White* court found "fatal error" in the jury instructions, requiring reversal.[103] The case also involved proto-*Bruton* problems, in that evidence competent against only one defendant but very damaging to the other was admitted, and the court observed, "In such case[s] it is very difficult for a juror to divest himself, under instructions, from the illegitimate effect of such evidence upon the party who ought not to be affected thereby."[104] Because the court already was reversing on other grounds, though, the court concluded, "[I]t is unnecessary to discuss these questions. This is a case where it is eminently fit that these plaintiffs in error should have separate trials."[105] The opinion never mentioned or considered antagonism.

---

[98] 81 Ill. 333 (Jan. 1876) (Dickey, J.).
[99] *Id.* at *2.
[100] *Id.* at *3.
[101] *Id.*
[102] *Id.* at *2.
[103] *Id.*
[104] *Id.* at *3.
[105] *Id.*

Although various other early cases appear repeatedly in Illinois' antagonistic defenses lineage—*Doyle v. People* (1893),[106] *Spies v. People* (1887),[107] *Johnson v. People* (1859),[108] *Maton v. People* (1854),[109] and *U.S. v. Marchant* (1827)[110]—they say nothing about antagonism and only cite the basic rule that severance is at the discretion of the trial court. Both *Doyle* and *Spies*—a major early conspiracy case arising from the infamous Haymarket Square bombing of 1886 that addressed severance only in passing—notably added the condition that there must be no abuse of discretion;[111] the earlier cases showed no awareness of any such qualification.[112] The main issue in *Doyle* concerned a jury instruction that identified by name codefendant Lafayette Le Masters, the only defendant who testified at trial, and allowed the jury to consider his interests in the case and his possible motivations for testifying in weighing his testimony's credibility.[113] Doyle contended that this drew attention to his failure to testify and improperly singled out Le Masters from other defendants; the court politely rejected Doyle's argument, explaining that Le Masters, as the only testifying defendant, was situated differently from all the others and that the court was only expressing the well-established rule that jurors may give testimony such weight as the circumstances justify.[114] In *Gillespie v. People* (1898),[115] a burglary case, the court, hesitant to derive any rule from *White*, noted that the *White* court, "under the very peculiar circumstances of the case, directed the circuit court to give the parties separate trials[,]" but observed that "whatever the correct rule may be," there was no basis for review absent abuse of discretion, and the court, citing *Maton*, *Johnson*, *Spies*, and *Doyle*, found no abuse of discretion.[116] Illinois thus ended the nineteenth century with rudimentary jurisprudence regarding severance, and nothing concerning antagonistic defenses.

The early twentieth century added little more. The next case in the antagonism lineage, *People v. Gukouski* (1911),[117] said nothing about antagonism, but cited and followed *Gillespie* and *Doyle* in repeating the basic rule on the trial court's discretion

---

106 147 Ill. 394, 35 N.E. 372 (Oct. 26, 1893) (Wilkin, J.).
107 122 Ill. 1, 12 N.E. 865 (Sept. 14, 1887) (Magruder, J.).
108 22 Ill. 314, 1859 WL 6884 (Apr. 1859).
109 15 Ill. 536, 1854 WL 4731 (June 1854).
110 25 U.S. 480, 1827 WL 3037 (Mar. 12, 1827).
111 Doyle, 147 Ill. at 397; Spies, 122 Ill. at 265.
112 Johnson, 22 Ill. 314; Maton, 15 Ill. 536; Marchant, 25 U.S. 480. Justice Joseph Story penned the *Marchant* opinion.
113 147 Ill. at 397.
114 *Id.* at 397-398.
115 176 Ill. 238, 52 N.E. 250 (Oct. 24, 1898) (Cartwright, J.).
116 *Id.* at 242-243.
117 250 Ill. 231, 95 N.E. 153 (Apr. 19, 1911) (Farmer, J.).

to sever and finding no abuse of discretion.[118] The case involved four Polish co-defendants, all members of a baker's union, who conspired to overturn a bakery wagon and attack the non-union wagon driver during a bakers' strike.[119] During the attack, the driver was shot and later died.[120] The main issue in the case concerned statements and confessions by each of the four defendants regarding who did the shooting, with three defendants tending to place the blame on one, the one shifting blame elsewhere.[121] There were questions as to whether translations of statements from Polish to English were accurate, plus whether the statements showed intent to murder.[122] The court concluded that in a conspiracy case, conspiracy to join in unlawful attack creates responsibility for the entire outcome, even if murder was not contemplated.[123] The issue of codefendant statements implicating another defendant was not raised. *People v. Covitz*,[124] an arson for insurance case at a woolen goods shop, saw two defendants, brothers, move for separate trials based upon a confession by a codefendant who allegedly would receive immunity for testifying for the prosecution, and on the codefendant's prior arson record and attempt to bribe a prosecutor not to indict the defendants.[125] The court explained that the evidence that tended to show a conspiracy to commit arson was competent as against all of them.[126] The court repeated the basic severance rule, cited *Gillespie*, *Doyle*, and *Spies*, and found no abuse of discretion.[127]

People v. Buckminster (1916),[128] another arson for insurance case, did not concern antagonistic defenses or claim to, but was the source of Illinois' pre-*Bruton* rule regarding codefendant confessions and statements that incriminate another defendant—what could and should have been an entirely separate strand of case law that later became entangled with antagonistic defenses. Buckminster's codefendant, ironically named Fink, made an extensive pretrial confession implicating Buckminster[129] but later testified at trial and denied making any confession.[130] The trial court admitted Fink's confession but instructed the jury to

[118] *Id.* at 232-233, 153
[119] *Id.* at 232.
[120] *Id.*
[121] *Id.* at 233-238.
[122] *Id.* at 238-239.
[123] *Id.* at 239-242.
[124] 262 Ill. 514, 104 N.E. 887 (Feb. 21, 1914) (Farmer, J.).
[125] *Id.* at 521-522.
[126] *Id.* at 547.
[127] *Id.* at 550-551.
[128] 274 Ill. 435, 113 N.E. 713 (Jun. 22, 1916) (Carter, J.).
[129] *Id.* at 437-442.
[130] *Id.* at 438.

disregard it as to Buckminster; this was the ruling at issue on appeal.[131] The *Buckminster* court discussed the existing rules on admitting a codefendant's confession as against another defendant, found no Illinois case addressing this specific situation, but held that the part of Fink's confession that implicated Buckminster should have been excluded; admission of that portion was not harmless error even where there was other strong evidence against Buckminster; and a limiting instruction could not cure the resulting prejudice.[132]

The next case to appear in the antagonistic defenses lineage, *People v. Bopp* (1917),[133] also concerned a separate issue—joint representation of multiple defendants by the same counsel—that became entangled with antagonistic defenses nevertheless. In *Bopp*, four young men in stolen cars, all with prison records and most on parole, fled after one of them fatally shot an investigating policeman.[134] Defendant McErlane, one of the parolees, was found with the murder weapon, a .38-caliber revolver, when arrested; defendant Bopp, another parolee, purchased a .38-caliber revolver and cartridges before the murder and had the cartridges when arrested.[135] Bopp was indicted for murder, McErlane as an accessory after the fact.[136] A codefendant testified that McErlane was driving and Bopp held the revolver when the shooting occurred.[137] At his separate trial, Bopp had no counsel but said he wished to hire McErlane's counsel, Williams, and requested a continuance to raise money for his defense.[138] The court, noting the state's considerable expense from maintaining the prosecution witnesses, ordered the trial to proceed and appointed Williams to also represent Bopp.[139] Williams objected that he was unfamiliar with Bopp's case and defense, and that McErlane had indicated that he and Bopp had conflicting interests in the case—in particular, that Bopp claimed McErlane might have fired the fatal shot.[140] Williams accepted his duty to represent Bopp if appointed, but requested a continuance to familiarize himself with Bopp's case and defense, particularly given the prosecution's intention to seek the death penalty.[141] The court, however, ordered the trial to proceed immediately.[142]

---

131 *Id.* at 442.
132 *Id.* at 444-447.
133 279 Ill. 184, 116 N.E. 679 (Jun. 1, 1917) (Dunn, J.).
134 *Id.* at 185-86.
135 *Id.* at 187, 188.
136 *Id.* at 186.
137 *Id.* at 187.
138 *Id.* at 189.
139 *Id.*
140 *Id.* at 189-91.
141 *Id.* at 190.
142 *Id.* at 191.

On appeal, the court held, "It was an abuse of discretion of the court thus to appoint counsel for the defense without giving him an opportunity for investigation or even to prepare his case."[143] The court explained,

> [T]he court should . . . appoint counsel who have no interest adverse to the prisoner which would interfere with a fair presentation of his defense, and time and opportunity should also be given to prepare for such defense. [Counsel] ask[ed] to be excused on the ground that the interest of his client (McErlane) in the trial was antagonistic to that of Bopp. The defenses of these two defendants were not the same. Each was an alibi, but each was dependent upon different testimony from the other. It might well be that testimony tending to exculpate one would tend to inculpate the other. Counsel was not obliged to disclose the facts which had come to his knowledge in his relation of attorney and could not properly do so.[144]

The court faulted the trial court for not accepting Williams' statement that he faced a conflict in representing both defendants, for requiring him to disclose the facts showing inconsistent defenses, for giving him no chance to investigate and prepare Bopp's case or prepare an affidavit for a continuance, and for assuming that his preparation for McErlane's separate trial "was sufficient preparation for the trial of Bopp's case."[145] More broadly, *Bopp* implicitly held that the same counsel should not represent two or more defendants with conflicting interests. As such, *Bopp* is the wellspring of a century's worth of Illinois case law on joint representation of criminal defendants. It is also the first Illinois case to use the word "antagonism" or "antagonistic" in a manner bearing even a remote relationship to the later rule on severance of defendants with antagonistic defenses. Obviously *Bopp* gives no such rule; it says nothing whatsoever about joint or separate trials, and given that Bopp and McErlane were not tried jointly, the issue of antagonistic defenses in a joint trial did not and could not arise. Yet *Bopp*, with its references to antagonism and, fatefully, to evidence exculpating one defendant but inculpating another, would later be taken out of the joint representation context and used to justify Illinois' supposed rule on antagonistic defenses.

The next several cases in the lineage concerned joint trials and sometimes also codefendant statements but said nothing about antagonistic defenses. In *People v.*

143 *Id.*
144 *Id.* at 191.
145 *Id.* at 192.

Sobzcak (1918),[146] three men held up a seventeen-year-old Chicago bank messenger as he made his afternoon rounds collecting deposits, then were jointly tried with Lexow, a "habitual criminal," who the other defendants alleged had told them that holding up the young messenger would be " 'like taking candy from a baby,'" which Lexow denied.[147] The three were found guilty; Lexow was not.[148] On appeal, the court rejected the defendants' argument that Lexow's habitual criminal status rubbed off on them.[149] *People v. Temple* (1920) involved the burglary and theft of four tires from an auto shop.[150] The appellate court held erroneous the trial court's denial of a defendant's requested instruction that the jury should consider that a codefendant, nominally a witness for the defense but actually a witness for the prosecution, turned state's evidence under a promise of leniency or immunity.[151] *People v. Lopez* (1921) concerned a grocery store robbery that resulted in murder.[152] Among other issues on appeal, Lopez claimed error from the admission of a codefendant's pretrial statement that Lopez had a gun at the scene of the crime, and from denial of a motion for a separate trial based upon the same statement.[153] The court concluded that Lopez, by not denying the statement when it was made in his presence, impliedly admitted its truth.[154] Regarding severance, the court cited *Covitz* for the trial court's discretion to sever and reiterated that the evidence at issue was properly admitted.[155]

People v. Cardinelli (1921) involved the armed robbery of a saloon and the double murders of the saloon owner and a patron.[156] Several young defendants, who pleaded guilty, made statements implicating Cardinelli, the older alleged ringleader of a "gang of baby bandits," and police officers testified regarding these statements at trial.[157] On appeal the court, citing *Buckminster*, held that Cardinelli had ultimately admitted nearly all of the codefendants' allegations, so there was no error in admitting the statements.[158] In *People v. Paisley* (1921), a father and two sons operated a bank while knowingly insolvent.[159] On appeal, the court briefly

146 286 Ill. 157, 121 N.E. 592 (Dec. 18, 1918) (Carter, J.).
147 *Id.* at 158-59, 160.
148 *Id.* at 161.
149 *Id.*
150 295 Ill. 463, 464, 129 N.E. 85 (Dec. 21, 1920) (Cartwright, C.J.).
151 *Id.* at 468-470.
152 296 Ill. 438, 439-40, 129 N.E. 791 (Feb. 15, 1921) (Stone, J.).
153 *Id.* at 447-50, 452-53.
154 *Id.* at 447, 449.
155 *Id.* at 452-53.
156 297 Ill. 116, 118-19, 130 N.E. 355 (Feb. 15, 1921) (Thompson, J.).
157 *Id.* at 118, 125-26.
158 *Id.* at 126. Cardinelli also cited Bopp regarding an insufficiently precise motion to strike testimony. *Id.* at 127.
159 299 Ill. 576, 578-79, 132 N.E. 822 (Oct. 22, 1921) (Thompson, J.).

rejected the father's motion for a separate trial, citing *Covitz* for the basic discretionary severance rule, *Gukouski* and *Temple* for the requirement that a severance motion set forth sufficient grounds supported by an affidavit, none of which the father provided.[160]

People v. Wood (1923) involved the armed robbery of a late-night gambling parlor that led to murder when the proprietor resisted. [161] Two codefendants made confessions to police implicating Wood; one codefendant ultimately pleaded guilty and testified at trial; the other codefendant's statement was admitted with a limiting instruction as to Wood.[162] Citing *Doyle* on joint trials; *Sobzcak*, *Covitz*, and *Gukouski* on discretion to sever; and *Paisley* on the requirement of a motion with grounds for a separate trial, the court held that Wood's severance motion was insufficient to show an abuse of discretion where the testifying codefendant's pretrial confession was not admitted and the other's was admitted with a limiting instruction.[163] *Wood* thus ventured into proto-*Bruton* territory, and it is questionable whether its holding regarding the curative effect of a jury instruction in the codefendant statement context would have passed muster under Illinois case law as it developed soon thereafter—but as with earlier opinions, it addressed antagonistic defenses not at all.

People v. Carmichael (1924) was, like *Bopp*, another case of young punks in a stolen car, one of them with a gun, murdering a police officer.[164] After they were caught, four of the five defendants offered written statements to the police, each one made out of the presence of the other defendants, which the prosecution offered in evidence.[165] Three statements said Carmichael did the shooting; Carmichael's statement said codefendant Shaheen was the shooter and indicated that all defendants intended to rob a roadhouse near where the shooting occurred.[166] Before deliberation, but not when the various statements were admitted in evidence, the jury was instructed that each statement was admissible only against the person who made it.[167] On appeal, the court cited *Buckminster*, *Temple*, and *Cardinelli* for the rule that one defendant's confession is inadmissible against another unless adopted by the other defendant(s), and again cited *Buckminster* in

---

160 *Id.* at 579-80. The Gukouski court merely mentioned examining the affidavit in that case (250 Ill. 231, 233); the Temple court found an affidavit insufficient and discussed why (295 Ill. 463, 464).

161 306 Ill. 224, 225-226, 137 N.E. 799 (Dec. 19, 1923) (Stone, J.).

162 *Id.* at 226-27, 229-30.

163 *Id.* at 229-30.

164 314 Ill. 460, 461-63, 145 N.E. 673 (Dec. 16, 1924) (De Young, J.).

165 *Id.* at 464.

166 *Id.*

167 *Id.* at 465.

holding that the limiting instruction regarding Carmichael's confession did not cure the prejudice to the other defendants.[168] Thus, *Carmichael* got into proto-*Bruton* territory but said nothing about antagonistic defenses.

FODDER FOR MISINTERPRETATION: *RUPERT* (1925) AND *SWEETIN* (1927)

People v. Rupert[169] would become the first really major building block in the antagonistic defenses lineage, though it was decided not on that basis but entirely on mishandling of codefendant statements. *Rupert* arose from a robbery resulting in murder involving codefendants Arnold Rupert and Jimmie Dean, two young African American defendants, who were both found guilty and convicted.[170] Rupert received the death penalty; Dean was sentenced to prison for life.[171]

The (white) murder victim, William Owens, showed he had $20-$30 in cash while paying for a meal at a saloon, then left shortly before midnight. His brother, at home not far away, heard a shot fired, then found Owens at his back door claiming "that two colored men had attacked him and tried to hold him up; that one held him and the little short fellow shot him."[172] Owens died the following day.[173] Both Rupert and Dean had been in the saloon when Owens was there. Dean left after Owens did; Rupert claimed to have been at the saloon when the shot was fired.[174] Rupert and Dean were both arrested the day after the victim died, each made a separate signed statement to police plus additional statements paralleling their signed statements, and both were tried together with separate court-appointed counsel.[175]

The opinion recounts, "Before the trial Rupert made a motion for a separate trial on the ground that all the evidence which would be produced by the people would not be applicable to him and Jimmie Dean; that Dean had made a statement to the police, and so far as the statement implicated Rupert, he would be unable to have a fair trial if jointly tried with Dean; that Rupert had also made a statement in regard to the crime to the police officers incriminating Dean. Rupert further stated to the court in his motion that if these statements were introduced in evidence

---

168 *Id.*
169 336 Ill. 38, 146 N.E. 456 (Feb. 17, 1925) (per curiam).
170 *Id.* at 39, 456.
171 *Id.*
172 *Id.* at 39-40, 456-57.
173 *Id.* at 40, 457.
174 *Id.*
175 *Id.* at 40, 42, 457, 458.

neither of the defendants would be able to procure a fair trial."[176] The statements themselves were not then before the court, and the court denied Rupert's motion.[177]

At trial, the prosecution introduced both statements in evidence, and each defendant objected to his codefendant's statement but was overruled.[178] Dean's statement alleged that he and Rupert left the saloon around midnight, following a man (Owens).[179] Dean knew Rupert intended to pull a stick-up.[180] Dean stopped walking, but Rupert continued toward the man. From about twenty feet away, Dean heard a shot, then saw Rupert run away. Dean also ran, ultimately back to the saloon. The next day, he met Rupert, who admitted the shooting.[181] Dean also identified the .38-caliber, nickel-plated Smith & Wesson revolver that police found as having been in Rupert's possession.[182]

For his part, Rupert alleged that Dean had asked him to loan Dean the revolver because a black man named Charles Yates was trying to kill him.[183] Rupert lent him the gun. The night of the shooting, Dean left the saloon while Rupert stayed there. An hour later, a shot was heard outside. The next day, Dean met Rupert and said he had something to tell him that nobody else could hear.[184] Dean confessed to the shooting after the other guy "made a gun play, and Dean had to get him." Dean didn't know whether he had killed the man, but knew he'd hit him before they both ran away. He returned the gun to Rupert. Rupert said the gun belonged to the saloon owner, who did not know Rupert had taken the weapon.[185]

The saloon owner testified that Rupert and Dean were both at the saloon before the shooting, that both were gone when the shooting occurred, that Rupert reappeared first, Dean later.[186] The owner acknowledged that the gun was his, that Rupert had worked for him, and that both Rupert and Dean knew where he kept it.[187] The saloon owner stated, over defense objections, that Rupert said he had given the gun to Dean for protection against Yates, that Rupert said Dean had

176 *Id.* at 40, 457.
177 *Id.*
178 *Id.*
179 *Id.* at 40-41, 457.
180 *Id.* at 41, 457.
181 *Id.*
182 *Id.*
183 *Id.*
184 *Id.* at 42, 457.
185 *Id.*
186 *Id.* at 42-43, 458.
187 *Id.* at 43, 458.

told him he shot the murder victim, and that the revolver was freshly discharged when Rupert returned it.[188]

That, basically, was the sum of the evidence in the case, aside from testimony of other witnesses who were there when the defendants gave their statements. Both defendants took the stand to testify in keeping with their statements, and each objected to the other defendant's incriminating testimony but were overruled.[189]

The *Rupert* court rejected the State's argument on appeal that separate trials are at the discretion of the trial court, observing, "It cannot be a matter of serious doubt that both defendants in this case were very much prejudiced by the fact that they did not have separate trials. The only incriminating evidence in the case against the defendants is to be found in the statement of the one against the other."[190] Noting that the State characterized each defendant's statement as a voluntary "confession," hence admissible, the court distinguished between confessions and self-exonerating statements, repeating the venerable rule from an earlier Illinois case, "'No man can confess for any one but himself.'"[191] The court remarked that the People had the "alleged confessions" and "well knew their contents and yet resisted the motion, necessarily knowing that they would rest almost their entire case as to each defendant upon the declaration of the other. They thereby deliberately led the court into error in overruling this motion."[192] The court opined,

> In the case of *People v. Buckminster*, . . . this court laid down the rule that where one of several defendants jointly indicted has made admissions or confessions implicating others, a severance should be ordered, unless the attorney for the state declares that such admissions or confessions will not be offered in evidence on the trial. It would have been better, as a matter of precaution, if Rupert had set forth in his motion the character or nature of the admission and confession of his codefendant, Dean, but the information was in the hands of the people, and the court should have taken the precaution to ascertain the nature of the incriminating evidence, or have taken the statement of Rupert as true that the alleged confession of Dean incriminated Rupert. This error was so serious that we must hold it was reversible error to overrule the motion for a severance.[193]

188 *Id.*
189 *Id.*
190 *Id.* at 44, 458.
191 *Id.*
192 *Id.* at 44-45, 458.
193 *Id.* at 45, 459.

The court added,

> The [trial] court also committed very serious error in admitting the alleged confession of each defendant against the other. The objections were very specific and covered every ground necessary for the protection of the defendants. *The court did not even limit, either in its rulings or in its instructions*, the declarations of either defendant to the one making them. It is argued that both defendants waived or cured this error by going on the witness stand and testifying to the same facts, in substance, alleged in their declarations. . . . Dean testified first, and Rupert had no alternative except to rest his case on the improperly admitted declaration of himself, counteracted by the improper declaration of Dean and Dean's testimony on the witness stand implicating Rupert, or take the witness stand himself. *The defendants were antagonistic to each other from the time they were arrested, and, as appears from the record, counsel for neither of them was able to protect his client against the statement of the other, which the court, over their objections, had improperly admitted in evidence.* It is so manifest that the defendants have not had a fair trial that we are not disposed to consider the fact that they went on the witness stand and testified in their own behalf, as off-setting the errors committed against them, or to hold that they waived the errors committed against them by testifying.[194]

The *Rupert* court thus considered the whole situation primarily as a violation of the *Buckminster* rule that a defendant's statement or confession implicating a codefendant requires either exclusion of that part of the statement from evidence or separate trials. The court's reasoning obviously concerned the codefendants' statements, not antagonistic defenses. Although the court remarked how the "defendants were antagonistic to each other from the time they were arrested," that is the only mention of antagonism in the whole opinion, followed shortly by the observation that defense counsel were unable to protect their respective clients from codefendants' *statements*, amidst a prolonged wider discussion of how the trial court erred by admitting the codefendants' *statements* and by failing to sever the trials based upon the *statements*. The court's declaration that there could be little doubt that both defendants were prejudiced by their joint trial, followed by, "The only incriminating evidence in the case against the defendants is to be found in the statement of the one against the other[,]" again focuses on the mishandled statements, not on antagonism in general. In short, *Rupert* was decided solely on the statements. If *Rupert*'s facts implicitly raised, or could have raised, the issue of antagonistic defenses, the holding clearly did not.

[194] *Id.* at 45-46, 458-59 (italics added).

In *People v. Sweetin*,[195] the next major building block, 32-year-old Elsie Sweetin was tried for the murder of her 41-year-old husband, Wilford Sweetin.[196] She and Wilford had been parishioners of the Methodist church of Ina, Illinois, where Lawrence M. Hight was pastor.[197] In July 1924, the Sweetins visited a neighboring town, where they had ice cream. Wilford thereafter became violently ill, with vomiting and severe stomach pain. Local doctors treated him for ptomaine poisoning. Over the next eleven days, he would appear to improve, then worsen again. He died at the end of July 1924. At a post-mortem, his doctors concluded that he died of cirrhosis of the liver, for which he had been treated previously.[198] There was gossip in the town regarding Elsie Sweetin and Pastor Hight, however. In mid-September 1924, Hight's wife died, apparently from ptomaine poisoning.[199] Six days later, Wilford's body was dug up, and tissue samples were sent to a forensic chemist in Chicago.[200] The chemist found sufficient arsenic to cause death.[201] That same day, local law enforcement officials in Ina visited the home of Pastor Hight, found a can of arsenic, and arrested and jailed him.[202] The "loquacious" Hight confessed and implicated Elsie Sweetin.[203]

At around five o'clock on the evening of September 22, 1924, local officials, acting without a warrant, took Sweetin into custody and brought her to the jail.[204] Sweetin, who had been sick for days, was examined by a physician who was also deputy sheriff, who prescribed her medicine that was administered to her through the night by another deputy sheriff.[205] She was given supper, then was

> questioned by the state's attorney and a newspaper reporter until about midnight, when she was taken to the sheriff's office in the courthouse, where, in her weakened condition, she was subjected to questions by reporters and officials until about 4 o'clock a. m., at which time, by direction of the state's attorney, Hight was brought from the county jail and placed in the room with her, and apparently they were left alone for a considerable time, although the officers and newspaper reporters were

---

195 325 Ill. 245, 156 N.E. 354 (Apr. 20, 1927) (Heard, J.)

196 *Id.* at 246, 355.

197 *Id.*

198 *Id.*

199 *Id.*

200 *Id.* at 246-47, 355.

201 *Id.*

202 *Id.* at 247, 355.

203 *Id.*

204 *Id.*

205 *Id.*

> listening in. Up to this time she had maintained her innocence of any complicity in the murder of her husband. She testified, and it is not contradicted, that Hight informed her that he had confessed the crime, implicating her, and that a mob was forming, and, unless she made a confession, or some statement that would satisfy the officers, the mob would take them both out and hang them, but that, if she would make a statement to satisfy the officers, they would both be removed to places of safety until the excitement had subsided. Thereupon the state's attorney was called in, and she made and signed a typewritten statement.[206]

Sweetin was then given breakfast and taken to a different jail where, between 11 p.m. and midnight, a woman newspaper reporter visited her to get her to repeat the story she had given to the state's attorney. Sweetin did so. The following day, Mr. Sweetin's father and the state's attorney and his wife all interviewed Sweetin around midnight, and she repeated the statement she had made to the state's attorney two days before.[207]

The subsequent trial largely hinged on Hight's mental state—his defense was insanity—plus the two codefendants' confessions and evidence of friendly but not romantic relations between Sweetin and Hight.[208] After hearing preliminary evidence, the trial court "properly" excluded Sweetin's original confession as improperly obtained and non-voluntary; as the *Sweetin* court noted, a prosecutor should never try to extract a confession from a defendant by unlawful means.[209] The trial court, however, admitted into evidence the two later iterations of Sweetin's confession, over her objections.[210] Sweetin took the stand and testified that she was in no way responsible for her husband's death, her first confession was influenced by fears of mob violence, she had merely repeated what Hight told her was necessary for her protection and safety, and her subsequent reiterations of her confession during the various late-night visits to her jail cell were motivated by the same fears.[211] She was convicted and sentenced to 35 years in prison.[212]

Citing various earlier cases from Illinois and neighboring states, the *Sweetin* court explained that if a "first confession was coerced by intimidation, fear, or other improper influence," then subsequent confessions of the same crime

---

206 *Id.* at 247-48, 355-56.
207 *Id.* at 248, 356.
208 *Id.* at 247, 355.
209 *Id.* at 248, 356.
210 *Id.* at 248-49, 356.
211 *Id.* at 249, 356.
212 *Id.* at 246, 355.

presumptively resulted from the same influence.[213] The court held that the evidence at hand failed to prove the contrary, making admission of Sweetin's subsequent confessions erroneous.[214] The court then described Sweetin's motion and affidavit for severance:

> Prior to the trial plaintiff in error filed her motion for a separate trial, supported by her affidavit, in which she stated, among other things, *that her defense and that of Hight were antagonistic to each other*, and that much of the evidence against him would be incompetent and prejudicial as to her; that he had made false confessions to the state's attorney, newspaper men, and others, out of her presence, implicating her; that Hight, while in jail at Nashville, was tried by a number of bishops and ministers of his church, at which time he made another false confession and accusation against her; . . . and that he had made various statements to the bishops, presiding elders, and other Methodist officials implicating her, and that the names of these persons were indorsed upon the indictment as witnesses; that, since his arrest, Hight, to get the favor of the State's attorney and other officials, became their willing tool, and aided them in every way in his power to procure evidence against her, and that, as the tool of these officials, he was at one time taken to her room in the jail, where he made threats, used persuasion, and represented to her that there was a mob gathering, and that she would be hanged unless she made some statement to induce the officers to remove them from the county; that, while she was confined in jail at Salem, Hight, intending to injure and entrap her, wrote letters addressed to her which were brought to her by the state's attorney; that she was not present at any of the confessions made by Hight; that such confessions would be competent as to Hight, but would be incompetent and prejudicial as to her.[215]

213 *Id.* at 249, 356.

214 *Id.*

215 *Id.* at 250, 356-57 (italics added). The opinion included a sample of Hight's "many confessions and statements, both oral and written, in which he implicated [Sweetin]"—a statement Hight signed after a higher-ranking regional Methodist church official visited Hight in jail and urged him to "get himself right with God":

"'Of my own free will I make the following statements to Rev. C. C. Hall: Mrs. Sweetin and I fell in love, and we intended to get married. Made arrangements to put husband, Wilford Sweetin, and my wife, Anna Hight, out of the way. She asked me what to get, and I got arsenic. The arsenic I bought in Benton July 22 I gave to Mrs. Elsie Sweetin. I never gave Sweetin any arsenic. I said I did because I didn't want to give her away. And after his death it was up to me to put my wife away, according to agreement. I didn't intend to do anything until we moved, but after she got sick I gave her arsenic.'" *Id.* at 251, 357.

For her part, Sweetin denied all Hight's allegations and testified that although Hight made romantic advances toward her, she spurned these but did not tell others on account of his position in the community and friendship with her family.[216]

Citing *Carmichael* and an earlier English case, the court explained that the trial court's limiting instruction that Hight's confessions were inadmissible as against Sweetin "could by no possibility eradicate the testimony from the minds of the jury" or cure the resulting prejudice.[217] Citing *Buckminster*, *Rupert*, *Carmichael*, *White*, and English and Canadian authorities, the court continued, "To obviate the evils arising from the possibility of the jury being misled by the confessions of a codefendant, the rule is general that, where one of several defendants jointly indicted has made admissions or confessions implicating others, a severance should be ordered, unless the attorney for the State declares that such admissions or confessions will not be offered in evidence on the trial. . . . The Constitution guarantees to every person accused of crime, whether innocent or guilty, a fair and impartial trial, and no person should be condemned to penal servitude who has been deprived, over his objection, of such trial upon evidence competent against him."[218] The court concluded, "[Sweetin] asked for a separate trial, and, for the reasons stated in her affidavit, it should have been accorded her."[219]

Thus, in considering the need for separate trials, the *Sweetin* court was clearly preoccupied with codefendant statements, plus related issues such as limiting instructions regarding those statements and the competence of the statements as to different defendants. The holding says nothing about antagonistic defenses. The entire opinion says almost nothing about them, either, except for the brief mention of one of the grounds for Sweetin's severance motion—"that her defense and that of Hight were antagonistic to each other." It could perhaps be argued, through a leap of logic, that the court's loose concluding statement—that Sweetin "asked for a separate trial, and, for the reasons stated in her affidavit, it should have been accorded her"—incorporated the antagonistic defenses ground in Sweetin's motion. Even under that expansive reasoning, however, the court's sweeping statement considered all of Sweetin's reasons together, not in isolation, so there is no reasonable way to argue that *Sweetin* held that antagonistic defenses, *alone*, justify severance. But later courts would miss that nuance.

---

216 *Id.*

217 *Id.*

218 *Id.*

219 *Id.* at 253, 357.

NO 'ANTAGONISM,' BUT SLIGHT INKLINGS EMERGE: ADDITIONAL CASES, 1927-1930

On the same day *Sweetin* was decided, the Illinois Supreme Court decided *People v. Allison,*[220] a case involving two codefendants charged with larceny of an automobile. *Allison* is the first Illinois case, or at least the first in the identifiable antagonism-severance lineage, to involve one of the classic situations of antagonistic defenses—where one defendant, or the other, or both, must be guilty, but each claims innocence—in the absence of incriminating pretrial statements or confessions by codefendants. Strikingly, in light of later assumptions regarding severance of antagonistic defenses, counsel never raised the issue of antagonism, and the *Allison* court found no problem with the defendants' antagonism and affirmed.

Homer Morville and James Allison were questioned by a police officer who saw them driving a stolen car at night with the headlights off and the taillight covered with a cloth.[221] The two men said they both owned the car, jointly.[222] Morville gave the officer a false name and a false phone number to call, then ran away while the officer was making the call.[223] Allison was taken to jail, where he gave a false name, but a police officer found his identification cards, with his real name, in his sock.[224] At trial, each defendant testified that he had nothing to do with stealing the car and never saw the car before his codefendant appeared with it and gave him a ride the night they were questioned, days after the theft.[225] "Allison was permitted to be cross-examined by Morville's counsel" after the prosecutor was finished with Allison;[226] Allison's counsel apparently did not seek to cross-examine Morville. Morville presented additional testimony from his employer and the employer's wife, both of whom testified that Morville was with them on the night the car was stolen, and Morville's employment records with the testifying employer were admitted into evidence without objection.[227] The jury found Allison guilty and Morville not guilty.[228]

On appeal, Allison argued that the trial court erred on four grounds: admitting the employment records, allowing Morville's counsel to cross-examine Allison and

220 325 Ill. 578, 156 N.E. 798 (Apr. 20, 1927) (Farmer, J.).
221 *Id.* at 579-80, 798.
222 *Id.* at 580, 798.
223 *Id.* at 580, 798-99.
224 *Id.* at 580, 799.
225 *Id.* at 581, 799.
226 *Id.*
227 *Id.* at 582-83, 799.
228 *Id.* at 579, 798.

base the cross-examination on the prosecutor's cross-examination, allowing Morville's counsel to act as a prosecutor of Allison, and giving erroneous instructions for the State.[229] In answering Allison's contentions, the court focused primarily on the alleged instructional errors and found none.[230] The court also noted that Allison never objected to admission of the employment records at trial.[231] As to Allison's arguments regarding Morville's counsel acting as a second prosecutor—which later would be one of the standard justifications for a rule requiring severing of antagonistic defenses both in Illinois and throughout the United States—the court observed,

> In the case at bar Allison and Morville were indicted jointly as principals. On the trial each of them testified as a witness in his own behalf and each sought to place the guilt on the other. So far as shown by the record, neither defendant nor his counsel knew what the other defendant was going to testify to until each testified on the witness stand. No motion for a separate trial was made and they were tried jointly. After Allison had testified and been cross-examined by the state's attorney, Morville's counsel also cross-examined him, and counsel for Allison say Morville's counsel usurped the functions of the prosecutor in his cross-examination, and further say they have been unable to find any case where the circumstances were similar to those on the trial of this case. It is not contended the people knew what the attitude of either defendant was to be on the trial as affecting his guilt or innocence. When Allison testified he clearly sought to throw the blame of guilty on Morville, and when Morville took the stand he returned the compliment. It is, of course, possible in any case where two men are jointly indicted for committing a crime, one of them may be guilty and one of them may not be guilty. They are competent witnesses to testify, and where, as here, each tries to show the other was guilty, and they are represented by different counsel who knew nothing of what the testimony of the other would be until they heard it from the witness stand, we do not think that justice or the law requires that the defendant who claims to be innocent shall not so state on the witness stand but shall submit to or not contradict the statement of the other defendant. We cannot say Morville's counsel did not have a right to cross-examine Allison and attempt to bring out facts which might weaken or destroy the effect of his testimony and that Allison's counsel did not have a right to do the same thing with Morville.[232]

229 *Id.* at 584, 800.
230 *Id.* at 584-86, 587-88, 800-801.
231 *Id.* at 584, 800.
232 *Id.* at 586-87, 800.

The court concluded, "It is true, the testimony of each defendant was very injurious to the other, but they created that situation themselves. It was the court's duty to see that neither of them was denied any legal right in presenting his defense and to instruct the jury as to the law."[233] The court held the trial fair, found no error, and affirmed.[234]

Thus—keep this in mind for later—*Allison* involved mutual finger-pointing by codefendants and cross-examination of a defendant by his codefendant's counsel, in a situation where at least one defendant almost certainly had to be guilty. To all this, the *Allison* court said: no problem, as long as each defendant has the same opportunity to testify, cross-examine, and otherwise implicate his codefendant.[235] Note also, of course, that there was no motion for severance.

People v. Nusbaum (1927) was a conspiracy and murder case involving several codefendants, including Eliza Nusbaum, apparently the wife of the victim.[236] All five alleged conspirators originally pleaded not guilty, but three of them later pleaded guilty and testified for the prosecution at the trial of the other two, including Nusbaum.[237] Apparently before trial, Nusbaum moved for a separate trial.[238] She contended that three conspirators had made confessions to Chicago police admitting that they conspired with her codefendant to murder the victim, but these confessions asserted that she was neither present nor participated in the crime.[239] She claimed that she would be prejudiced if she were tried with the other defendants, and that the only evidence of her participation in any capacity was in her codefendants' statements, which were incompetent against her.[240] This motion was denied, and Nusbaum was convicted and sentenced to life in prison; her codefendant received the death penalty.[241] Nusbaum appealed, claiming error in the denial of severance among other arguments.[242]

---

233 *Id.* at 588, 801-02.

234 *Id.*

235 Interestingly, this is somewhat similar to the reasoning Judge Posner applied much later in *United States v. Zafiro*, 945 F.2d 881, 886 (7th Cir. 1991).

236 326 Ill. 518, 519-21, 158 N.E. 142 (Jun. 22, 1927) (De Young, J.).

237 *Id.* at 519.

238 *Id.* at 520.

239 *Id.*

240 *Id.* at 520-21.

241 *Id.* at 520, 521.

242 *Id.* at 521.

The appellate court noted that the evidence from the case clearly showed that Nusbaum was a conspirator, even if not present at the actual murder.[243] The court rejected her arguments on inadmissible codefendant statements because they tended to show her participation in the conspiracy.[244] Regarding Nusbaum's claim that she feared her convicted codefendant who extorted money from her for years, "and that in consequence their defenses were antagonistic and she should have had a separate trial," the court observed that her severance motion and affidavit gave no indication of fear, duress, or a defense based on those grounds or any other basis to claim antagonism.[245] Citing *Maton*, *Johnson*, *Spies*, *Doyle*, *Gukouski*, *Covitz*, *Sobzcak*, and *Wood*, the court repeated the standard rule—"the denial of a motion for a separate trial will not be reviewed unless there has been a clear abuse of discretion"—adding, "No definite rule can be laid down as to when separate trials should be granted upon [a joint] indictment."[246] The court held there was no abuse or error and affirmed.[247] Aside from the brief references in passing to antagonistic defenses, which were clearly driven by the appellant's pleading and indicate, along with *Sweetin*, that attorneys in the wake of *Rupert* had come to have a generalized sense that "antagonistic defenses" was a new magic word that required severance even if the Illinois courts had never said so, the *Nusbaum* court said nothing further about antagonistic defenses and nothing noteworthy on codefendant statements, and specifically declined to proclaim a rule on severance.

The next few cases that appear in the antagonistic defenses lineage follow *Nusbaum* in merely reiterating the discretionary severance rule, finding no abuse of discretion, and saying little or nothing about antagonistic defenses. *People v. Corbishly* (1927) cited *Covitz* and *Gukouski* for the standard rule;[248] *People v. Birger* (1928) cited *Covitz*, *Gukouski*, *Gillespie*, and *Doyle*;[249] *People v. Lawson* (1928) cited *Covitz* and *Birger*.[250] *Corbishly* never mentioned antagonism or codefendant statements. Birger claimed that he and his codefendant's "defenses were antagonistic," a claim thrown in haphazardly among a mixed bag of other arguments including a warning about codefendant statements.[251] The court answered that no defendant offered any evidence; the prosecution, as promised, offered no codefendant-incriminating statements; and the codefendants' opening

---

243 *Id.* at 521-22.
244 *Id.* at 524-25.
245 *Id.* at 522.
246 *Id.* at 523.
247 *Id.* at 523, 528.
248 327 Ill. 312, 335-36, 158 N.E. 732 (Oct. 22, 1927) (Duncan, J.).
249 329 Ill. 352, 367-68, 160 N.E. 564 (Feb. 24, 1928) (De Young, J.).
250 331 Ill. 380, 393, 163 N.E. 149 (Jun. 23, 1928) (Duncan, J.).
251 Birger, 329 Ill. at 367.

statements included nothing indicating "that the individual defenses were antagonistic."[252] Thus, the *Birger* court, responding to Birger's claim, explicitly only said that there was no antagonism, and did not say whether this had any significance; implicitly, it may have indicated agreement that antagonism had some significance, but not how much, and it mentioned antagonism only in passing, gave no clear holding, cited no authorities, and stated no rule on the topic. Similarly, in a brief paragraph the *Lawson* court stated, "There was no showing . . . that the defense[s were] antagonistic[,]" then explained why the defenses and testimony were in harmony.[253] By making this observation immediately after its statement of the general discretionary severance rule, *Lawson* made it appear more clearly than in *Birger* that antagonistic defenses somehow mattered to the severance decision, but again, no authorities were cited, no rule was given, and it is impossible to know whether the court was merely rejecting an argument about antagonistic defenses without crediting it.

The next case in the lineage, *People v. Giardiano* (1928),[254] never mentioned antagonism, only codefendant statements. Giardiano moved for severance based upon codefendants' confessions; the prosecutor promised that any confessions offered into evidence "would not mention or involve" Giardiano, and he kept his word.[255] The *Giardiano* court observed, "Hence the rule applied in [*Sweetin*] and invoked by the plaintiff in error, that where one of several defendants jointly indicted has made admissions or confessions implicating codefendants, a severance should be ordered unless the state's attorney declares that such admissions or confessions will not be offered in evidence on the trial, has no application to the instant case."[256] The court then stated the general discretionary severance rule, citing *Birger*, *Covitz*, *Gukouski*, *Gillespie*, and *Doyle*, and found no abuse of discretion.[257] Notably, the court correctly defined the rule from *Sweetin* as concerning incriminating codefendants' statements and confessions, not antagonistic defenses.

The next case also never mentioned antagonism, and also cited *Sweetin*, as well as *Rupert*, as authority regarding codefendants' confessions. In *People v. Bolton* (1930), Bolton's codefendant, Johnson, made a confession to police that incriminated Bolton.[258] The trial court denied Bolton's pretrial motion for a separate trial even

252 *Id.*
253 Lawson, 331 Ill. at 393.
254 332 Ill. 476, 163 N.E. 798 (Oct. 25, 1928) (De Young, C.J.).
255 *Id.* at 480.
256 *Id.* at 480-81.
257 *Id.* at 481.
258 339 Ill. 225, 227, 171 N.E. 152 (Apr. 17, 1930) (Stone, J.).

without an objection from the State.[259] At trial, the court also denied Bolton's request that any reference to him in Johnson's statement be omitted, so a police officer testified that Johnson had told him how Bolton took the lead and held the gun in a stick-up of a Chicago couple.[260] Bolton's counsel then requested, and the court gave, an instruction that Johnson's confession was not binding on Bolton.[261] The appellate court held that Bolton should have received a separate trial, citing *Sweetin*, *Rupert*, *Buckminster*, and (curiously) *White* for the "rule long in effect in this state" that statements by defendants incriminating codefendants required severance unless the prosecution agreed to exclude the statements.[262] Thus, *Bolton*, like *Giardiano*, concerned codefendant confessions, not antagonistic defenses, and the *Bolton* court correctly understood *Sweetin* and *Rupert*, like *Buckminster*, to be about codefendant confessions.

ORIGINAL SINS: *FISHER*, *PAYNE*, *LEHNE*, AND THE EMERGENCE OF THE ILLINOIS ANTAGONISTIC DEFENSES 'RULE,' 1930-35

Given that earlier opinions correctly identified *Sweetin* and *Rupert* as early-day *Bruton* cases involving codefendant confessions, while no opinion had stated a rule on antagonistic defenses (although *Birger* and *Lawson* may have drifted dangerously close), it is striking that the next case in the lineage misread *Sweetin* to have been primarily about antagonistic defenses and pushed Illinois case law closer to an antagonistic defenses severance rule built on air, with no proper foundation in earlier opinions. *People v. Fisher*[263] was a relatively lengthy, major opinion consuming more than thirty pages of the Illinois reporter and involving many issues requiring a detailed recital of facts, in which the severance issue was a relative sideshow basically comprising only a single paragraph and page.[264] The case involved a heavily armed bank robbery in which a bank guard was killed.[265] Five of six indicted robbers were caught, one was tried separately, and the other four were tried together, with three receiving the death penalty, one sentenced to life in prison.[266] Among the issues the court had to address on appeal were whether confessions were extracted by beatings or otherwise involuntary,[267] whether the jury was improperly controlled or exposed to outside information

259 *Id.*
260 *Id.* at 228.
261 *Id.*
262 *Id.* at 229.
263 340 Ill. 216, 172 N.E. 743 (Jun. 20, 1930) (Stone, J.).
264 *Id.* at 226-27.
265 *Id.* at 219-20.
266 *Id.* at 219.
267 *Id.* at 226, 227-232.

(they were allowed to have a radio in the jury room, for instance),[268] and the admissibility of relatively sophisticated expert testimony on forensics and ballistics regarding the weapons and rounds that killed the bank guard,[269] along with other alleged evidentiary or instructional errors.[270]

The *Fisher* court addressed the severance issue first, noting that "[t]he ground on which the separate trial was sought was that each of the other defendants had made a confession implicating Fisher."[271] Fisher contended that his case thus came within "the rule laid down in [*Sweetin*] and [*Rupert*]"[272]—indicating that Fisher's counsel recognized that both cases concerned codefendant statements. The court answered, very directly but incorrectly, "In the Sweetin Case the main ground for the motion was that the defenses of the two defendants were antagonistic. No such ground is stated in the motion in the instant case."[273] Regarding *Rupert*, the court declared, "In the Rupert Case each defendant made a statement in which he exonerated himself and implicated the other in the crime."[274] The court then distinguished *Rupert* because all the *Fisher* defendants had, in their confessions, not only implicated each other but implicated themselves, and were substantially in agreement. The *Fisher* court cited *Birger*, *Lopez*, and *Covitz* for the general discretionary severance rule, and *Bolton*, *Buckminster*, and a few non-lineage cases for Illinois' proto-*Bruton* rule—that "where a motion for separate trial is made on the ground of confessions of others implicating the mover, a severance should be ordered unless the state's attorney declares that the admissions or confessions will not be offered in evidence on the trial or unless there be eliminated from the confessions any reference to the codefendant."[275] [This seems to be the first time a redaction option was added to the *Buckminster* rule, at least in the antagonistic defenses lineage.] The court concluded, "This case differs on the facts from any of the cases above cited. In this case the defenses were not antagonistic, and confessions were made by each in substance identical with the others[.]"[276]

---

268 *Id.* at 242-48.

269 *Id.* at 236-42.

270 Defense counsel also contested a variance between the indictment and proof where the indictment gave the victim as "Martin V. French" when the proof showed his name to be "Martin B. French," *id.* at 234, argued that the prosecutor's closing remarks were prejudicial, *id.* at 248, and claimed insufficient evidence, id. at 248-49.

271 *Id.* at 226.

272 *Id.* at 227.

273 *Id.*

274 *Id.*

275 *Id.*

276 *Id.*

Thus the *Fisher* court incorrectly summarized *Sweetin* as being argued and decided on antagonistic defenses. It did not mischaracterize *Rupert* that way—the court said nothing about antagonism in the *Rupert* context and appears to have recognized correctly that *Rupert* was fundamentally about codefendant statements—but the distinguishing point it extracted from *Rupert*, focusing on the conflict between the two defendants, together with the two references to antagonism in the opinion, would be used by later courts to summarily define *Rupert*, too, as an antagonistic defenses case. Unlike a good many other decisions that followed, defense counsel could not be blamed for introducing the notion of antagonism where it did not belong in *Fisher*; rather, it appears that the *Fisher* court, confronting a long, complex, difficult case and opinion, hoped to quickly and efficiently dispatch a relatively minor issue by briefly and succinctly summarizing and distinguishing *Rupert* and *Sweetin*, two relatively complex cases that had not yet been analyzed, distilled, and defined. This worthy goal entailed risks, however, as the *Fisher* court in its haste got *Sweetin* plain wrong and defined *Rupert* in a manner dangerously open to later misinterpretation. So *Fisher* was an important milestone in the development of Illinois' rule on antagonistic defenses, and helped to establish a longstanding pattern of courts sweeping a nuisance side-issue under the rug by using overly brief, excessively succinct, and fundamentally misleading summaries of complex earlier decisions.

The next two cases in the antagonistic defenses lineage never mentioned or involved antagonism. *People v. Sullivan* (1931) involved codefendants' statements, as well as the risk of prejudice from the notoriously bad character of one defendant rubbing off on others.[277] The *Sullivan* court quoted *Wood* citing *Sobczak*, *Covitz*, *Gukouski*, and *Doyle* for the general rule on discretionary severance and quoted *Fisher* at length regarding incriminating codefendants' confessions and how a motion for severance should be granted unless the prosecutor agrees not to introduce such a statement in evidence " 'or unless there be eliminated from the confessions any reference to the codefendant.' "[278] The prosecutor substituted "the other person" for "Richard Sullivan" throughout the confession; the *Sullivan* court found no error.[279] *People v. Hotchkiss* (1931) involved a defendant's complaint of likely prejudice from joint trial with a codefendant who previously had been convicted of a felony.[280] The court cited *Fisher*, *Giardiano*, *Birger*, and *Nusbaum* on discretionary severance, *Sobzcak* on joint trial with an habitual criminal with a prior felony conviction not requiring severance absent a showing of prejudice.[281]

---

277 345 Ill. 87, 99, 177 N.E. 733, 738 (Jun. 18, 1931) (Dunn, J.).
278 *Id.* at 99-100, 738.
279 *Id.*
280 347 Ill. 217, 220, 179 N.E. 524, 525 (Dec. 17, 1931) (Orr, J.).
281 *Id.* at 220-221, 525.

The next case in the lineage, *People v. Rose*,[282] involved antagonism, but antagonism of a different sort. In *Rose*, two African American men held up a carload of five white boys at gunpoint, then shot and killed a railroad company security officer when he came to investigate.[283] At trial, the court appointed a pair of attorneys to jointly represent both defendants. The joint counsel moved for separate trials, submitting affidavits to show that one defendant, Rose, would argue that he was present and saw his codefendant, Eckford, fire the fatal shot, whereas Eckford would argue that he was not present. The court denied the motion.[284] At trial, Eckford testified that he was not present; Rose did not testify.[285]

The Illinois Supreme Court observed,

> While the inconsistency of the defense did not appear on the trial for the reason that Rose did not testify, the situation might well be that that inconsistency did not appear by reason of the embarrassing situation in which the attorneys were placed. As stated in their brief, "defendants' counsel were put to the task of presenting two inconsistent defenses to the same jury. It could not be done. Counsel followed their best judgment and put Eckford on the witness stand and did not permit Rose to testify. It may be that in doing so counsel did not perform their full duty to defendant Rose."[286]

The *Rose* court quoted at length from *Bopp* regarding the duty of counsel to have no interest adverse to a client, including the part where the counsel in *Bopp* " 'asked to be excused on the ground that the interest of his client (McErlane) in the trial was antagonistic to that of Bopp.' "[287] The court reversed, concluding, "Every defendant who is unable to employ counsel for his defense has a right to have an attorney appointed by the court who can, and will upon the trial, present to the court and jury the defendant's full defense, untrammeled by any conflicting interests of a codefendant."[288] Although the actual reversal was of the trial court's denial of Rose's motion for a severance,[289] *Rose* was, and the court obviously understood it to be, a case regarding joint representation of multiple defendants with conflicting interests. The court said nothing about the separate issue of joint

282 348 Ill. 214, 180 N.E. 791 (Apr. 23, 1932) (Heard, J.) (Orr, J. dissenting).
283 *Id.* at 215.
284 *Id.* at 216.
285 *Id.* at 217, 791.
286 *Id.*
287 *Id.*
288 *Id.* at 218, 791.
289 *Id.*

trial of antagonistic defendants with separate counsel, and the word "antagonistic" only arose in the quote from *Bopp*—the only authority cited in *Rose.*

Nearly five years after *Fisher*, however, the Illinois antagonistic defenses "rule" reemerged in what would become its classic form—a statement of the "rule" briefly, in passing, in a case in which it did not apply and thus required no holding. In *People v. Payne* (1935), a conspiracy case penned by Justice Shaw, six codefendants were charged with a murder that occurred during an armed robbery.[290] On appeal, Payne contended, inter alia, that codefendant Rich, who pleaded guilty, testified to "certain acts and conversations" of other codefendants when Payne was not present, causing prejudice that sufficiently justified his motion for a separate trial.[291] The court explained that Rich's testimony indicated a conspiracy of which Payne was a member, so his absence during the conversations was immaterial.[292] Probably no more needed to be said on the topic, but the court, wishing to neatly and succinctly summarize relevant rules, group-cited *Fisher*, *Lawson*, *Birger*, *Corbishly*, *Wood*, and *Gukouski* for the general rule on discretionary severance, adding, "The right to a severance depends upon whether the defense of one defendant is so antagonistic to the defense of other defendants that a severance is necessary to assure a fair trial."[293] Justice Shaw apparently drew upon and extended *Fisher*'s mischaracterization of *Sweetin*, plus the ambiguous references to antagonism in cases such as *Lawson* and *Birger*, to abruptly create a new "rule" without a holding, seemingly unaware that the "rule" was new, actually unsupported by earlier authorities, and unnecessary for deciding *Payne.*

Notably, *Payne*'s sweeping but inaccurate general proclamation on the appropriate grounds for severance was at least implicitly exclusive. Although in declaring that the right to severance depends upon antagonistic defenses, it could perhaps be read to say only that antagonistic defenses are one significant factor among many other possible factors supporting severance, the easier, more obvious reading is that antagonistic defenses are the sole, *exclusive* basis for severance. Later courts mostly followed the latter interpretation. Also notably, *Payne*'s formulation of the "rule" indicated that there are degrees of antagonism, and that severance only was required where defenses were "so antagonistic" that only separate trials would assure fairness. The latter part of the rule might not be that helpful in operational terms, because it says, more or less, that severance is necessary where it's necessary; but it does at least establish that only a serious level of antagonism, not just any antagonism, is required. Later courts would miss that distinction. So

290 359 Ill. 246, 248, 194 N.E. 539 (Feb. 15, 1935) (Shaw, J.).

291 *Id.* at 253.

292 *Id.* at 253-54.

293 *Id.* at 253.

Justice Shaw's well-intended effort to helpfully clarify an area of law backfired, and instead set loose a process that would breed complications and confusion down the road. For although the *Payne* court's new "rule" might have been wrong and juridically unfounded, and did not precisely define antagonism or the extent of antagonism necessary to require separate trials, its language was, or appeared to be, quite simple and straightforward—just the sort of thing courts love, especially when they are trying to sweep aside a nuisance issue as quickly and efficiently as possible. As such, *Payne*'s language would take deep root in Illinois jurisprudence over the next half century, as many later courts joined Justice Shaw in assuming the antagonism-severance rule into existence.

Less than a week after *Payne*, Justice Shaw offered another major opinion concerning antagonistic defenses that succeeded in mischaracterizing *Sweetin*, *Rupert*, and *Rose* while pushing Illinois further along toward the "rule" that *Payne* had assumed into existence. In *People v. Lehne*, a wife and her lover, Lehne, allegedly conspired to kill her husband, whom Lehne shot one night while he slept.[294] Both wife and Lehne made extensive statements to police after their arrest regarding the planning of the murder, statements that were parallel overall but contradicted each other on particular points.[295] In particular, the wife denied intending that her lover shoot her husband and claimed that Lehne did all the planning.[296] The wife made her statement outside the presence of Lehne, but after it was sworn and notarized, Lehne was brought in and the statement was read to him as he followed along with a typed transcript, making pencil marks in eight places where his story differed.[297] Lehne then dictated his statement to police in the wife's presence, with the wife denying portions of his statement.[298] At trial, both defendants testified on their own behalf as well as introducing witnesses.[299] The wife and Lehne both objected to the introduction of his statement, and Lehne also objected to the introduction of the wife's statement.[300] The wife's objection was based on a claim that she had not acquiesced to Lehne's statement but had substantially denied it all.[301] The trial court admitted Lehne's statement but required the deletion of various portions where the wife specifically denied

294 359 Ill. 631, 633, 195 N.E. 468 (Feb. 21, 1935) (Shaw, J.).
295 *Id.* at 633-643, 470-474.
296 *Id.*
297 *Id.* at 636, 471.
298 *Id.* at 637-643, 471-474.
299 *Id.* at 643-644, 474.
300 *Id.* at 644, 474.
301 *Id.*

what Lehne said.[302] The jury convicted both defendants of murder and selected the death penalty for both.[303]

On appeal, the *Lehne* court noted that the only issues in the case were whether the trial court had erred by (1) denying the wife's motion for a separate trial, (2) admitting her statement as against Lehne, and (3) admitting Lehne's statement as against both defendants.[304] The court determined that the answer to the first question hinged on the second and third.[305] Although Lehne invoked *Buckminster* for the principle that no one may confess for another and no one should be subject to conviction based upon the statement of another made outside his presence, the court observed that Lehne had full opportunity to contradict the wife's statement but generally did not and effectively adopted and confirmed it.[306] The court also found the trial court's deletions from Lehne's statement appropriate as to both defendants.[307]

The *Lehne* court then turned to the question of severance and noted that it was determined by the holding on the defendants' statements.[308] Citing *Birger*, the court explained, "The general rule is that persons jointly indicted shall be jointly tried . . ., and it is only in those cases where fairness to one or more defendants requires it that a severance motion is imperatively required."[309] The court also cited *Birger*, *Covitz*, *Gukouski*, *Gillespie*, *Doyle*, and *Fisher* regarding the trial court's discretion to sever,[310] then expounded:

> Any set of circumstances which is sufficient to deprive a defendant of a fair trial if tried jointly with another or others is sufficient to require a separate trial, and on the other hand any reasons falling short of this measure do not necessarily require a severance. On this principle it was held by us in People v. Rupert . . . *that a severance should have been granted where the defenses of the defendants were antagonistic and each had made a statement denying his own guilt and accusing his codefendant*; these statements constituting the principal evidence relied on by the people. In People v. Sweetin, . . . *we reached the same conclusion, and for the same reason.* In that case the defendants were jointly indicted for the murder, by arsenic poisoning, of Mrs.

302 *Id.* at 644-645, 474.
303 *Id.* at 633, 469.
304 *Id.* at 647, 475.
305 *Id.*
306 *Id.* at 647-648, 475-476.
307 *Id.* at 649, 476.
308 *Id.*
309 *Id.*
310 *Id.* at 649-650, 476.

> Sweetin's husband, which it was shown might have been committed by either one of them. Each defendant denied guilt, blaming the other, and the codefendant Hight signed a confession admitting the murder of his own wife, denying the one for which he and Mrs. Sweetin were being tried, and affirmatively asserting that he had delivered the arsenic to her. So, also, in People v. Rose, . . . we decided that fairness required a separate trial. Rose and Eckford were jointly indicted for murder, and a motion for a separate trial was made by Rose. The affidavit of his attorneys supporting this motion stated that Eckford would testify that he was not present at the time of the shooting and that Rose would testify that the shot was, in fact, fired by Eckford. We held that upon this showing a severance should have been granted even though the inconsistency did not actually arise on the trial by reason of the failure of Rose to testify. We found that his failure to testify may well have been caused by the very failure to grant him a separate trial and the consequent embarrassment to the attorneys in attempting to present inconsistent defenses to the same jury. The judgment was reversed for that reason. These are the principal cases relied upon by the defendants here, and to them more might be added. All are illustrative of the principle uniformly adhered to by this court, i.e., that a separate trial should be granted when fairness so requires. The case at bar presents no such requirement. Neither defendant had any defense antagonistic to the codefendant.[311]

This tour-de-force of mischaracterization of earlier authorities deserves to be quoted and analyzed at length. The *Lehne* court came closest to saying something accurate about *Rupert*, but as we have seen, the *Rupert* court for its holding relied entirely upon *Buckminster* and its appropriate rule that incriminating statements by a codefendant required severance of defendants unless the prosecutor agreed to delete all incriminating portions or to not introduce the incriminating statement at trial.[312] Although the *Rupert* court certainly did notice that the defendants (not the "defenses of the defendants" as the *Lehne* court stated) were antagonistic to each other, that their respective statements each exonerated the declarant and implicated the other, and that these statements were the prosecution's only substantial incriminating evidence, the *Rupert* court made its decision based on mishandling of the statements under *Buckminster*, not on some general rule regarding antagonistic defenses.[313] The *Sweetin* court said nothing about antagonistic defenses; Pastor Hight did not defend by denying guilt and blaming Elsie Sweetin but rather confessed to poisoning his wife, admitted complicity in

311 *Id.* at 650-651, 476-477.

312 *See Rupert* at 45-46, 458-459; *Buckminster* at 447.

313 *See Rupert* at 45-46, 458-459.

the death of Mr. Sweetin, and defended by claiming insanity; there is no indication in the opinion that Elsie Sweetin ever blamed Hight for the death of her husband; and the *Sweetin* holding hung on mishandling of a codefendant's statements (as well as shocking abuses in the procurement of defendant statements), not on antagonistic defenses.[314] *Lehne*'s misreading of *Rupert* and *Sweetin* appears to have derived more from *Fisher* than from actual readings of *Rupert* and *Sweetin*. The only mention of antagonism in *Rose* came in the quote from *Bopp*, and *Rose*, like *Bopp*, was decided on the basis of a defendant's right to unconflicted counsel, not on antagonistic defenses.[315] *Lehne* completely missed or ignored the key nuance that *Rose*, unlike *Lehne*, involved joint representation.[316] Moreover, *Lehne* never needed a lengthy exegesis on antagonistic defenses; the defenses clearly were not antagonistic, but were in "complete accord" as to the essential facts, as the court observed, so the holding did not, and did not need to, define antagonistic defenses.[317] There is also no indication in the *Lehne* opinion that the defendants ever raised the issue of antagonistic defenses; their arguments appear to have been focused solely on admission of the statements.[318] One of the few things *Lehne* got right was its repeated iteration of the general rule "that a separate trial should be granted when fairness so requires"[319]—a clean statement of the principle at stake uncluttered by confused babble about antagonistic defenses.

On the same day as *Lehne*, in a per curiam decision, the Illinois Supreme Court decided *People v. Albers* (1935), a case involving bitter factional strife between rival coal miners' unions that led to a drive-by shooting in which a rifle bullet passed through the wall of a house and killed a schoolgirl as she did her homework.[320] As in *Fisher*, defendants alleged that their confessions were procured by force.[321] Also among the forty assigned errors, the defendants contended that one defendant's confession should not have been admitted as against codefendants who had not adopted it.[322] The court cited *Birger*, *Lopez*, *Sullivan*, and *Hotchkiss* on discretionary severance, *Fisher* for pretrial defendant statements that implicate other defendants requiring severance unless the statements are excluded or redacted, and found no abuse of discretion where the statements were redacted pursuant to a stipulation.[323] In response to defendants' argument that their case came under "the

---

314 *See Sweetin* at 252-253.
315 *See Rose* at 217-218, 791.
316 *See* Lehne at 647, 475.
317 *Id.* at 651, 477.
318 *Id.* at 644-645, 647; 474, 475.
319 *Id.* at 651, 477.
320 360 Ill. 73, 74-75, 195 N.E. 459 (Feb. 21, 1935) (per curiam).
321 *Id.* at 76, 78-82.
322 *Id.* at 74, 82.
323 *Id.* at 83-84.

rules laid down . . . in . . . Sweetin . . . and . . . Rupert," the court closely followed language in *Fisher* (though without citing it as support), stating, "In the Sweetin Case the principal ground for severance was that the defenses of the two accused were antagonistic."[324] The court notably focused on the actual defenses at trial rather than the allegedly involuntary confessions in finding "no such conflict here."[325] After finishing its brief discussion of *Sweetin* and antagonism, the court explained regarding *Rupert*, "Each defendant in the Rupert Case cleared himself and implicated the other. Here the defendants who confessed did not try to throw the blame on the shoulders of the others. The statement of each confessing defendant was used only against its maker unless some other defendant had adopted it in whole or in part. . . . The rule laid down in the Rupert Case is not controlling in this case."[326]

Thus *Albers* followed *Fisher* in incorrectly defining *Sweetin* as a case decided on antagonistic defenses, but the court correctly recognized antagonistic defenses (as offered at trial) to constitute an entirely separate category from conflicting pretrial codefendant statements. The *Albers* court also apparently followed *Fisher* in categorizing *Rupert* not as an antagonistic defenses case, but as a codefendant statements case, albeit one in which each declarant exculpated himself and implicated his codefendant. In other words, although later courts would define the mutual self-exoneration and finger-pointing that occurred in *Rupert* as the defining characteristic of antagonistic defenses, *Fisher* and *Albers* (and *Rupert*) did not. Notably, both defense counsel and the court seem to have understood that *Sweetin* and *Rupert* laid down *rules* (plural), not the same rule—contrary to *Lehne*. Although the *Albers* court erred regarding *Sweetin* and missed crucial nuances in *Rupert* by following *Fisher*'s hyper-abbreviated and misleading summaries of those cases' holdings, it avoided stating a general antagonism-severance rule, as in *Payne*, or attaching *Sweetin* and *Rupert* to that rule, as *Lehne* had and later opinions would.

The next case in the lineage, *People v. Patris* (1935), which involved the bombing of a Chicago beauty parlor,[327] never mentioned or addressed antagonism, was only concerned with codefendants' confessions or admissions, and did not conflate the two categories. The court cited *Buckminster*, *Sweetin*, *Fisher*, and *Carmichael* for the rule that codefendants' incriminating statements required severance "unless the state's attorney declares that the admissions or confessions will not be offered in

---

324 *Id.* at 84.

325 *Id.* at 84. Intriguingly, the court noted, "The fact that all defendants were tried together seemingly did not distress their counsel, as they all joined, at times, in representing all the defendants, even going to the extent of examining each other's clients." *Id.*

326 *Id.*

327 360 Ill. 596, 597, 196 N.E. 806 (Jun. 14, 1935) (Jones, J.).

evidence upon the trial or unless there be eliminated from the confessions any reference to the codefendant applying for a severance."[328] The court held that the trial court had violated this rule by admitting the codefendant's prejudicially incriminating confession with only a limiting instruction as to Patris, and reversed.[329] *Patris*, apparently, correctly understood *Sweetin* and *Fisher*, like *Buckminster* and *Carmichael*, to be about codefendants' statements, not antagonistic defenses.

In *People v. Siegal* (1935), which involved the kidnapping for ransom of a Toledo, Ohio businessman in Chicago, the Court also never mentioned antagonism and only discussed and rejected claims of prejudice from a defendant's confession that was admitted with "x" substituted for the codefendants' names.[330] The court cited no authority beyond the Illinois kidnapping statute.[331] *Siegal* is noteworthy chiefly for its reflection on the other, usually forgotten side of the joinder-severance equation:

> The people's rights in criminal prosecutions are to be observed as much as the defendants' rights. Both parties are clothed with certain privileges and presumptions and they must be duly regarded. It would be unjust and unreasonable to universally permit separate trials of persons who are jointly charged with a crime, and the better practice is not to permit it unless it shall appear from a showing made to the court that a denial of a severance would work prejudice to some one or more of the parties.[332]

ENTRENCHING THE RULE: *BETSON* AND *MINNECCI*, 1936

The next case in the lineage, *People v. Betson* (1936), involved the kidnapping for ransom of a Peoria physician.[333] Among 27 assigned errors, the defendant contended that the trial court improperly denied his motion for severance and erroneously admitted a codefendant's confession; because the only basis for Betson's severance motion was a vague intimation of prejudice from

328 *Id.* at 601, 808.

329 *Id.* at 600-02.

330 362 Ill. 389, 390-95, 200 N.E. 72, 73-74 (Dec. 19, 1935) (Jones, J.; Shaw, J., dissenting).

331 *Id.*

332 *Id.* at 393, 74. In a much later case, *People v. Hill*, 65 Ill.App.3d 879, 382 N.E. 2d 881 (Nov. 17, 1978) (Trapp, J.), Judge Craven wrote a dissent describing what he found to be a disturbing case of apparently inconsistent or incorrect verdicts arising from separate trials of joint wrongdoers—perhaps the worst potential result of severing otherwise appropriately joined codefendants. *See* Hill at 889-90, 887-88 (Craven, J., dissenting).

333 362 Ill. 502, 503-04, 200 N.E. 594 (Feb. 14, 1936) (Orr, J.).

codefendants' statements, these constituted the same error in different clothing.[334] Regarding severance, the court found that Betson's "motion and affidavit did not disclose that his defense was to be antagonistic to that of his codefendants," noting further, "The record is conclusive that there was no antagonistic defense for the reason that no affirmative defense was offered by any of the other defendants."[335] Citing *Nusbaum*, the court stated, "This court, unless the facts were not then known, will not reverse a judgment and order a separate trial unless all the reasons therefor were presented to the consideration of the trial court."[336] The court found no abuse of discretion in the denial of severance because Betson's motion and affidavit were "insufficient in law" but added gratuitously, "The right to a severance must rest upon the ground that the defense to be offered by one defendant is so antagonistic to the defense to be offered by the remainder of the defendants that severance is necessary to insure a fair trial. [Citing *Lawson*, *Fisher*, and *Payne*.]"[337] The court then discussed how the codefendant confessions at issue were appropriately redacted.[338]

It is unclear from the opinion whether Betson ever raised the issue of antagonistic defenses, or whether the court injected that concept. Even assuming that severance under Illinois law depended entirely upon antagonistic defenses, however, the *Betson* court never had to go beyond its determination that Betson's severance motion and affidavit did not show antagonistic defenses. *Betson* took *Payne*'s "rule" and extended it, making it explicitly exclusive by saying the right to severance "must rest upon the ground" of antagonistic defenses, indicating that no other ground could justify severance. Thus *Betson* sharply rigidified a rule it did not need to state.

Betson also added or reinforced some other noteworthy, sometimes countervailing tendencies in Illinois' developing antagonism-severance rule. As in *Albers*, the court defined antagonistic defenses by the defenses actually offered at trial, not by the content of codefendants' pretrial statements—a distinction that later would be lost as courts indiscriminately lumped codefendant statements together with antagonistic defenses or treated the former as a subcategory of the latter. *Betson* also reinforced the sufficient grounds and affidavit requirement that surfaced earlier in *Temple*, *Paisley*, *Wood*, and *Nusbaum*, but added the condition, "unless the facts were not then known"—a significant qualification for trial fairness that would be lost, then rediscovered and expanded much later.

---

334 *Id.* at 507-08.
335 *Id.* at 507.
336 *Id.* at 507-08.
337 *Id.* at 508.
338 *Id.* at 508-09.

People v. Minnecci (1936),[339] decided the same day as *Betson*, further entrenched Illinois' antagonism-severance rule while further erasing or obscuring the precedential tracks leading to it. In *Minnecci*, a case involving three codefendants whose robbery of a haberdasher's shop resulted in the proprietor's murder, defendant Minnecci claimed that he was prejudiced by pretrial statements of his two codefendants.[340] The court found no prejudice where the codefendants never accused Minnecci of guilt either in their statements or at trial.[341] The court also noted that Minnecci moved for severance but made no showing in support of the motion.[342]

In support of its holding, the court cited *Birger* for the general rule of joint trial, *Lehne* for the rule that the need for severance "is governed by the facts in each case . . . and is addressed to the sound discretion of the trial judge."[343] The court then declared, without citing any additional authority,

> Any set of circumstances which is sufficient to deprive a defendant of a fair trial if tried jointly with another or others is sufficient to require a separate trial, and, on the other hand, any reasons falling short of this measure do not make a severance necessary. In the absence of a showing to the trial court as to how the defendant would be prejudiced by a joint trial, he is not in position to complain of the action of the trial court on writ of error. However, we have examined the point on its merits. The rule is that where there is more than one defendant and the defenses are antagonistic, and one defendant accuses the other, so that it will be impossible for the defendant who asked a severance to have a fair trial, the severance should be granted.[344]

Unlike *Betson*, *Minnecci* apparently ignored the sweeping antagonism-severance rule in *Payne*. Instead, the *Minnecci* court seems to have derived its own sweeping general statement of the rule by distilling the somewhat rambling discussion of *Rupert*, *Sweetin*, and *Rose* in *Lehne*, which (incorrectly) linked severance to antagonistic defenses in all three cases. Probably for that reason, unlike *Payne*'s implicitly exclusive and *Betson*'s explicitly exclusive iteration of the rule, *Minnecci*'s version was nonexclusive—it required severance *if* there were antagonistic

339 362 Ill. 541, 200 N.E. 853 (Feb. 14, 1936) (Farthing, J.).
340 *Id.* at 542.
341 *Id.* at 545. The three defendants' combined statement was introduced and admitted in evidence without objection. *Id.* at 544.
342 *Id.* at 544-545.
343 *Id.* at 545.
344 *Id.* at 545.

defenses, not *only if* there were, allowing other possible grounds for severance. *Minnecci*'s version also included other appropriate qualifications, such as the degree of antagonism condition—"so that it will be impossible for the defendant who asked a severance to have a fair trial"—which may have been consciously or unconsciously derived all or in part from *Payne*, and the closely related "and one defendant accuses the other" condition, which clearly came from *Lehne*.

The conditions in *Minnecci*'s iteration of the antagonism-severance rule can be read at least a few different ways, with varying plausibility. It could indicate that antagonistic defenses, one defendant accusing the other, and the impossibility of a fair trial are all separate necessary factors that are cumulatively sufficient to require severance; that antagonistic defenses and one defendant accusing the other are separate necessary factors that together make a fair trial impossible and require severance; that antagonistic defenses and one defendant accusing the other are actually the same factor, with one defendant accusing the other being part of the definition of antagonistic defenses, and that the presence of that factor necessarily entails that a fair trial would be impossible, or in other words is sufficient in itself to require severance; or that antagonistic defenses and one defendant accusing the other are the same factor, but the impossibility of a fair trial is an additional, independent necessary factor for severance.

Whichever reading of *Minnecci* might be correct, by all readings, and regardless of whether one defendant accusing the other is seen as a separate necessary factor or part of the definition of antagonism, it is required for severance. *Minnecci*'s one-defendant-accusing-the-other ingredient thus helps to define either antagonism or degree of antagonism by indicating that lesser levels of antagonism do not require severance. *Minnecci*'s rule iteration does not address whether antagonistic defenses are limited to defenses presented at trial or also include codefendant statements, an issue on which later courts would reach varying conclusions; because Minnecci's codefendants did not accuse him either in statements or at trial, the court did not have to decide that issue. Of course, whatever the *Minnecci* court meant to say, its rule was built on no legitimate precedential foundation.

Minnecci's statement regarding the defendant's obligation to make a showing of prejudice to the trial court added to the case law regarding sufficient grounds and affidavits, but was never cited for that purpose, perhaps because although the court could have decided the case on that issue, it did not. *Minnecci* also kept, nearly verbatim, *Lehne*'s statement regarding "Any set of circumstances . . . ," an overarching statement of principle which kept the whole purpose of the severance rule—fairness—in proper perspective, but which many later courts either forgot or overlooked.

THE LONG-FORGOTTEN 'FOUNTAINHEAD': *BRAUNE*, 1936

People v. Braune (1936),[345] which decades later would be called "the fountainhead" of Illinois antagonistic defenses jurisprudence, was a case involving ugly facts that was decided almost entirely on its facts, with little reference to existing law. Codefendants Frank R. Braune and Maurice L. Dale, both physicians, were charged with killing Marie Dwyer by performing a criminal abortion on her.[346] Both were found guilty of manslaughter.[347]

Dwyer was Dr. Dale's patient, and, as the opinion stated in delightfully circumspect Victorian fashion, "also kept company with him."[348] As a result, she became pregnant, which they discovered in January 1935. On February 18, 1935, they went to Dr. Braune's office, where he examined Dwyer. Dwyer and Dale returned to Braune's office on February 21 and 22. On the latter date, the prosecutor alleged, Dale procured from Braune an abortion on Dwyer. While using a forceps to remove placental tissue, Braune inadvertently also caught a loop of intestinal tissue, then severed the intestine while using a scissors to cut loose the tissue held in the forceps. Braune and Dale then found that the severed tissue was intestine, attempted to put the severed ends back together, and took Dwyer to a hospital for surgery to reconnect her intestine. She died a few days later.[349]

---

345 363 Ill. 551, 2 N.E.2d 839 (Jun. 10, 1936) (Jones, J.).

346 *Id.* at 552, 839.

347 *Id.* The *Chicago Daily Tribune* ran more than 20 articles on the Braune-Dale case from 1935-36, though some were quite brief. See *Doctor Accused After Operation Released in Bail*, CHI. DAILY TRIB., Feb. 26, 1935, at 12; *Seek 2 Doctors After Girl Dies of Operation*, CHI. DAILY TRIB., Feb. 27, 1935, at 2; *Two Physicians Seized at Quiz on Girl's Death*, CHI. DAILY TRIB., Feb. 28, 1935, at 5; *Free 2 Doctors on $20,000 Bond in Girl's Death*, CHI. DAILY TRIB., Mar. 1, 1935, at 15; *Physician's Aid Relates Story of Girl's Death*, CHI. DAILY TRIB., Mar. 3, 1935, at 13; *Quiz 3 Today in Girl's Death Laid to an Illegal Operation*, CHI. DAILY TRIB., Mar. 4, 1935, at 11; *Seek Indictment of 2 Physicians in Girl's Death*, CHI. DAILY TRIB., Mar. 5, 1935, at 9; *Study Doctor's Books in Quiz on Abortion Ring*, CHI. DAILY TRIB., Mar. 6, 1935, at 16; *Seeks to Indict 2 Doctors Today in Death of Girl*, CHI. DAILY TRIB., Mar. 7, 1935, at 3; *Vote to Indict Two Doctors in Abortion Death*, CHI. DAILY TRIB., Mar. 8, 1935, at 13; *Indicted Doctor Named by Nurse in Abortion Quiz*, CHI. DAILY TRIB., Mar. 9, 1935, at 6; *50 Doctors May Lose Licenses in Abortion Ring*, CHI. DAILY TRIB., Mar. 10, 1935, at 21; *Doctors Freed on $50,000 Bond in Murder Case*, CHI. DAILY TRIB., Mar. 12, 1935, at 15; *Seize Abortion Doctor on New Murder Charge*, CHI. DAILY TRIB., May 1, 1935, at 18; *Fainting Juror Brings Mistrial in Abortion Case*, CHI. DAILY TRIB., June 6, 1935, at 10; *Abortion Death Evidence Given by Doctor's Aid*, CHI. DAILY TRIB., June 7, 1935, at 10; *2 Doctors Open Abortion Trial Defense Today*, CHI. DAILY TRIB., June 8, 1935, at 13; *Finish Evidence in Murder Trial of Two Doctors*, CHI. DAILY TRIB., June 12, 1935, at 10; *Two Abortion Doctors Guilty; Get 1 to 14 Years*, CHI. DAILY TRIB., June 13, 1935, at 1; *Sentence Two Physicians in Abortion Death*, CHI. DAILY TRIB., June 29, 1935, at 6; *Police Arrest Dr. F. F. Braune on New Charge*, CHI. DAILY TRIB., Feb. 4, 1936, at 6; *Sues Doctors for $10,000 in Girl's Abortion Death*, CHI. DAILY TRIB., Feb. 25, 1936, at 2; *Two Physicians Win New Trial in Death of Girl*, CHI. DAILY TRIB., June 11, 1936, at 11.

348 *Id.*

349 *Id.* at 552, 839-40.

The defendants had separate counsel, and before trial, Braune moved to sever their trials, including a detailed verified petition giving his version of events.[350] Braune claimed that on his first examination of "Miss Dwyer" he found that she had been pregnant for about three months, but it appeared that the foetus was dead and that Dwyer was the "victim of a 'missed abortion[.]'"[351] Braune decided he would have to anesthetize Dwyer for an examination to be certain of her condition and that of the foetus, and that if the foetus was dead, it would have to be removed to avoid serious consequences and risk of death to Dwyer.[352] Braune's petition "set forth with great particularity" what happened on February 22, when Dwyer was anesthetized.[353] Braune averred that Dwyer's "uterus had become so boggy and impaired that it ruptured, admitting into it the intestine, and that the latter was severed before he was aware of the rupture[,]" and that "the diseased and impaired condition of her genital organs was due to efforts of Dr. Dale to abort her[.]"[354] Braune also alleged that Dwyer's general physical condition was "greatly depleted" due to a head injury that left her incapable of any employment.[355] Braune's petition further averred that Dwyer's condition as an invalid resulted from a fall, and

> While she was in such state of invalidism said Dale caused her to become pregnant, and thereupon he sought to persuade her against her better instincts to bring about a condition, or to have a condition brought about in her uterus and genital organs which would result in her miscarriage; that her condition during the months of December, 1934, and January, 1935, was one of extreme suffering and ill-health; that during said months said Dale was with her a great deal and sought to and did tamper with her genital organs, and at divers times used a catheter on her; that he prescribed and gave her medicines which had an injurious effect upon her internal organs, and some of which medicines were intended to bring about a miscarriage; that she suffered excruciating pain at times in the lower pelvis, and that her suffering and despondency finally became so unbearable that she attempted suicide on January 11, 1935, in the office of

---

350 *Id.* at 552-553, 840.
351 *Id.* at 553, 840. A "missed abortion" occurs when a fetus dies in the uterus but is not expelled for two months or more, which can lead to health complications for the mother. *See* http://medical-dictionary.thefreedictionary.com/missed+abortion.
352 *Id.*
353 *Id.*
354 *Id.*
355 *Id.*

> said Dale and had to be taken to the Cook County Hospital for treatment.[356]

Braune's petition warned that Dale would testify in his own behalf and that their "defenses [would] be directly and diametrically conflicting and antagonistic to each other and it would be impossible for him to secure a fair and impartial trial jointly with Dale."[357]

The court denied Braune's motion, whereupon Dale similarly moved for severance, alleging that the facts stated in Braune's petition were prejudicial to him, denying the truth of any of Braune's averments that implicated him in the crime, warning that Braune would testify in his own behalf to the facts alleged in his petition, and contending that "because they are codefendants he cannot cross-examine Braune as he would desire to do in view of their antagonistic defenses; and that he cannot obtain a fair and impartial trial if they are tried jointly."[358] The prosecutor replied that the defenses merely indicated that each counsel would involve the other physician-codefendant, and " '[t]he court by proper instructions can certainly caution the jury.' "[359] The court also denied Dale's motion.[360]

The *Braune* court cited *Paisley* for the rule that a severance motion must set out sufficient grounds, *Hotchkiss* and *Nusbaum* for the rule that a court decides such a motion on the grounds advanced at the time the motion was made.[361] The court politely but somewhat incredulously rejected the State's argument that the defendants' petitions "did not state any facts or any theories which disclose that the defenses would be inconsistent[,]" pointing to the grisly facts stated in Braune's petition regarding the serious physical harm and excruciating pain Dwyer suffered from Dale's alleged earlier abortion attempts, all of which Dale denied.[362] The court cited *Patris* regarding a trial court's judicial, but not arbitrary, discretion to grant or deny a severance.[363] The court then explained,

> It was apparent from the petitions that an actual and substantial hostility existed between the defendants over their lines of defense. Each was protesting his innocence and condemning the other. Each declared the other would take the witness stand and testify to a state of facts which

356 *Id.* at 554-555, 840-841.
357 *Id.*
358 *Id.* at 553-554, 840.
359 *Id.* at 554, 840.
360 *Id.*
361 *Id.*
362 *Id.* at 554-555, 840-841.
363 *Id.* at 555, 841.

> would be exculpatory of the witness and condemnatory of his codefendant. Criminations and recriminations were the inevitable result. Ordinarily the right of one defendant to cross-examine his codefendant does not exist. However, there is an exception to the rule, based on justice and necessity. Where one defendant has given testimony which tends to incriminate the other defendant, the latter, especially where he had no prior notice of such incriminating testimony, may cross-examine the former; but we know of no decided case where such a situation had been brought to the attention of the court prior to the trial and a severance was denied.[364]

The court distinguished *Allison*, in which each codefendant testified in his own behalf and blamed the other, and one defendant's counsel cross-examined the other defendant after the prosecution's cross-examination.[365] The *Braune* court explained, "Neither defendant knew what the other defendant would testify to until each testified on the witness stand. No motion for separate trial had been made."[366] And although "it was claimed that he usurped the functions of a prosecutor in his cross-examination[,]" the *Allison* court "held that where codefendants are represented by different counsel, who knew nothing of what the testimony of the other would be until they heard it from the witness stand, justice requires that the defendant who claims to be innocent shall have the right of cross-examination."[367] In *Braune*, where the antagonism was firmly pointed out before trial, there was no such risk of surprise.

The court observed that the trial court "did not hold the petitions were insufficient to set forth the antagonism of defenses[,]" but instead ruled, "'While the petition avers the interests of defendants are antagonistic, I believe the interests of each may be protected by admonitions or instructions to the jury as matters arise requiring protection against any clash of interests.'"[368] The *Braune* court, however, declared,

> It is our belief that no judge, however learned and skillful, could have protected the defendants in this case against their own hostility. The record shows in many instances that the defendants' witnesses were subjected to searching and critical cross-examinations by counsel for the antagonistic codefendant. Frequently it extended beyond the field covered

364 *Id.*
365 *Id.* at 556, 841.
366 *Id.*
367 *Id.*
368 *Id.*

> by the state's attorney and in some cases went into matters never inquired of by him.[369]

The court noted that Braune and three of his witnesses were cross-examined by Dale's counsel; Dale and four of his witnesses were cross-examined by Braune's counsel. The court recounted, "It was in one of these cross-examinations that the facts relating to Miss Dwyer's attempted suicide in Dale's office and their differences in religious beliefs were injected into the case. Irrelevant matters, such as the change of name of Dale, were brought out by counsel for Braune."[370] Although the prosecution did not cross-examine a character witness Dale called, a long-time practicing physician and professor of pediatrics at the University of Illinois who knew Dale when he attended the university, had known him for years thereafter, and testified to his "general reputation for being a peaceable and law-abiding citizen," Braune's counsel did cross-examine the witness solely to bring out the fact that Dale had changed his name, and that when the witness was Dale's teacher, he had known Dale as "Udelsky."[371] This, together with the court's circumspect reference to "religious differences," suggests that Braune's counsel was determined to hammer home to the jury that Dale was a Jew who had changed his name, and so inflame any open or latent anti-Semitism jurors might harbor and add interfaith miscegenation to an already scandalous (for the times) story involving forbidden extramarital sex and cohabitation, bastardy, abortion, and attempted suicide.[372] The court concluded, in what would—much later—become famous and oft-cited language, "The trial was in many respects more of a contest between the defendants than between the people and the defendants. It produced a spectacle where the people frequently stood by and witnessed a combat in which the defendants attempted to destroy each other."[373] Citing *Minnecci* not specifically regarding antagonism, but only for the sound general rule that "Any set of circumstances which is sufficient to deprive a defendant of a fair trial if tried jointly with another is sufficient to require a separate trial[,]" the court held, "The situation presented to the court upon the applications for separate trials required the granting of the petitions."[374]

---

369 *Id.*

370 *Id.*

371 *Id.* at 556-557, 841-842.

372 As an example of how different times, and religious and sexual mores, were back then, during the 1920s, an interfaith extramarital affair that produced an illicit son threatened to ruin the career of America's best-known and best-loved composer of classical music, George Gershwin, and had to be carefully hushed up. *See* JOAN PEYSER, THE MEMORY OF ALL THAT: THE LIFE OF GEORGE GERSHWIN 109-111 (2006).

373 *Id.* at 557, 842.

374 *Id.* The court also noted "other errors appearing in this record may be hereafter avoided[,]" including, inter alia, evidence that the prosecutor contemplated a bastardy charge against Dale, or

FORGETTING *BRAUNE*: 1938-1944

After *Braune*, there was no new case in Illinois' antagonistic defenses lineage for nearly two years until *People v. Kozlowski* (1938), in which two defendants were tried jointly and convicted of armed robbery and a third pleaded guilty in a separate trial.[375] At trial, Kozlowski moved for severance because his two codefendants were charged with being habitual criminals, because "the respective defenses were antagonistic," and because the other two had made statements tending to incriminate him.[376] In a very brief paragraph, the court cited *Patris* on joint trial and discretionary severance, found Kozlowski's habitual criminals argument meritless, stated, "Boreman's defense was not antagonistic to that of this defendant" without citing authority, and affirmed.[377] Three years later, *People v. Mutter* (1941), another arson-for-insurance case involving two brothers like *Covitz*, was decided.[378] *Mutter*, like *Kozlowski*, ignored *Braune*. The court cited *Wood* and *Corbishly* regarding joint trial, *Kozlowski* on discretionary severance.[379] Rejecting Max Mutter's complaint of improper denial of severance, the court observed, "Generally, if one defendant makes confessions implicating the other defendant or defendants, a severance should be ordered [citing *Bolton*] and, likewise, where the defense of one defendant is so antagonistic to the defense of the others that a severance is necessary to insure a fair trial. [Citing *Payne*.]"[380] The court found "neither of those elements . . . present" where no defendant confessed or offered an antagonistic defense.[381] The court also cited *Gillespie* regarding testimony competent against one defendant but incompetent against another and held that the trial court handled any such situations appropriately.[382] *Mutter* discussed and dismissed severance in one paragraph and is noteworthy mostly for revealing the court's understanding that antagonistic defenses and codefendant statements are two distinct categories.

Braune made a brief, minor reappearance in 1942 in *People v. Meisenhelter*.[383] *Meisenhelter* involved a group of union officials and members who conspired to,

that Dale refused to marry Dwyer, and other evidence regarding, apparently, the equipment and techniques used for the abortion. *Id.* at 557, 842.

375 368 Ill. 124, 125, 13 N.E.2d 174 (Feb. 16, 1938) (Farthing, C.J.).

376 *Id.* at 125.

377 *Id.* at 126, 175-76.

378 378 Ill. 216, 217-25, 37 N.E.2d 790 (Nov. 18, 1941) (Farthing, J.).

379 *Id.* at 227-228.

380 *Id.* at 795.

381 *Id.*

382 *Id.* at 796.

383 381 Ill. 378, 388-89, 45 N.E.2d 678, 684 (Nov. 17, 1942) (Stone, C.J.).

and did, bomb an oil pipeline built with non-union labor.[384] On appeal of the bombing case, which was tried separately from the conspiracy charges, the defendants, citing *Patris*, complained of prejudice from statements of a codefendant who pleaded guilty.[385] The State, citing *Minnecci* and *Betson*, countered that the defendants showed no prejudice and "the verified motion did not disclose that the defenses . . . were antagonistic."[386] The court cited *Braune* and *Patris* on discretionary severance, *Braune* and *Minnecci*, *Paisley*, *Hotchkiss*, and *Nusbaum* for the requirement that a severance motion set out appropriate grounds for the trial court to consider.[387] The court relied on *Minnecci* regarding joint trial, the defendant's obligation to show prejudice from a joint trial, the "any set of circumstances" sufficient to deny a fair trial language originally from *Lehne*, and, most significantly, "Where defenses are antagonistic and one defendant accuses the other, thus making it impossible for the defendant asking for a severance to have a fair trial, the severance should be granted."[388] The court explained that the severance motions did not show how the complaining defendants' defenses were antagonistic to the defense of the codefendant who made the statements at issue, and also pointed out that the trial court properly deleted the names of defendants in the separate conspiracy trial, and that the codefendant in question was not even a defendant in the bombing case.[389] The court lengthily quoted *Siegal* regarding how courts must protect the people's rights along with the defendants' rights in considering severance motions, noted that no antagonistic defenses arose at trial, and held that denial of the severance motions was no error.[390] In the appeal of the related conspiracy convictions, the court quoted the same language from *Siegal*, cited *Minnecci* regarding the trial court's discretion to sever, and stated, "There was no showing made on the application for severance that the defenses of the different defendants were antagonistic."[391] In addition to mentioning *Braune* for the last time until 1975, *Meisenhelter* is noteworthy for suggesting that it was relevant whether or not antagonistic defenses actually surfaced at trial—later cases would deny that—and for seemingly moving toward lumping codefendant statements together with antagonistic defenses more than earlier cases had done.

People v. Serritello (1944)[392] entirely concerned codefendant confessions, never mentioned or otherwise addressed antagonism, and did not conflate the two

---

384 *Id.* at 381-82, 680-81.
385 *Id.* at 387-88, 683.
386 *Id.* at 388, 683.
387 *Id.* at 388-389, 684.
388 *Id.* at 388-89, 683-84.
389 *Id.* at 389, 684.
390 *Id.* at 389-390, 684.
391 People v. Meisenhelter, 317 Ill.App. 511, 516-17, 47 N.E.2d 108 (Feb. 24, 1943) (Hayes, J.).
392 385 Ill. 554, 53 N.E.2d 581 (Jan. 20, 1944) (Murphy, J.).

categories. The only evidence linking codefendant Clow to a burglary was his and Serritello's joint possession of stolen items after the burglary, and Serritello's written confession.[393] The court cited *Patris* and *Sweetin* on discretionary severance, and those two cases plus *Fisher*, *Buckminster*, *Carmichael*, and *Betson* on how to handle codefendants' confessions.[394] Although the prosecution deleted Clow's name and replaced it with "Blank" whenever it was mentioned as Serritello's written confession was offered in evidence solely against Serritello, the court held that the confession nevertheless prejudiced Clow, and reversed his conviction.[395]

COMPOUNDING CONFUSION: *BARBARO* AND THE EXPLICIT RECATEGORIZATION OF INCRIMINATING CODEFENDANT STATEMENTS AS ANTAGONISTIC DEFENSES, 1946

The next case in the lineage, *People v. Barbaro* (1946),[396] is another codefendant-statements case, but the court transformed it into an antagonism case by needlessly invoking the language of antagonism and mixing it with the proto-*Bruton* issue, as *Serritello* had avoided. *Barbaro* involved a complex lattice of multiple interconnected codefendant statements and confessions. Like *Serritello*, *Barbaro* was a burglary case in which the two defendants were found in joint possession of stolen goods, and the only evidence linking the defendants to the burglary were their codefendants' statements, along with their own statements.[397] Each defendant made multiple statements to police, some while separate from each other, some allegedly in each other's presence, some allegedly under either a promise of immunity or threats by police.[398] Prosecution witnesses testified regarding the defendants' statements without redaction of references to the codefendants, though the court gave limiting instructions.[399] The prosecution sought to rely on evidence that at one of four separate conferences with local authorities, both defendants, in each other's presence, had made confessions implicating themselves individually and each other, but the court concluded that the "insuperable difficulty of separating such confessions from those made out of

393 *Id.* at 555-58, 581-83.

394 *Id.* at 556-57, 558, 582-583.

395 *Id.* at pp. 557-558, 582-583.

396 395 Ill. 264, 69 N.E.2d 692 (Nov. 20, 1946) (Wilson, J.).

397 *Id.* at 266-69, 693-94.

398 *Id.* Defendant Ferne Barbaro testified that the county sheriff of rural Saline County, Illinois, and the police chief and fire chief of Marion, Illinois, scolded her for being a white woman in the company of a black man (codefendant Preston Williams), talked to her in a vulgar manner, promised to let her go if she made a statement implicating Williams, and threatened to see that she "took a trip" if she did not. *Id.* at 267-268, 694.

399 *Id.* at 271, 695.

the presence of each other remain[ed]" for the jury.[400] The court accordingly reversed and remanded for separate trials for both defendants.[401]

Barbaro thus was a case involving, and decided on, improper admission and use of conflicting codefendants' confessions causing prejudice that overwhelmed any mitigative efforts. The *Barbaro* court, however, needlessly injected antagonism into the equation. The court cited *Serritello*, *Patris*, *Fisher*, and *Sweetin* on joint trial and discretionary severance, then continued,

> The right to a severance must rest upon the ground that the defense to be offered by one defendant is so antagonistic to the defense to be offered by the other defendant that a severance is necessary to insure a fair trial. [Citing *Betson*.] Accordingly, it has been generally held that when a motion for a separate trial is made on the ground that a confession by a codefendant implicates the petitioner, a severance should be ordered unless the State's Attorney declares that the admissions or confessions will not be offered in evidence upon the trial, or unless there be eliminated from the confessions any reference to the codefendant applying for a severance. [Citing *Serritello*, *Fisher*, and *Bolton*.] The reason for the rule is that it is practically impossible to remove by instruction the prejudicial effect of the confessions against the defendants implicated. [Citing *Sweetin*.][402]

By this language, the *Barbaro* court fell into the trap the *Betson* court inadvertently set a decade earlier when it incorrectly declared that antagonistic defenses constituted the sole, exclusive ground for separate trials. For if that was true, then anything sufficient to justify severance, by definition, necessarily had to be redefined as antagonistic defenses. Thus, notwithstanding that Illinois had a reasonably successful rule—the *Buckminster* rule, as later expanded and modified—regarding the handling of incriminating codefendant statements that predated all the later confused babble about antagonistic defenses, *Barbaro* began the process of twisting definitions to try to force what had been the separate, distinct category of codefendant statements under the rubric of antagonistic defenses to conform with *Betson*'s misstatement of the law. Although this process was never entirely completed, and later courts occasionally could not help but stumble upon the realization that the categories were fundamentally different while some other courts considering codefendant statements ignored antagonism altogether, most opinions in the antagonism lineage would dutifully declare that incriminating

---

400 *Id.*

401 *Id.* at 273, 696.

402 *Id.* at 270-71, 695.

codefendant statements were a subcategory of antagonistic defenses—indeed, the dominant subcategory—creating further complication and confusion down the road.

As an example of this confusion, the *Barbaro* court went on to observe, "A fair summary of the evidence adduced leads to the conclusion that the defenses of the two defendants were, in fact, antagonistic to each other."[403] The court explained that the People's evidence showed Barbaro implicating codefendant Williams, but Barbaro testified that she did so only because of promises and threats by local officials, thus calling into question the prosecution's evidence; similarly, the People's evidence disclosed that Williams admitted participation in the crimes at Barbaro's suggestion, but Williams denied this on the stand.[404] The court missed the key point that these examples show that although the defendants' defenses both contradicted the People's evidence, they were in fact not antagonistic to each other. A defendant's defense normally refers to the defense that a defendant proposes to, or actually does, offer at trial, not the state of the evidence before trial, particularly the prosecution's evidence. A defendant, and defense counsel, have control over the defense offered, including choosing not to offer a defense at all; they do not control the overall state of the evidence, which can of course affect the plausibility of whatever defense the defendant selects. But *Barbaro* itself clearly shows that part of a defendant's defense can be challenging the validity of pretrial statements or confessions. Such pretrial statements or confessions thus necessarily do not define defendants' defenses. Yet numerous later Illinois courts would follow the *Barbaro* court in this misunderstanding, all for the purpose of dutifully misconstruing incriminating codefendant statements as a subcategory of antagonistic defenses.

The next opinion, *People v. Tabet* (1948), merely mentioned the appellants' antagonism arguments while rejecting them for failure to specify grounds or show antagonism (citing *Woods* and *Paisley*).[405] Similarly, in *People v. Mosher* (1949), the court quickly dismissed Mosher's severance argument regarding his codefendant's confession by noting there was nothing in the record to indicate that the statement in question was a confession or was "in any manner antagonistic to [Mosher]."[406] In *People v. Varela* (1950), Varela argued that he inevitably would be prejudiced by joint trial with a jail-breaker and " 'confessed'" murderer, Najera, who had drawn much public attention, and that Najera's confession implicated

403 Id at 271, 695.
404 *Id.* at 272, 695-96.
405 402 Ill. 93, 101, 83 N.E.2d 329, 333-34 (Nov. 18, 1948) (Simpson, J.).
406 403 Ill. 112, 115-16, 85 N.E.2d 658 (Mar. 24, 1949) (Daily, J.) (citing *Albers* and *Payne* on discretionary severance; Mosher relied on *Mutter*).

Varela.[407] The court noted that it was apparent from the record "and fully conceded that the defenses of the two defendants are not antagonistic" because Varela had entirely adopted Najera's confession (citing *Lehne* and *Fisher*).[408] The court rejected the appellant's reliance on *Barbaro* because "there the defenses were antagonistic."[409] The court also held that the trial court had given appropriate limiting instructions (citing *Mutter* and *Gillespie*), and that no prejudice was shown.[410]

THE FIRST CLASSIC POSTWAR STATEMENT OF THE 'RULE': *LINDSAY*, 1952

Not until 1952, in *People v. Lindsay*,[411] did the Illinois Supreme Court substantially add to the state's supposed antagonism-severance rule. The defendants' motions for severance argued that codefendants had made incriminating statements, plus what was already becoming standard boilerplate to the effect that a joint trial could not be fair and impartial and "the defenses of the codefendants were antagonistic and against the petitioner for those reasons."[412] The court cited *Fisher* regarding incriminating codefendant statements normally requiring severance unless the prosecution excluded or redacted the statements, but explained that the various defendants all admitted substantially the same set of facts, "[t]he motions for severance in no place show or point out in what manner the defenses of the various defendants were antagonistic to each other," and that as in *Fisher*, rather than exonerating themselves, each defendant in his statement implicated both himself and his codefendants, so the trial court was justified in denying the severance motions.[413]

Lindsay thus only involved codefendant statements and had no reason to address antagonism at all except inasmuch as codefendant confessions had come to be wrongly perceived as a subcategory of antagonism, and defense counsel had begun to claim "antagonism" with greater abandon. Although *Lindsay* did not cite *Barbaro* or that opinion's outright conflation of incriminating codefendant statements with antagonistic defenses, *Lindsay*'s discussion of the codefendant statements in close conjunction with antagonistic defenses implied the same conflation of categories; the defendants' severance motions clearly and explicitly conflated them.

---

407 405 Ill. 236, 247-48, 90 N.E.2d 631, 636 (Jan. 18, 1950) (per curiam).
408 *Id.* at 248, 636-637.
409 *Id.* at 248, 637.
410 *Id.*
411 412 Ill. 472, 107 N.E.2d 614 (Jun. 4, 1952) (per curiam).
412 *Id.* at 481, 619.
413 *Id.* at 481-482, 619.

Lindsay's master summary of the entire Illinois severance rule did not clearly conflate the two categories, however, and it is noteworthy that in what was intended to be a relatively complete, comprehensive statement of all parts of the rule, the court never specifically mentioned codefendant statements. Rather than giving one segment of the rule at a time, followed by authority specific to that point, the court offered the entire rule as a package, followed by a cluster of authorities not linked to any specific point and including the recent decisions in *Tabet* and *Varela* that barely mentioned antagonism. The court borrowed the *Minnecci* version and ignored the *Payne/Betson* version in proclaiming:

> The general rule is that persons jointly indicted shall be jointly tried. Except in those cases where fairness to one or more defendants requires that a severance be granted, the matter lies in the discretion of the trial judge and the question of abuse of such discretion depends upon the facts of each case. It is incumbent upon a defendant, moving for a separate trial, to show how he would be prejudiced by a joint trial. If he fails so to do, he cannot on review complain of the acts of the trial court in denying his motion. *Where defenses are antagonistic and one defendant accuses the other, thus making it impossible for the defendant asking for a severance to have a fair trial, the severance should be granted.* However, a motion for a severance must set out the grounds showing the reason for granting the severance. The trial court passes upon the motion on the grounds advanced at the time it is made. Any set of circumstances sufficient to deprive a defendant of a fair trial if tried jointly with another is sufficient to require a separate trial. The granting of a severance and separate trial is within the sound discretion of the court but it is a judicial and not an arbitrary discretion. [Citing *Fisher*, *Albers*, *Minnecci*, *Meisenhelter*, *Tabet*, and *Varela*.][414]

The *Lindsay* court thus followed *Minnecci*, and not *Betson*, in stating the antagonism rule non-exclusively: the court states that a severance should be granted where defenses are antagonistic and one defendant accuses the other, but does not state that is the only situation were a severance is justified. The *Minnecci/Lehne* language, "Any set of circumstances sufficient to deprive a defendant of a fair trial if tried jointly with another is sufficient to require a separate trial," is also non-exclusive and implies that there could be many situations justifying severance. It also implies that facts could arise that would entitle a defendant to a severance even if that defendant failed to establish the need for a severance the usual way by a pretrial

414 *Id.* at 480-81, 618-19 (italics added). Surprisingly few later cases noticed the condition that *Lindsay* borrowed from *Minnecci*—that "one defendant accuses the other." *See* People v. Beard, 35 Ill.App.3d 725, 733 342 N.E.2d 343, 349 (Feb. 10, 1976) (Rechenmacher, J.); People v. Murphy, 93 Ill.App.3d 606, 609, 417 N.E.2d 759, 762 (Feb. 20, 1981) (Mejda, J.).

motion—thus implicitly challenging the court's own recitation that "It is incumbent upon a defendant, moving for a separate trial, to show how he would be prejudiced by a joint trial. If he fails so to do, he cannot on review complain of the acts of the trial court in denying his motion."

Lindsay altered *Minnecci*'s language in subtle but significant ways that tended to rigidify the rule. For example, where *Minnecci* said that a defendant who fails to show prejudice from a joint trial to the trial court "is not in position to complain" about denial of severance—and the *Minnecci* court then went ahead to consider the issue on its merits anyway—*Lindsay* said that such a defendant "cannot on review complain" about the denial. More crucially, *Lindsay* at least partly restricted the potential openness and ambiguity in *Minnecci's* version of the key segment of the rule. Where *Minnecci* said, "The rule is that where there is more than one defendant and the defenses are antagonistic, and one defendant accuses the other, so that it will be impossible for the defendant who asked a severance to have a fair trial, the severance should be granted," *Lindsay* said, "Where defenses are antagonistic and one defendant accuses the other, thus making it impossible for the defendant asking for a severance to have a fair trial, the severance should be granted." *Lindsay* thus removed any possible ambiguity regarding the impossibility of a fair trial as an independent factor; the *Lindsay* version makes it clear that factor is established if the others are. Thus, where *Minnecci*'s "so that it will be impossible" language implied a requirement of a sufficient degree of antagonism, *Lindsay*'s "thus making it impossible" language created an automatic definition. *Lindsay*'s deletion of *Minnecci*'s comma between "Where defenses are antagonistic" and "and one defendant accuses the other" also tends to restrict the possible meanings of *Minnecci* by suggesting more strongly that the two factors may really be one and the same. Whether the *Lindsay* court intended these changes in meaning is another question; mostly likely the court thought it was conveying the exact same message as *Minnecci.*

A SIMPLE RULE, OFT REPEATED: *GRILEC, HENDERSON*, AND THEIR NUMEROUS PROGENY, 1954-1980

The next case in the antagonism lineage to follow *Lindsay*, *People v. Grilec*,[415] came almost two years later and ironically seemed oblivious to the *Lindsay* court's conscientious efforts at rule construction. In *Grilec*, in a very brief, almost throwaway paragraph at the very end of an opinion focused mostly on statements used to prove a conspiracy, the court cited *Barbaro* and *Mutter* generally on joint trial and discretionary severance before observing, without further citation of authority, "The record here discloses not only that the defenses of Grilec and his

[415] 2 Ill.2d 538, 119 N.E.2d 232 (Mar. 17, 1954) (Bristow, J.).

codefendant Milosic were not antagonistic, but, on the contrary, they were wholly consistent and harmonious. The paramount inquiry or test is, are the defenses of such an antagonistic nature that a severance is imperative to insure a fair trial. We are of the opinion the trial court did not err in denying plaintiff in error's motion for a severance."[416] *Grilec* thus said almost nothing, and effectively decided nothing, regarding antagonistic defenses—other than that the defenses obviously were not antagonistic, which made the statement of the antagonism severance rule entirely gratuitous. That is, it would have been entirely sufficient for the court to say in effect, as other courts sometimes did, "You do not have a legitimate antagonistic defenses argument," without adding, "But if you had a legitimate argument, here's what we would have done."

Grilec followed earlier opinions in referring to a single severance rule that lumped together antagonistic defenses, problems relating to codefendant statements and confessions, and any other conceivable grounds for severance all under the rubric of antagonism. Notably, though, the *Grilec* court hedged its bets by stating the supposed rule in a not-entirely-exclusive fashion: although the "paramount inquiry" concerned antagonism, that implicitly left room for lesser inquiries bearing on the issue of severance, too. The *Grilec* court thus steered ambiguously between the non-exclusive phrasing in *Mutter*—"Generally . . . a severance should be ordered [both where a defendant's statement implicates another defendant] and, likewise, where the defense of one defendant is so antagonistic to the defense of the others that a severance is necessary to insure a fair trial" (recognizing codefendant statements and antagonistic defenses as separate, distinct categories)[417]—and *Babaro*'s exclusive phrasing: "The right to a severance must rest upon the ground that [one defendant's anticipated] defense . . . is so antagonistic to the [other's] defense . . . that a severance is necessary to insure a fair trial."

Grilec was one in a long line of Illinois cases that found no antagonism and hence really did not have to use or apply Illinois' supposed antagonism-severance rule, but merely mentioned it in passing in dismissing a weak severance argument. This makes it perhaps slightly ironic that *Grilec*'s phrasing became a classic statement of the Illinois severance "rule" that reappeared in dozens of subsequent opinions through 1985 and was especially popular with later courts seeking to dismiss the issue of antagonism briefly. Those using the distinctive phrase "paramount inquiry" are easiest to identify,[418] but *Grilec* also sired a sublineage using the

416 *Id.* at 546-47, 236.

417 Mutter, 37 N.E.2d at 795.

418 Grilec "paramount inquiry" progeny: People v. Wilson, 29 Ill.2d 82, 193 N.E.2d 449, 454 (Sept. 27, 1963) (per curiam) (citing Grilec); People v. Brinn, 32 Ill.2d 232, 204 N.E.2d 724 (Jan. 21,

alternate construction "primary question" through *People v. Henderson*, which cited two of *Grilec*'s early progeny to state, "The primary question is whether the defenses of the several defendants are so antagonistic that a fair trial can be assured only by a severance."[419] *Henderson*, like most of *Grilec*'s progeny, was a

1965) (Solfisburg, J.) (quoting Grilec); People v. Connolly, 33 Ill.2d 128, 131, 210 N.E.2d 523, 525 (Sept. 28, 1965) (Hershey, J.) (citing Wilson (1963)); People v. Bracken, 68 Ill.App.2d 466, 470, 216 N.E.2d 176, 178 (Feb. 10, 1966) (Dempsey, J.) (codefendants' statements) (citing Grilec); People v. Gendron, 41 Ill.2d 351, 357, 243 N.E.2d 208, 212 (Nov. 22, 1968) (Ward, J.) (quoting Wilson (1963) quoting Grilec); People v. Ramey, 115 Ill.App.2d 431, 437, 253 N.E.2d 688, 692 (Oct. 15, 1969) (Leighton, J.) (citing Grilec); People v. Canaday, 49 Ill.2d 416, 425, 275 N.E.2d 356, 361 (Sept. 30, 1971) (Ward, J.) (quoting Grilec); People v. Wilson, 12 Ill.App.3d 59, 297 N.E.2d 790 (May 16, 1973) (Burman, P.J.) (citing Canaday); People v. Brown, 27 Ill.App.3d 569, 327 N.E.2d 51 (Apr. 23, 1975) (Hallett, J.) (citing/quoting Canaday); People v. Lee, 46 Ill.App.3d 343, 360 N.E.2d 1173, 1177 (Mar. 11, 1977) (Alloy, J.) (quoting Canaday quoting Gendron); People v. Colon (69 Ill.App.3d 1021, 387 N.E.2d 956 (Mar. 20, 1979) (Woodward, J.) (citing Canaday); People v. Lee, 86 Ill.App.3d 922, 929, 408 N.E.2d 335, 341 (Jul. 21, 1980) (O'Connor, J.) (mis-citing Yonder for "Of paramount concern is whether their defenses are so antagonistic that a severance is imperative to a fair trial."); People v. Lee, 87 Ill.2d 182, 429 N.E.2d 461 (Nov. 13, 1981) (Simon, J.) (reversing appellate court's decision in Lee (1980) (citing Gendron (1968) for "paramount inquiry").

[419] 37 Ill.2d 489, 492, 229 N.E.2d 519 (May 18, 1967) (House, J.). Henderson's "primary question" sublineage includes: People v. Henderson, 37 Ill.2d 489, 229 N.E.2d 519 (May 18, 1967) (House, J.) (citing Wilson (1963), Connolly); People v. Trigg, 97 Ill.App.2d 261, 271, 240 N.E.2d 130 (Jun. 10, 1968) (Burman, P.J.) (citing Henderson, Connolly) (slightly alternate construction); People v. Bernette, 45 Ill.2d 227, 241, 258 N.E.2d 793, 800 (Mar. 24, 1970) (per curiam) (citing Henderson, Connolly, and Wilson); People v. Brooks, 51 Ill.2d 156, 166, 281 N.E.2d 326 (Mar. 30, 1972) (Ryan, J.) (citing Henderson); People v. Holtz, 19 Ill.App.3d 781, 789, 313 N.E.2d 234, 241 (May 17, 1974) (Drucker, J.) (citing Henderson and Brooks); People v. Daniels, 35 Ill.App.3d 791, 796, 342 N.E.2d 809, 812 (Jan. 28, 1976) (Johnson, P.J.) (citing Bernette); People v. Hoover, 35 Ill.App.3d 799, 342 N.E.2d 795 (Jan. 28, 1976) (Adesko, J.) (citing Connolly); People v. Appold, 39 Ill.App.3d 814, 815-16, 350 N.E.2d 511, 512 (July 01, 1976) (Trapp, P.J.); People v. Davis, 43 Ill.App.3d 603, 609-10, 357 N.E.2d 96, 101 (Oct. 26, 1976) (Downing, J.) ("Our supreme court has said numerous times that in determining whether a severance should be granted, the primary question is whether the defenses of the defendants are so antagonistic that a fair trial can be assured only by a severance. [Citing Canaday, Yonder, Gendron, Henderson, Brinn, and Betson (1936)]"); People v. Rudolph, 50 Ill.App.3d 559, 569, 365 N.E.2d 930 (Jun. 27, 1977) (Goldberg, P.J.) (citing Bernette and Allen); People v. Jayne, 52 Ill.App.3d 990, 1005, 368 N.E.2d 422, 433 (Sept. 2, 1977) (Bua, J.) (citing Daniels); People v. Nickson, 58 Ill.App.3d 470, 482, 374 N.E.2d 804, 812 (Mar. 13, 1978 (Goldberg, P.J.) (citing Brooks); People v. Mertens, 77 Ill.App.3d 791, 396 N.E.2d 595 (Oct. 30, 1979) (Lindberg, J.) (citing Brooks); People v. Jones, 82 Ill.App.3d 386, 399, 402 N.E.2d 746, 755 (Mar. 14, 1980) (Mejda, J.) (citing Canaday and Davis); People v. Crowder, 99 Ill.App.3d 500, 511, 425 N.E.2d 994, 1001 (Jul. 29, 1981) (Lindberg, J.) (citing Mertens (1979)) (court found no abuse of discretion on denial of severance but reversed and remanded for denial of appellant's motion to voir dire the jury); People v. Griggs, 104 Ill.App.3d 527, 432 N.E.2d 1176 (Feb. 22, 1982) (McGloon, J.) (alternate construction); People v. Morrow, 104 Ill.App.3d 995, 1006, 433 N.E.2d 985, 994 (Mar. 09, 1982) (Stamos, P.J.) (citing Wilson (1963) (alternate construction); People v. Ruiz, 94 Ill.2d 245, 257, 447 N.E.2d 148, 152-53 (Dec. 17, 1982) (Ryan, C.J.) (citing Brooks, Bernette, and Gendron); People v. Columbo, 118 Ill.App.3d 882, 939-40, 455 N.E.2d 733, 775 (Jun. 24, 1983) (Wilson, P.J.) (codefendant statements) (citing Henderson); People

codefendant statements case that had nothing to do with antagonistic defenses but for earlier opinions' improper conflation of the two categories. *Grilec* itself was not cited after 1976,[420] but it passed its torch to progeny cases—such as *People v. Wilson*

---

v. Conley, 118 Ill.App.3d 122, 454 N.E.2d 1107 (Sept. 23, 1983) (Sullivan, J.) (quoting alternative construction in Morrow (1982)); People v. Hargis, 118 Ill.App.3d 1064, 1074-75, 456 N.E.2d 250, 255 (Nov. 03, 1983) (Mills, J.) (quoting Ruiz (1982)); People v. Griffin, 124 Ill.App.3d 119, 124, 463 N.E.2d 1055 (May 14, 1984) (Harrison, J.) (citing Canaday (1971)). There were also numerous cases that used alternative constructions derived from Grilec/Henderson: People v. Allen, 36 Ill.App.3d 821, 825, 344 N.E.2d 825, 828 (Mar. 04, 1976 (Dempsey, J.) (citing Grilec for "Persons jointly indicted for the commission of a crime should be tried together unless their defenses are of such an antagonistic nature that a severance is necessary to insure a fair trial."); People v. Henderson, 39 Ill.App.3d 164, 351 N.E.2d 225 (Jun. 03, 1976) (Dempsey, J.) (companion case to Allen (1976)) (citing Grilec for, "The governing principle is that persons jointly indicted should be tried together unless their defenses are so antagonistic that a severance is necessary to insure a fair trial."); People v. Morrow, 40 Ill.App.3d 1020, 353 N.E.2d 354, 357 (Aug. 2, 1976) (Simon, J.) (citing Gendron for "The resolution of a motion for severance turns on whether the defenses are of such an antagonistic nature that defendants cannot receive fair trial when tried together."); People v. Miner, 46 Ill.App.3d 273, 283, 360 N.E.2d 1141 (Feb. 28, 1977) (Karns, J.) (citing Brooks (1972) for "Separate trials are required only when the defenses of the defendants are so antagonistic that a fair trial can be assured only by a severance"); People v. Vinson, 49 Ill.App.3d 602, 364 N.E.2d 364, 367 (May 23, 1977) (O'Connor, J.) (citing Brooks for "Generally, co-defendants are tried jointly unless their defenses are so antagonistic that a severance is required to assure the defendants a fair trial."); People v. Ballard, 65 Ill.App.3d 831, 840, 382 N.E.2d 800, 807-08 (Oct. 20, 1978) (Woodward, J.) (citing Henderson (1976) for "The governing principle is that persons jointly indicted should be tried together unless their defenses are so antagonistic that a severance is necessary to insure a fair trial."); People v. Moore, 65 Ill.App.3d 712, 719, 382 N.E.2d 810, 815-16 (Nov. 2, 1978) (Boyle, J.) (citing Brooks (1972) and Brown (1975) for "It is axiomatic that co-defendants should be tried jointly together unless their defenses are so antagonistic that a severance must be granted to insure the defendants of a fair trial. "); People v. Cain, 70 Ill.App.3d 1, 6, 388 N.E.2d 54 (Feb. 26, 1979) (Buckley, J.) (citing Barbaro and Jayne for "joint trials are favored unless the defenses of the co-defendants are so antagonistic that a joint trial would prevent the co-defendants from receiving a fair trial."); People v. Mumford, 70 Ill.App.3d 395, 405, 387 N.E.2d 910, 917-18 (Mar. 19, 1979) (Goldberg, P.J.) (quoting Canaday quoting Gendron: "It has been repeatedly held that the issue here is ' "* * * whether the defenses are of such an antagonistic nature that a severance is imperative to secure a fair trial." ' "); People v. Lumpkin, 105 Ill.App.3d 157, 166, 433 N.E.2d 1369, 1376 (Apr. 01, 1982) (Jones, J.) (citing Canaday (1971) and Davis (1976) for "[A] severance should be granted where the defendants' defenses are so antagonistic that severance is the only way of assuring a fair trial"); People v. Kinion, 105 Ill.App.3d 1069, 435 N.E.2d 533, 538 (May 05, 1982) (Stouder, J.) (citing Canaday (1971) for "The benchmark by which the determination of prejudice is made in the more common instance involving co-defendants is whether defenses are so antagonistic that severance is imperative to require a fair trial."); People v. Guyon, 117 Ill.App.3d 522, 453 N.E.2d 849 (Aug. 24, 1983 (McGillicuddy, J.) (citing Canaday (1971) and Brooks (1972) for "It is well established in Illinois that separate trials are required only where the defenses of the codefendants are so antagonistic that a fair trial cannot be assured without a severance.").

420 See People v. Allen (36 Ill.App.3d 821, 825, 344 N.E.2d 825, 828 (Mar. 04, 1976 (Dempsey, J.) and People v. Henderson (39 Ill.App.3d 164, 351 N.E.2d 225 (Jun. 03, 1976) (Dempsey, J.).

(1963),[421] *People v. Connolly* (1965),[422] *People v. Gendron* (1968),[423] *People v. Canaday* (1971),[424] and from the *Henderson* sublineage, *People v. Bernette* (1970)[425] and *People v. Brooks* (1972)[426]—that were frequently cited even though they, too, generally said very little about the issue of antagonistic defenses and usually only concerned codefendant statements.

Even as *Lindsay*, *Grilec*, *Henderson*, and their multitudinous progeny were helping to erase the traditional and appropriate distinction between severance based on antagonistic defenses and severance based upon incriminating codefendant statements, other cases within the antagonistic defenses lineage, and even more outside of it, continued to treat codefendant statements as a separate category and ignored antagonistic defenses jurisprudence or treated it separately. *People v. Johnson* (1958)[427] was not one of those, though it came close. In a purely codefendant statements case that cited *Lindsay* strictly regarding incriminating confessions and analogized closely to a codefendant statements case that never mentioned antagonism and showed that it was not necessary to do so,[428] the *Johnson* court held that under the circumstances, the prosecution's substitution of "Blank" for a defendant's name did not sufficiently overcome the prejudicial impact from introducing a codefendant's incriminating confession and concluded, "It is clear from the foregoing that there was hostility between the two defendants, and that their defenses to the crime were antagonistic and incompatible."[429] It is unclear from the *Johnson* opinion, but it appears entirely possible that defense counsel did not even raise the issue of antagonism and that the court may have gratuitously introduced the concept.

People v. Clark (1959),[430] however, only mentioned antagonism briefly at the beginning of the opinion to note that the trial court had allowed the public defender to withdraw as Clark's counsel because his defense was antagonistic to those of his publicly defended codefendants—entirely appropriate in the context of joint representation—but never once mentioned antagonism again in a lengthy discussion of proper handling of incriminating codefendant statements that ironically cited many of the usual suspects regarding the antagonistic defenses rule:

---

421 29 Ill.2d 82, 193 N.E.2d 449 (Sept. 27, 1963) (per curiam).

422 33 Ill.2d 128, 210 N.E.2d 523 (Sept. 28, 1965) (Hershey, J.).

423 41 Ill.2d 351, 243 N.E.2d 208 (Nov. 22, 1968) (Ward, J.).

424 49 Ill.2d 416, 275 N.E.2d 356 (Sept. 30, 1971) (Ward, J.).

425 45 Ill.2d 227, 258 N.E.2d 793 (Mar. 24, 1970) (per curiam).

426 51 Ill.2d 156, 281 N.E.2d 326 (Mar. 30, 1972) (Ryan, J.).

427 13 Ill.2d 619, 150 N.E.2d 597 (May 21, 1958) (Hershey, J.).

428 People v. Hodson, 406 Ill. 328, 94 N.E.2d 166.

429 *Id.* at 623-24.

430 17 Ill.2d 486, 162 N.E.2d 413 (Nov. 18, 1959) (Daily, J.).

Patris, *Sweetin*, *Lindsay*, *Minnecci*, *Lehne*, *Barbaro*, *Bolton*, *Meisenhelter*, and even *Johnson* (1958)—proving that this could be done.[431] *Clark* (1959) would go on to be a frequently cited authority, often cited together with authorities regarding antagonistic defenses in later cases that were really only codefendant statements cases.[432] A later example of a purely codefendant statements case that appears in the antagonism lineage is *People v. McVay* (1981),[433] which noted in passing merely that a codefendant's pretrial statements were "antagonistic to McVay's position at trial and that they readily lead to an incriminating conclusion against him," but otherwise never mentioned antagonism, stated no rule on it, and recognized and relied upon relatively pure codefendant statements authorities.[434] *People v. Strayhorn* (1965)[435] is an interesting example of an opinion that still understood the categories of incriminating codefendant statements and antagonistic defenses to be separate and discussed and rejected each ground in the same opinion—though it ironically cited *Clark* (1959) for the rule that "where it appears that the defenses of the co-defendants are antagonistic, or that confessions made by an accomplice outside of the presence of a defendant may be admitted in evidence, the motion for severance should be allowed."[436]

SOMETHING OUT OF NOTHING: *EARL* AND *YONDER* AS AUTHORITIES FOR THE 'RULE,' 1966-1980

People v. Earl (1966)[437] was a very brief, relatively minor murder case that involved codefendant statements and never mentioned antagonism. The court analogized to *Lindsay*, and cited some other opinions outside the antagonism lineage, in affirming.[438] *Earl* is only interesting at all in this context because despite its total silence regarding antagonism, it became, indirectly, the supposed source for a frequent iteration of the Illinois rule on severance of antagonistic defenses.

The murder victim in *Earl* was found badly beaten and later died.[439] After his arrest, Earl's codefendant, Cocroft, made a statement that he was with Earl when

---

431 *Id.* at 489-92.

432 *Clark* (1959) was cited 14 times in the antagonistic defenses lineage through 1985 (*Strayhorn*, *Bernette*, *Clark* (1970), *Clark* (1972), *Brooks*, *Rosenborgh*, *Allen*, *Davis*, *Lee* (1981), *Cart*, *Edwards*, *Racanelli*, *Sullivan* (1985), and *Trass*) and four times afterward, showing remarkable longevity and persistence, especially for a sound precedent.

433 98 Ill.App.3d 708, 424 N.E.2d 922 (July 28, 1981) (Alloy, J.)

434 *Id.* at 716, 716-18, 927, 927-28 (citing *Clark* (1959), *Sweetin*, *Buckminster*, *Serritello*, *Ross*, *Mosher*, and *Bruton*).

435 35 Ill.2d 41, 219 N.E.2d 517 (Nov. 19, 1965) (Klingbiel, C.J.).

436 *Id.* at 43-45, 519-20.

437 34 Ill.2d 11, 213 N.E.2d 556 (Jan. 25, 1966) (Hershey, J.).

438 *Id.* at 13-14, 557.

439 *Id.* at 12-13, 557.

Earl put a revolver to the victim's neck, the victim then cut Earl with a knife, Earl took the victim a distance away, Cocroft heard fighting, and Earl then reappeared with the victim's coat and "a handful of change."[440] Cocroft said he had no role in the beating or its aftermath.[441] Earl contended that Cocroft's statement was so prejudicial as to require a separate trial unless the State either did not introduce the statement in evidence or deleted all references to Earl.[442] Citing *Lindsay* only for the general rule on joint trial and finding *Lindsay* closely similar, the court explained that Cocroft's written statements were made in Earl's presence, and Earl received copies at the arraignment, so there was no surprise; Earl's own statement contained the same facts; and the trial court, at a bench trial, ruled that Cocroft's statements were not admissible against Earl.[443] Finding no abuse of discretion regarding severance, the court then continued on to address briefly a few other unrelated issues in an opinion that took less than two pages of the Northeastern Reporter.[444]

Earl was thus a minor case with little to say about codefendant statements and effectively nothing to say about antagonistic defenses. It was appropriately ignored as a source of precedent for more than three years until it reemerged in *People v. Yonder.*[445] In *Yonder*, which involved an ugly, brutal home-invasion-style robbery and was a more significant and notorious case than *Earl* in general, defendant Yonder's sanity was one of the primary issues for the court, among others.[446] In a side argument, though, both codefendants contended "that they were entitled to separate trials, and that the trial court's failure to grant their motions for severance deprived them of a fair trial and denied [codefendant] Guido the right to call Yonder as a witness."[447] The court declared,

> The granting of a separate trial is not a matter of right but falls within the sound discretion of the trial court which must consider whether the defenses of those being jointly tried are so antagonistic that a fair trial can be had only by severance. [Citing *Earl.*] In reviewing the trial court's decision on this issue, we will look only to the petitions filed by the

440 *Id.* at 13, 557.

441 *Id.*

442 *Id.*

443 *Id.* at 13-14, 557.

444 *Id.* at 14-15, 557-558. The Earl court cited Albers (1935) on an unrelated point regarding voluntary confessions. *Id.* at 15, 558. The only other notable aspect of the case is that it was a pre-Miranda case in which the defendant made a statement without being advised of his right to counsel. *Id.*; see also Miranda.

445 44 Ill.2d 376, 256 N.E.2d 321 (May 28, 1969) (House, J.).

446 *Id.* at 383-385, 325-327, and generally.

447 *Id.* at 385-386, 327.

> defendants and the matters alleged therein, and not to the subsequent happenings at trial. The petitions allege that each defendant will incriminate the other, that Yonder's admission of guilt but allegation of insanity will dilute Guido's defense of innocence, that Guido will not be able to put Yonder on the stand as a witness on Guido's behalf as that he may be exculpated, and that the jury will be allowed to hear inadmissible and inflammatory evidence concerning Yonder's conduct during the robbery. It is our opinion that the above allegations were mere apprehensions and that the trial court did not abuse its discretion in denying the defendants' motions for severance.[448]

The *Yonder* court said no more regarding severance or antagonistic defenses than this scant paragraph, and cited no authority other than *Earl*. *Earl* supported the boilerplate statements about no right to separate trial and severance being at the trial court's discretion; it did not in any way support the statement about antagonistic defenses. *Earl* also said nothing about a reviewing court considering only the defendants' petitions and not "subsequent happenings at trial," nor the insufficiency of "mere apprehensions" of antagonism at trial, and the *Yonder* court did not indicate that it did, but rather pulled those rules entirely out of a hat with no overt precedential substantiation. Had the *Yonder* court looked to the case from the antagonism lineage that the *Earl* court consulted (and to give them the benefit of the doubt, perhaps they did)—*Lindsay*—the court would have found a rule requiring severance of antagonistic defenses along with language stating that the defendant must show how he would be prejudiced by a joint trial and may not complain on appeal of the trial court's denial of his motion if he fails to do so.[449] The latter language gives at least partial, implicit support to *Yonder*'s statements on looking only to the petitions and ignoring subsequent happenings at trial and mere apprehensions of antagonism—though *Lindsay* also included, and *Yonder* left out, the overarching rule that "Any set of circumstances sufficient to deprive a defendant of a fair trial if tried jointly with another is sufficient to require a separate trial."[450] *Yonder*'s failure to include that part of the Illinois tradition helped lead to confusion down the road, as courts focused on the contents of pretrial motions more than the fairness of the trials that followed. Regardless, though, *Yonder* was a case in which antagonistic defenses were a sideshow at best, apparently thrown in somewhat haphazardly by appellants' counsel and certainly addressed cursorily and in passing by the court, making *Yonder* a weak and relatively unsuitable source of precedential authority on severance and antagonistic defenses.

---

448 *Id.* at 386, 327.
449 Lindsay (1952) at 481, 619.
450 *Id.*

Nevertheless, *Yonder* became an oft-cited authority both on severance of antagonistic defenses[451] and on looking only to the pretrial petitions and ignoring both mere apprehensions of antagonism and subsequent happenings at trial.[452]

[451] Cases citing *Yonder* for a rule requiring severance of antagonistic defenses: People v. Muersch, 4 Ill.App.3d 1003, 1007, 282 N.E.2d 767, 770 (Apr. 10, 1972) (Burke, J.) (citing Earl and Yonder) (addressing issue briefly in passing); People v. Jackson, 24 Ill.App.3d 700, 706, 321 N.E.2d 420 (Nov. 27, 1974) (Hallett, J.) (citing Yonder and Earl) (addressing issue briefly in passing); People v. Falconer, 33 Ill.App.3d 563, 565-566, 338 N.E.2d 216, 218 (Nov. 17, 1975) (Dixon, J.) (citing Yonder) (addressing issue briefly in passing); People v. Davis, 43 Ill.App.3d 603, 610, 357 N.E.2d 96, 101 (Oct. 26, 1976) (Downing, J.) (citing Yonder along with Canaday, Gendron, Henderson, Brinn, and Betson) (considering issue at length); People v. Hunter, 61 Ill.App.3d 588, 376 N.E.2d 1065, 1071 (Jun. 02, 1978) (Green, P.J.) (citing Yonder and Gendron to support brief observation in passing on no showing of antagonistic defenses); People v. Clark, 71 Ill.App.3d 381, 398, 389 N.E.2d 911, 923 (May 04, 1979) (Seidenfeld, J.) (citing Yonder); People v. Malaszenko, 76 Ill.App.3d 1, 393 N.E.2d 1350 (Aug. 30, 1979) (Jiganti, P.J.) (citing Yonder in passing); People v. Jones, 81 Ill.App.3d 724, 726, 401 N.E.2d 1325, 1327 (Mar. 12, 1980) (Green, J.) (citing Yonder among others) (considering issue in depth); People v. Lee, 86 Ill.App.3d 922, 929, 408 N.E.2d 335, 341 (Jul. 21, 1980) (O'Connor, J.) (misattributing Grilec formulation of rule to Yonder) (considering issue in depth); People v. Poree, 119 Ill.App.3d 590, 595, 456 N.E.2d 950, 954 (Nov. 18, 1983) (Mejda, J.) (citing Yonder and Murphy (1981)). People v. Brown, 27 Ill.App.3d 569, 576, 327 N.E.2d 51, 55 (Apr. 23, 1975) (Hallett, J.) quoted Earl but avoided citing it for the antagonism rule and instead cited Canaday (1971); People v. Columbo, 118 Ill.App.3d 882, 939, 455 N.E.2d 733, 775 (Jun. 24, 1983) (Wilson, P.J.) cited Earl only for the basic abuse of discretion standard of reversal.

[452] Cases citing *Yonder* for reasons other than antagonism-severance rule: People v. Davis, 43 Ill.App.3d 603, 610, 357 N.E.2d 96, 101 (Oct. 26, 1976) (Downing, J.) (mere apprehension insufficient); People v. Miner, 46 Ill.App.3d 273, 283, 360 N.E.2d 1141, 1149 (Feb. 28, 1977) (Karns, J.) (mere apprehension insufficient); People v. Lee, 46 Ill.App.3d 343, 360 N.E.2d 1173, 1177 (Mar. 11, 1977) (Alloy, J.) (look only at petitions not subsequent happenings); People v. Scales, 47 Ill.App.3d 755, 764, 362 N.E.2d 691 (Mar. 24, 1977) (Stengel, P.J.) (mere apprehension insufficient) (in passing); People v. Vinson, 49 Ill.App.3d 602, 364 N.E.2d 364, 367 (May 23, 1977) (O'Connor, J.) (discretion to sever); People v. Jones, 81 Ill.App.3d 724, 726, 728, 401 N.E.2d 1325, 1327, 1328 (Mar. 12, 1980) (Green, J.) (considering and extending Yonder in concluding that a reviewing court may consider statements of counsel in addition to petitions at hearing on severance motion); People v. Lee, 86 Ill.App.3d 922, 930, 408 N.E.2d 335, 341 (Jul. 21, 1980) (O'Connor, J.) (look only at petitions not subsequent happenings, but court also aware of need to sever anytime prejudice appears); People v. McMullen, 88 Ill.App.3d 611, 613, 410 N.E.2d 1174, 1176 (Sept. 24, 1980) (Mills, P.J.) (State argues pretrial motion demonstrating prejudice required, court follows Jones (1980) in also considering statements of counsel at pretrial motion hearing); People v. Powell, 95 Ill.App.3d 93, 98, 419 N.E.2d 708, 712 (Apr. 09, 1981) (Webber, J.) (look only at petitions not subsequent happenings); People v. Brophy, 96 Ill.App.3d 936, 945, 422 N.E.2d 158 (May 28, 1981) (Linn, J.) (defendant must demonstrate prejudice before trial); People v. Lee, 87 Ill.2d 182, 186, 429 N.E.2d 461, 463 (Nov. 13, 1981) (Simon, J.) (defendant must demonstrate prejudice before trial); People v. Ruiz, 94 Ill.2d 245, 257, 447 N.E.2d 148, 152 (Dec. 17, 1982) (Ryan, C.J.) (no automatic right to separate trial); People v. Columbo, 118 Ill.App.3d 882, 939-940, 941, 455 N.E.2d 733, 775, 776 (Jun. 24, 1983) (Wilson, P.J.) (look only at petitions not subsequent happenings, mere speculation as to antagonism insufficient); People v. Molstad, 101 Ill.2d 128,

Although *Yonder* said and decided little on the issue, what it did say was relatively short, snappy, and superficially easy to understand, and as usual, later opinions favored that sort of language over more complicated analysis. Also, although *Yonder* was something of a junk precedent regarding severance of antagonistic defenses, its popularity might have been enhanced because the United States Supreme Court denied certiorari, even though that decision almost certainly had nothing to do with *Yonder*'s brief paragraph on severance and antagonistic defenses.[453]

Even as so many courts dutifully repeated the version of the rule stated in *Grilec*, *Henderson*, or *Yonder*, other opinions, perhaps wisely, mentioned antagonism only briefly or in passing,[454] or avoided stating a rule on antagonistic defenses or mentioning them at all.[455]

136, 461 N.E.2d 398, 403 (Feb. 01, 1984) (Clark, J.) (mere apprehension insufficient); People v. Daugherty, 102 Ill.2d 533, 544, 545, 468 N.E.2d 969, 974-975 (Jun. 29, 1984) (Simon, J.) (distinguishing Yonder regarding mere apprehension insufficient, slightly bending rule on look only at petitions not subsequent happenings); People v. Zambetta, 132 Ill.App.3d 740, 745, 477 N.E.2d 821, 825 (Apr. 29, 1985) (Strouse, J.) (mere apprehension insufficient); People v. Duncan, 133 Ill.App.3d 489, 478 N.E.2d 1125, 1130-1131 (May 16, 1985) (Stouder, J.) (mere apprehension insufficient); People v. Bean, 109 Ill.2d 80, 100, 485 N.E.2d 349, 358 (Oct. 03, 1985) (Simon, J.) (look only at petitions not subsequent happenings); People v. Byron, 116 Ill.2d 81, 92, 506 N.E.2d 1247, 1251 (Feb. 20, 1987) (Goldenhersh, J.) (mere apprehension insufficient); People v. Collins, 186 Ill.App.3d 35, 45, 541 N.E.2d 1308, 1314 (Jun. 30, 1989) (Manning, P.J.) (mere apprehension insufficient); People v. Rice, 286 Ill.App.3d 394, 402, 675 N.E.2d 944, 950 (Dec. 30, 1996) (O'Brien, J.) (look only at petitions not subsequent happenings, but court also aware of need to sever anytime prejudice appears).

453 In my experience, lower courts, in their quest for safety from reversal by higher courts, sometimes make more out of "cert. den." than it likely warrants. In *People v. Baer*, 35 Ill.App.3d 391, 400, 342 N.E.2d 177, 184 (Jan. 9, 1976) (Sullivan, J.), the court cited *People v. Rosenborgh*, 21 Ill.App.3d 376, and its cert. denied status, for the severance rule that "the test is whether the defense of one of the defendants is so antagonistic to the other as to deny a fair trial." Ironically, *Rosenborgh* nowhere mentioned antagonism or an antagonistic defenses severance rule; it only addressed codefendant statements as an independent issue and cited *Bruton* and *Clark* (1959) in one very brief paragraph. *See Rosenborgh* at 688. See also POSNER, HOW JUDGES THINK, *supra* note 6, at 50 (discussing ambiguity of certiorari petition denials).

454 People v. Pulaski, 15 Ill.2d 291, 155 N.E.2d 29 (Nov. 26, 1958) (Hershey, J.); People v. Aldridge, 19 Ill.2d 176, 180, 166 N.E.2d 563, 565 (Mar. 31, 1960) (Schaefer, J.); People v. Williams, 30 Ill.2d 166, 167, 195 N.E.2d 715, 715-16 (Jan. 22, 1964) (House, J.); People v. Arnold (91 Ill.App.2d 282, 233 N.E.2d 764 (Jan. 22, 1968) (Smith, P.J.)); People v. Ross, 41 Ill.2d 445, 244 N.E.2d 608 (May 29, 1968) (Kluczynski, J.); People v. Rhodes, 41 Ill.2d 494, 498, 244 N.E.2d 145, 147 (Jan. 29, 1969) (House, J.); People v. Humphrey, 129 Ill.App.2d 404, 414, 262 N.E.2d 721, 726 (Oct. 2, 1970) (Abrahamson, J.); People v. Watkins, 3 Ill.App.3d 560, 564, 278 N.E.2d 156 (Jan. 31, 1972) (Seidenfeld, J.); People v. Rahn, 15 Ill.App.3d 170, 304 N.E.2d 161 (Nov. 7, 1973) (Trapp, J.); People v. Williams, 39 Ill.App.3d 449, 350 N.E.2d 135 (June 9, 1976) (Adesko, J.); People v. Williams, 52 Ill.App.3d 81, 367 N.E.2d 167 (Aug. 9, 1977) (Stamos, J.); People v. Bailey, 60 Ill.App.3d 1046, 1053, 377 N.E.2d 273, 278 (May 25, 1978) (Dieringer, J.); People v. Muellner, 70

CROSS-CONTAMINATION: JOINT-REPRESENTATION CASES IN THE ANTAGONISTIC DEFENSES LINEAGE, 1953-1980

As we have seen, *Bopp* (1917) implicitly indicated that defendants with conflicting interests should not be represented by the same counsel, and *Rose* (1932), following *Bopp*, stated explicitly, "Every defendant who is unable to employ counsel for his defense has a right to have an attorney appointed by the court who can, and will upon the trial, present to the court and jury the defendant's full defense, untrammeled by any conflicting interests of a codefendant." Neither case said anything about antagonistic defenses outside the joint-representation context.

The next major joint representation case to appear in the antagonism lineage was *People v. Dolgin* (1953), which involved two codefendants jointly indicted for forgery and counterfeiting to evade Illinois' cigarette tax.[456] Among other issues on

Ill.App.3d 671, 388 N.E.2d 851 (Mar. 21, 1979) (Karns, J.); People v. Hunter, 61 Ill.App.3d 588, 376 N.E.2d 1065 (Jun. 2, 1978) (Green, P.J.); People v. Johnson, 74 Ill.App.3d 1037, 393 N.E.2d 40 (July 19, 1979) (Linn, J.); People v. Goodman, 75 Ill.App.3d 369, 372, 393 N.E.2d 1233, 1236 (Aug. 9, 1979) (Karns, J.); People v. Jones, 82 Ill.App.3d 386, 402 N.E.2d 746 (Mar. 14, 1980) (Mejda, J.); People v. Stevenson, 90 Ill.App.3d 903, 413 N.E.2d 1339 (Nov. 20, 1980) (Jiganti, J.); People v. Manna, 96 Ill.App.3d 506, 421 N.E.2d 542 (Apr. 30, 1981) (Nash, J.); People v. Cart (102 Ill.App.3d 173, 429 N.E.2d 553 (Dec. 2, 1981) (Nash, J.); People v. Griggs, 104 Ill.App.3d 527, 432 N.E.2d 1176 (Feb. 22, 1982) (McGloon, J.); People v. Olbrot, 106 Ill.App.3d 367, 435 N.E.2d 1242 (May 3, 1982) (O'Connor, J.); People v. Jones, 116 Ill.App.3d 233, 451 N.E.2d 1358 (July 14, 1983) (Johnson, J.); People v. Fuller, 117 Ill.App.3d 1026, 454 N.E.2d 334 (July 19, 1983) (Perlin, J.); People v. Sanford, 116 Ill.App.3d 834, 452 N.E.2d 710 (July 29, 1983) (Mejda, J.); People v. Jackson, 119 Ill.App.3d 951, 458 N.E.2d 59 (Dec. 8, 1983) (Johnson, J.); People v. Duncan, 133 Ill.App.3d 489, 478 N.E.2d 1125 (May 16, 1985) (Stouder, J.); People v. Visnack, 135 Ill.App.3d 113, 481 N.E.2d 744 (May 21, 1985) (Stamos, P.J.); People v. Morrison, 137 Ill.App.3d 171, 484 N.E.2d 329 (Aug. 19, 1985) (Campbell, J.); People v. Walker, 136 Ill.App.3d 177, 483 N.E.2d 301 (Aug. 27, 1985) (Barry, J.).

455 People v. Berry, 37 Ill.2d 329, 226 N.E.2d 591 (May 18, 1967) (Klingbiel, J.); People v. Rhodes, 41 Ill.2d 494, 498, 244 N.E.2d 145, 147 (Jan. 29, 1969) (House, J.) (appellant raised, but court gave no rule on, antagonism); People v. Clark, 130 Ill.App.2d 558, 562, 265 N.E.2d 191, 194 (Nov. 18, 1970) (Davis, P.J.) (same as *Rhodes*); People v. Clark, 50 Ill.2d 292, 278 N.E.2d 782 (Jan. 28, 1972) (Underwood, C.J.) (codefendant statements case resulting in reversal never mentioned antagonism); People v. Merritt, 16 Ill. App. 3d 72, 305 N.E.2d 579 (Nov. 28, 1973) (Dieringer, J.); People v. Rosenborgh, 21 Ill.App.3d 676, 315 N.E.2d 545 (Jul. 12, 1974) (Lorenz, J.); People v. Howard, 34 Ill.App.3d 145, 149, 340 N.E.2d 53, 56 (Nov. 14, 1975) (Lorenz, J.); People v. Bradford, 84 Ill.App.3d 493, 411 N.E.2d 869 (June 2, 1980) (McGloon, J.); People v. Nash, 90 Ill.App.3d 612, 413 N.E.2d 16 (Nov. 5, 1980) (Downing, J.); People v. Bluitt, 98 Ill.App.3d 19, 424 N.E.2d 62 (July 09, 1981) (Linn, J.); People v. Moore, 115 Ill.App.3d 266, 450 N.E.2d 855 (May 31, 1983) (McGloon, J.); People v. Racanelli, 132 Ill.App.3d 124, 476 N.E.2d 1179 (March 15, 1985) (Mejda, P.J.) (Pincham, J., dissenting); People v. Sullivan, 136 Ill.App.3d 293, 483 N.E.2d 324 (Aug. 28, 1985) (McNamara, J.); People v. Williams, 136 Ill.App.3d 126, 483 N.E.2d 306 (Aug. 30, 1985) (Barry, J.).

456 415 Ill. 434, 437, 114 N.E.2d 389, 391 (May 20, 1953) (Fulton, J.).

appeal, including alleged juror tampering and attempted bribery, Dolgin claimed he was denied trial counsel of his own choice.[457] Both codefendants were represented by the same counsel until the eve of trial, and on the day before trial, both defendants moved to continue the trial until after the upcoming November elections because their case had become a " 'political football.' "[458] The trial court denied the motion, which gave no other grounds and did not mention antagonistic defenses.[459] On the day of the trial, the joint counsel moved to sever the trials on the ground that a prosecution witness would testify against one defendant and so negatively impact the other defendant. The court denied the motion. Counsel then sought to withdraw as counsel for one of the defendants "on the ground that Lieb's and Dolgin's defenses would be antagonistic." The court denied this motion, also.[460] Another attorney then filed a motion to continue the case and to intercede on Dolgin's behalf, arguing that Dolgin needed separate counsel and that the new attorney needed additional time to prepare the case.[461] The court denied the continuance but allowed the new attorney to step in to represent Dolgin, and the trial went forward.[462] Lieb was acquitted, but Dolgin was convicted and sentenced to prison.[463]

Regarding Dolgin's argument that he was denied his constitutional right to counsel of his choice, the court reasoned that because the only ground for the original counsel's motion to withdraw was antagonistic defenses, the argument could "have merit only if the defenses of Lieb and [Dolgin] were, in fact, antagonistic."[464] The court's review of the record, however, found "nothing to indicate any incompatibility of interest."[465] Although the court obviously mentioned antagonism, this was purely in the context of conflicting interests requiring representation by separate counsel; *Dolgin* was in no way concerned with the question of separate trials for codefendants with antagonistic defenses. The court did, notably and unfortunately, use the term "antagonistic" in conjunction with the low-level definition "any incompatibility of interest," which would cause confusion in later joint-representation cases. *Dolgin*'s statement specific to the facts of that case—the joint counsel's suspicious last-minute motion to withdraw as counsel for one defendant on the sole, particular ground of antagonistic defenses could only have merit if there were antagonistic defenses—would also later be

457 *Id.* at 445-46, 394-95.
458 *Id.* at 446-47, 395.
459 *Id.* at 447, 395.
460 *Id.*
461 *Id.* at 447, 395-96.
462 *Id.* at 447, 396.
463 *Id.* at 437, 391.
464 *Id.* at 448, 396.
465 *Id.*

mistranslated in *People v. Banks* (1968), a case involving separate trials but not joint representation, as "Only when the interests of the joint defendants are in fact antagonistic must the court grant separate trials. [Citing *Dolgin.*]"[466] The *Banks* court showed no awareness that *Dolgin* was a joint representation case, or that joint representation was a different issue. The same was true of *People v. Battle* (1969), which in rejecting a weak severance argument cited *Dolgin* along with *Banks* for, "Joint defendants will be entitled to a severance of their trials only where it is shown that their individual defenses are in fact antagonistic to each other."[467]

In *People v. Clark* (1959), the court allowed the public defender to withdraw as Clark's counsel because his "defense was antagonistic to those of [his codefendants]."[468] In *People v. Wolff* (1960), the court found no basis for the court-appointed attorney's claim of conflicting interests between the two defendants, and antagonism was never mentioned.[469]

People v. Friedrich (1960) is a highly anomalous joint-representation case that did not offer any holding on severance for antagonistic defenses because the trial court granted such a severance.[470] The joint counsel for two defendants informed the court that he foresaw antagonistic defenses by his two clients and requested either a severance of their trials or withdrawal of his representation from one or the other.[471] The trial court, responding to what became a rather complicated equation, and due to concerns that it would be unethical to allow the counsel to represent both defendants even in separate trials if there were indeed a conflict of interest between them, ruled that the counsel in question could only represent defendant Friedrich if Friedrich and his codefendant (Zahler) agreed to be tried jointly and stipulated that they did not have conflicting interests or defenses.[472] Although Friedrich later had a separate trial at which he was convicted, he was forced to go to trial with a counsel different from the original counsel of his choice.[473]

Although noting the trial court's earnest effort to protect the defendant's right to a counsel free of conflicts, the *Friedrich* court explained, perceptively,

---

[466] 103 Ill.App.2d 180, 186, 243 N.E.2d 669, 672 (Dec. 10, 1968 (McNamara, J.).
[467] 116 Ill.App.2d 375, 383, 254 N.E.2d 90, 95 (Nov. 12, 1969) (Burke, J.)
[468] 17 Ill.2d 486, 487, 162 N.E.2d 413, 415 (Nov. 18, 1959) (Daily, J.).
[469] 19 Ill.2d 318, 321-323, 167 N.E.2d 197, 198-199 (May 18, 1960) (Daily, J.).
[470] 20 Ill.2d 240, 248, 169 N.E.2d 752, 755 (Sept. 29, 1960) (Hershey, J.).
[471] *Id.* at 244-246, 755.
[472] *Id.* at 245-48, 755-56.
[473] *Id.* at 242, 250, 753, 758.

> The grounds which require a sverance are different from those which prevent an attorney from representing conflicting interests. A severance should be granted where the defenses are antagonistic or the circumstances are such that it would be unfair to require a joint trial. [Citing *Lindsay*.] We believe the facts set forth in Zahler's motion were sufficient to show that he could not obtain a fair trial if tried jointly with defendant and, therefore, were sufficient to require a severance.[474]

The court, noting the trial court's agreement that severance was justified but faulting its imposition of a requirement that the codefendants must have separate counsel even in separate trials, held that there was nothing to suggest that there would have been any ethical violation in allowing the original chosen counsel to represent both defendants in separate trials.[475] Thus, for the trial court to require Friedrich to retain a different attorney deprived him of his right to counsel.[476]

So *Friedrich*, a complicated opinion regarding a muddled situation, clearly offered no holding on severance for antagonistic defenses; it did not need to. Rather, it assumed the rule in *Lindsay*, and distinguished that from the rule for joint representation by counsel. Its comments regarding severance for antagonistic defenses were unquestionably dicta, and it is noteworthy that the court identified two grounds for severance—(1) antagonistic defenses and (2) circumstances making a joint trial unfair—and selected the latter, not the former, in concluding that severance was appropriate. It was also avoided by later cases in the antagonism lineage.[477]

Although *Friedrich* may have muddied the waters, *People v. Chapman* (1965)[478] was the first joint representation case to lump the joint-representation conflicting interests rule together with the antagonistic defenses rule and so blur the boundaries between the two properly distinct categories. Regarding the appellant's claim of conflicting interests between himself and his jointly represented codefendant, plus a gratuitous argument that " 'co-defendants in a criminal case are necessarily adverse to one another,' "[479] the court noted, "It is only when the interests of the joint defendants are *in fact* antagonistic that the court must grant

---

474 *Id.* at 251, 758.
475 *Id.* at 252, 759.
476 *Id.* at 255, 760.
477 *Friedrich* was only cited briefly in *Arnold* (1968) at 285, 765 ("Circumstances which warrant the appointment of separate counsel do not necessarily mandate separate trial and vice-versa.") and *Lee* (1980) at 930, 341 (necessity of separate counsel, alone, does not also require separate trials).
478 66 Ill.App.2d 124, 214 N.E.2d 313 (December 27, 1965) (Kluczynski, J.)
479 *Id.* at 127, 315.

separate trials or require separate legal representation. [Citing *Dolgin* at 448.]."[480] *Dolgin*, however, never said anything about when to sever trials, either at page 448 or anywhere else. The court went on to cite *Wolff*, *Rose*, and *Bopp* on conflicting interests before determining that there was nothing in the record suggesting any "adverse or antagonistic" interests between the codefendants, or anything "that could indicate such incompatibility or conflict."[481] In addition to raising the antagonism-severance rule entirely unnecessarily, *Chapman* dangerously mixed together such potentially different concepts as "adverse," "antagonistic," "incompatibility," and "conflict" indiscriminately.

Just as the contagion of the antagonistic defenses rule jumped inappropriately into the joint representation lineage in *Chapman*, predictably, it jumped back to the antagonistic defenses lineage from *Chapman*. *People v. Van Hyning* (1966)[482] concerned only a severance argument based upon codefendants' statements, not joint representation, but the court observed, "The question of joint or separate trials for defendants—who are jointly indicted—has given rise to many problems," added, "However, the law is rather clear" [always a dangerous statement for a court to make], then quoted *Chapman* at length, including irrelevant language from *Wolff*, *Rose*, and *Bopp* regarding conflicting interests in the joint representation context along with *Chapman*'s misstatement of the *Dolgin* holding: " 'It is only when the interests of the joint defendants are in fact antagonistic that the court must grant separate trials or require separate legal representation.' "[483] *Van Hyning* thus inappropriately mixed together not only antagonistic defenses and codefendant statements, but joint representation, also—a sort of trifecta of precedential confusion. The *Chapman* language also reappeared in later joint representation cases.[484]

The *Chapman-Van Hyning* transaction occurred within Illinois' mid-level appellate court system. Yet the antagonism-severance rule jumping to the joint-representation lineage also occurred at the Illinois Supreme Court level, and without reliance on *Chapman*, in *People v. McCasle* (1966), a joint representation case in which the appellant contended that the trial court should have appointed separate counsel for him on its own motion.[485] The *McCasle* court politely answered, in a single paragraph dismissing a clearly weak argument, that there was no inconsistency in the codefendants' defenses and no impropriety in the public

480 *Id.*
481 *Id.*
482 72 Ill.App.2d 168, 219 N.E.2d 268 (Jun. 23, 1966) (Davis, J.).
483 *Id.* at 177-178, 272.
484 *See* People v. Dickens, 19 Ill.App.3d 419, 311 N.E.2d 705, 708 (May 21, 1974) (Eberspacher, J.); People v. Holman, 43 Ill.App.3d 56, 59, 356 N.E.2d 1115, 1117 (Oct. 26, 1976) (T.J. Moran, P.J.).
485 35 Ill.2d 552, 556, 221 N.E.2d 227, 230 (Nov. 14, 1966) (Underwood, J.).

defender's joint representation of both codefendants.[486] The court added in passing, "As a general rule, jointly indicted defendants should be jointly tried unless their defenses are antagonistic, and a severance is neither required nor authorized where their defenses are not inconsistent. [Citing *Wilson*, *Brinn* (1965), *Aldridge* (1960), and *Grilec*, none of which involved joint representation.]"[487] This brief, well-intended reference to the supposed general rule on severance of antagonistic defenses led to *McCasle*'s use as an authority in *People v. James* (1970), a severance case not involving joint representation, where the court cited *McCasle* in stating, "A severance should only be granted where the defenses are antagonistic or inconsistent"[488]—notably rearranging and garbling *McCasle*'s language to suggest that antagonism and inconsistency meant the same thing, such that merely inconsistent defenses required severance.

Later joint representation cases also recycled *McCasle*'s language about antagonistic defenses. *People v. Smith* (1974) used it verbatim;[489] *People v. Holman* (1976), a combined joint representation and antagonistic defenses case in which the appellants faulted the trial court both for not appointing separate counsel and for not severing their trials based upon one defendant's pretrial statement that incriminated the other, cited both *McCasle* and *Chapman* in stating an exclusive version of the rule: "The court must grant separate trials or require separate legal representation only when the defenses of joint defendants are so antagonistic that a fair trial would be otherwise impossible."[490] As in *Van Hyning*, the *Holman* court in its brief discussion finding no error tended to conflate joint representation with antagonistic defenses and codefendants' statements.[491]

People v. Ware (1968) was a joint representation case that resulted in a reversal for denial of right to counsel after one defendant pleaded guilty and testified at trial that his jointly-represented codefendant, who had pleaded not guilty, had participated in the crimes charged.[492] The court recited, "Co-defendants have a right to separate counsel if their positions are antagonistic. [Citing *Dolgin*.] Here, there was complete antagonism between the positions of the defendant[s.]"[493] In offering its tacit definition of complete antagonism, the *Ware* court, appropriately, considered only the joint representation context. Opinions after *Ware*, however, went in different directions regarding at what stage of the sentencing process one

---

486 *Id.*
487 *Id.*
488 130 Ill.App.2d 532, 263 N.E.2d 705, 708 (Nov. 04, 1970) (Abrahamson, J.).
489 19 Ill.App.3d 138, 145, 310 N.E.2d 818, 823 (May 02, 1974) (Smith, P.J.).
490 43 Ill.App.3d 56, 59, 356 N.E.2d 1115, 1117 (Oct. 26, 1976) (T.J. Moran, P.J.).
491 *Id.* at 59-60, 1117-1118.
492 39 Ill.2d 66, 67, 233 N.E.2d 421, 422 (Jan. 19, 1968) (Ward, J.).
493 *Id.* at 68, 422.

codefendant testifying against a jointly represented codefendant constituted antagonistic interests and required separate representation,[494] as well as whether complete antagonism was required. *Ware*, of course, never said complete antagonism was required and merely found it in the facts of *Ware*, but some later courts missed that nuance and built "complete antagonism" into the *Ware* "rule."

The antagonism-severance rule further infected the case law on joint representation in *People v. Bass* (1968), a joint representation case in which the appellant contended that the trial court had a sua sponte duty either to appoint separate counsel or sever the trials.[495] The *Bass* court answered that it "fail[ed] to perceive any conflict between the interests of the co-defendants," noting, "In the instant case, it has not been demonstrated that the interests of the co-defendants were conflicting or antagonistic. Neither Robbins nor Bass was attempting to establish his defense by implicating the other—a classic example of conflicting and antagonistic interests which would justify a severance."[496] Aside from this slightly gratuitous reference to antagonism, there was no further discussion of antagonism; the court followed *McCasle* and affirmed.[497] Notably, the level of antagonism mentioned in *Bass*—each defendant actively implicating the other—was much higher than the level of conflicting interests that would justify separate counsel in a joint representation case.

Yet the mention of antagonism in cases such as *Bopp* and *Dolgin*, together with the pulling in of the antagonism-severance rule in *Friedrich* and *Chapman* and, particularly, the references to antagonism in fact, complete antagonism, or mutual finger-pointing in *Chapman*, *Ware*, and *Bass*, inevitably caused confusion about the

---

494 *See* People v. Johnson, 46 Ill.2d 266, 267-68, 265 N.E.2d 869, 870 (Sept. 22, 1970) (Crebs, J.) (distinguishing Ware and finding no divided allegiance of counsel where a jointly represented codefendant "obtained complete immunity and dismissal of the charges against him" before testifying); People v. Forbis, 12 Ill.App.3d 536, 539-40, 298 N.E.2d 771, 774 (Jul. 05, 1973) (Craven, P.J.) (distinguishing Ware and finding no attorney conflict where a jointly represented codefendant pleaded guilty and was sentenced before testifying, and "obtained complete immunity and dismissal of the charges against him" before testifying and so "had nothing to gain"); People v. Augustus, 36 Ill.App.3d 75, 76-77, 343 N.E.2d 272, 273 (Feb. 18, 1976) (Jones, J.) (finding attorney conflict under same situation as in Forbis); People v. Halluin, 36 Ill.App.3d 556, 344 N.E.2d 579 (Mar. 12, 1976) (Moran, J.) (reviewing the dispute at length, rejecting reasoning in *Forbis*, finding antagonistic interests between defendants where attorney could not wholeheartedly impeach testifying client on behalf of client on trial, and holding that the "confidentiality of attorney-client communications persists after sentencing of the client") (Also noting, "Most of the cases verbalizing the 'antagonistic position' principle are ones in which certain situations were found not to involve antagonistic positions.").

495 101 Ill.App.2d 259, 261, 243 N.E.2d 305, 307 (Sept. 19, 1968) (Sullivan, J.).

496 *Id.* at 262, 307.

497 *Id.* at 263, 308.

appropriate standard for determining when conflicting interests of codefendants required separate representation. The standard for antagonistic defenses was supposed to be relatively high; the standard for conflicting interests in the joint representation context, relatively low. Yet the intrusion of terms and concepts from the antagonistic defenses context into the joint representation context left later courts struggling with where to set the standard and how to define antagonistic or conflicting interests. As with the antagonistic defenses lineage, it was easy for this process to become garbled.

For instance, in *People v. Durley* (1972), in what would become a standard appellate technique, Durley intertwined ineffective assistance of counsel and antagonistic defenses arguments by contending that his trial counsel was ineffective for failing to seek an evidentiary hearing regarding his clients' antagonistic defenses.[498] The court briefly discussed and dismissed Durley's arguments, citing *Dolgin* to state, *non-exclusively*, "It is unquestioned that co-defendants should have a right to separate counsel if their positions are antagonistic," but finding no demonstration of conflicting interests to support the bare allegations in the petition.[499] Two years later, however, in *People v. St. Pierre* (1975), a joint representation case in which the court rejected St. Pierre's claim of conflicting interests from his codefendant's statement that St. Pierre stabbed the victim given that St. Pierre himself testified at trial that he stabbed the victim,[500] the court, citing *Durley* and *Ware*, declared, *exclusively*, "The rule is well settled that separate counsel is required only where the interests of co-defendants are in fact antagonistic," and found that the defendants "did not have antagonistic defenses."[501] The *St. Pierre* court thus took what was fact-specific language in *Dolgin*—for *Dolgin*'s motion for substitution of counsel based solely and specifically on antagonistic defenses to have merit, there obviously had to be antagonistic defenses—and *Durley*'s non-exclusive statement of the rule—jointly represented codefendants are entitled to separate counsel *if* they have antagonistic positions—and changed that into an exclusive rule—separate counsel *only if* there were antagonistic interests. The court also muddled antagonistic interests together with antagonistic defenses. In *People v. Barren* (1975), the court gave a non-exclusive version: "[C]onflict of interest exists where one attorney represents two or more co-defendants whose defenses are antagonistic to each other, and in such case, they are entitled to separate counsel. [Citing *Johnson* (1970); *Ware*.]"[502] The court thus identified antagonistic defenses as a situation where conflicting interests existed, but did not say that was the only such

---

498 53 Ill.2d 156, 157-58, 290 N.E.2d 244, 245 (Nov. 30, 1972) (Davis, J.).

499 *Id.* at 160, 246.

500 25 Ill.App.3d 644, 651, 324 N.E.2d 226, 231 (Jan. 22, 1975) (Johnson, J.).

501 *Id.*

502 32 Ill.App.3d 78, 81, 335 N.E.2d 779, 782 (Oct. 06, 1975) (Alloy, J.).

situation. In *People v. Benka* (1983), the court offered a different non-exclusive version of the *Chapman* rule—"[D]efendants should have separate trials and separate representation where the defenses are antagonistic"[503]—which probably unintentionally added the idea that the same counsel should never represent two defendants with antagonistic defenses, even in separate trials.

People v. Dickens (1974) was strictly a joint representation case in which counsel made the losing argument that joint representation by the public defender constituted ineffective assistance per se.[504] The court likely could have dismissed this weak argument more summarily, but instead quoted *Chapman* at length, including its exclusive "only when" version of the severance/separate representation rule.[505] The court also distinguished *Johnson* (1970) and *Ware*, noting that the *Ware* court found " 'complete antagonism'" between the defendants, but in *Dickens* "there was no showing that the[] defenses were completely antagonistic."[506] Later, the court held that because "there was no showing of an actual conflict of interest between the defendants," the ineffective assistance claim was without merit.[507] Although the *Dickens* court merely stated that the defenses in *Dickens* were not completely antagonistic while distinguishing *Ware*, later cases would infer that *Dickens* set a rule requiring complete antagonism of defenses.

As with antagonistic defenses, in the joint representation context, statements of a rule on antagonism were usually gratuitous, because usually there was clearly no conflict in the defenses. For instance, in *People v. Brown* (1976), on the day of trial, the privately retained joint defense counsel moved to withdraw as counsel for either defendant "on the ground that a conflict of interest was present due to potentially antagonistic defenses."[508] The *Brown* court reviewed earlier joint representation opinions as well as antagonistic defenses or severance cases such as *Canaday* and *Humphrey* before finding the defendants' defenses "consisistent and complementary, not antagonistic."[509] The court of course gave no holding regarding severance of antagonistic defenses, but only borrowed the reasoning about them from earlier opinions. *People v. Jones* (1976) involved the stock argument that a joint trial counsel's failure to move for a severance denied his clients effective assistance of counsel.[510] The court cited *McCasle* along with *Muersch* (1972), a minor case that said almost nothing about antagonistic defenses

503 117 Ill.App.3d 221, 225, 453 N.E.2d 71, 74 (Aug. 18, 1983) (Van Deusen, J.).
504 19 Ill.App.3d 419, 422, 311 N.E.2d 705, 708 (May 21, 1974) (Eberspacher, J.).
505 *Id.* at 423, 708.
506 *Id.* at 422-23, 708.
507 *Id.* at 423, 708-09.
508 36 Ill.App.3d 416, 418, 343 N.E.2d 700, 701 (Mar. 10, 1976) (Stouder, J.).
509 *Id.* at 702-03, 419-20.
510 40 Ill.App.3d 850, 858, 353 N.E.2d 375 (Apr. 28, 1976) (Johnson, P.J.).

and nothing about joint representation, for the antagonism-severance rule, and found no inconsistency in the defenses.[511] In *People v. Clark* (1976), by contrast, the court credited the defendants' argument that their joint counsel's failure to request a severance denied them effective assistance of counsel;[512] the court held that although it benefitted one defendant to have a second defendant's confession read with the defendants' names deleted, it would have benefitted a third defendant to have the names included.[513] *Clark* is also notable for being seemingly the first case in which counsel used the term "mutually antagonistic," a term of art in many other jurisdictions that never caught on in Illinois.[514] Similarly, in *People v. Ishman* (1978), a joint representation case, a defendant moved for and was granted a severance based upon " 'irreconcilable differences'" in his and other codefendants' defenses, which appears to be the first and only importation of another term of art common in other jurisdictions into Illinois case law.[515]

In *People v. Wilder* (1977), the court rejected Wilder's argument that she received ineffective assistance of counsel because the public defender represented both her and another defendant in separate trials, noting that the other defendant never testified against her and observing, "Clearly such a conflict exists where one defendant testifies at the trial of the other or at a joint trial in a manner antagonistic to the interests of the other defendant, or where two defendants assert antagonistic defenses at a joint trial. There is no inherent conflict of interest where several defendants are represented by the same counsel and assert inconsistent defenses at separate trials so long as one does not testify against the other. [Citing *Johnson* (1970), *Ware*, *McCasle*, and *Halluin* (1976), along with *Wilson* (1963).]"[516] In its examples, *Wilder* revealed an understanding that antagonistic interests and antagonistic defenses could represent different categories.

---

511 *Id.*

512 42 Ill.App.3d 472, 475, 355 N.E.2d 619, 621 (Sept. 29, 1976) (Alloy, P.J.).

513 *Id.* at 474, 476, 620, 622.

514 For the federal circuits, see generally Dewey, *supra* note 58. The category is also common in many other states.

515 61 Ill.App.3d 517, 518-19, 378 N.E.2d 179 (May 11, 1978) (Eberspacher, P.J.). Similarly, in *People v. Holtz*, one of *Henderson*'s progeny, a defendant claimed, seemingly for the first time in Illinois jurisprudence (and unsuccessfully), that his and a codefendant's defenses were " 'mutually exclusive' "—which, along with "mutually antagonistic" and "irreconcilable," is the third (and most common) of the three standard terms of art used to justify severing conflicting codefendants in federal jurisprudence and in most other states. *See* People v. Holtz, 19 Ill.App.3d 781, 313 N.E.2d 234 (May 17, 1974) (Drucker, J.); People v. Brown, 27 Ill.App.3d 569, 574, 327 N.E.2d 51, 54; Dewey, *supra* note 58, generally. Illinois courts steadfastly resisted incorporating these new and foreign terms, however.

516 48 Ill.App.3d 13, 14-15, 362 N.E.2d 436, 437-38 (Apr. 25, 1977) (Reardon, J.).

People v. Meng (1977)[517] was a joint representation case that recognized that its holding was limited to the joint representation context and distinguished that context from that of antagonistic defenses. The defendants were two teen-aged boys accused of burgling the home of a recently deceased friend.[518] Both defendants were represented by the county public defender, although each was separately represented by a different attorney from the public defender's staff. Meng contended that he was denied effective assistance of counsel because of a potential conflict of interest for the public defender that arose due to " 'antagonism"' between his defense and that of his codefendant.[519] In addressing this issue, the court reviewed *Ware*, *Johnson*, and *Augustus* (1976),; it also noted the holding in *Dickens* (supposedly) requiring a " 'complete antagonism"' of defenses to show an actual, rather than merely a potential, conflict of interest to require separate counsel.[520] The *Meng* court followed other authorities in holding that the possibility of conflicting interests was enough to trigger Illinois' per se separate counsel rule, and the court declined to follow *Dickens*.[521] The court specifically declined to decide whether the codefendants' conflicting defenses justified a severance, as the defendants had requested before trial.[522] Justice Karns dissented, arguing that the only issue worthy of consideration was whether Meng's severance motion should have been granted, and concluding that it was appropriately denied.[523] Karns called for sticking to *Dickens*' supposed rule, and he quoted at length from *Chapman*, including *Chapman*'s mischaracterization of the holding in *Dolgin*.[524]

Various other joint representation cases mentioned antagonism or antagonistic defenses or positions only briefly or in passing.[525] Others (perhaps wisely) never mentioned the issue or term at all.[526]

---

517 54 Ill.App.3d 357, 369 N.E.2d 549 (Oct. 21, 1977) (Eberspacher, J.).

518 *Id.* at 359, 550.

519 *Id.* at 360, 551.

520 *Id.* at 363-64, 553. Notably, although *Dickens* did require an actual conflict of interests, it did not hold that complete antagonism was required; it used that language only in distinguishing *Ware*. See discussion *supra*.

521 *Id.* at 364, 553.

522 *Id.*

523 *Id.* at 366, 555 (Karns, J., dissenting).

524 *Id.*

525 *See* People v. Robinson, 42 Ill.2d 371, 375, 247 N.E.2d 898, 900 (Mar. 27, 1969) (Ward, J.); People v. Cheatham, 6 Ill.App.3d 1079, 1081-82, 286 N.E.2d 597, 598-99 (Aug. 16, 1972) (Abrahamson, J.); People v. Robinson, 17 Ill.App.3d 310, 314-15, 308 N.E.2d 88 (Jan. 18, 1974) (English, J.); People v. Hastings, 72 Ill.App.3d 816, 390 N.E.2d 1273 (May 21, 1979) (McGloon, J.).; People v. Williams (94 Ill.App.3d 241, 418 N.E.2d 840 (Mar. 12, 1981) (Linn, J.).

526 *See* People v. Forbis, 12 Ill.App.3d 536, 298 N.E.2d 771 (Jul. 05, 1973) (Craven, P.J.); People v. Richardson, 16 Ill.App.3d 830, 831-33, 306 N.E.2d 886, 888-889 (Jan. 30, 1974) (Dixon, J.); People

A BELATED FIRST EFFORT TO DEFINE ANTAGONISM AND THE REDISCOVERY OF *BRAUNE*: *DAVIS*, 1976

After more than thirty years of peaceful slumber following *Meisenhelter* (1942),[527] *Braune* reappeared in Illinois' antagonistic defenses lineage in *People v. Brown* (1975),[528] a relatively brief, minor rape case. The most notable thing about *Brown* regarding antagonistic defenses is that Brown's counsel and the court both treated antagonistic defenses as an entirely separate issue, discussed in an entirely separate part of the opinion, from that of improper questioning of witnesses by a codefendant's counsel, for which issue alone *Braune* was cited and distinguished.[529]

---

v. Husar, 22 Ill.App.3d 758, 318 N.E.2d 24 (Sept. 10, 1974) (Leighton, J.); People v. Augustus, 36 Ill.App.3d 75, 343 N.E.2d 272 (Feb. 18, 1976) (Jones, J.).

527 *Braune* was mentioned briefly in the context of criminal abortion in *People v. Fedora*, 393 Ill. 165, 184, 65 N.E. 2ed 447 (Jan. 23, 1946), a murder case that had nothing to do with abortion or severance and is thus outside the antagonism lineage. At least one other intervening case also perhaps, by its language, reflected an awareness of *Braune* (or else perhaps of *De Luna v. United States*, 308 F.2d 140 (5th Cir. 1962), the case that was the "fountainhead" of all federal jurisprudence on antagonistic defenses and likely drew nationwide judicial attention) : *People v. Higginbotham*, 56 Ill.App.2d 140, 205 N.E.2d 273 (Mar. 11, 1965), which was penned by Presiding Justice Smith, perhaps the most captivating literary stylist ever to sit on any Illinois appellate court, and thus may deserve quoting at some length:

We begin with the general proposition that co-indictees should be tried together. [Citing *Lindsay* (1952).] Most propositions have exceptions and this one is no different. If co-defendants do in fact have antagonistic defenses, such as each pointing a self-exonerating finger at the other, they obviously can't be tried together, if we are to avoid the spectacle of the prosecution sitting back while defendants engage each other in combat. Too, separate trials are sometimes had where one has confessed and implicated the other. A cautionary instruction to give effect to the confession only as to the confessor may serve only to emphasize the very matter the jury is told to forget, as in the story, by Mark Twain, of the boy told to stand in a corner and not think of a white rabbit.

This latter circumstance is not present, and the only question is whether their respective defenses were antagonistic. The two victims testified that both defendants robbed them. In defense, defendants both denied it, and neither said the other did. The co-defendant stated that he and the victims exchanged the amenities of the day-it happened to be January 1-while Higginbotham testified that he was out of carshot and didn't know what co-defendant was saying or doing. This is certainly not a 'He did it, I didn't' defense, rather a 'I didn't do it, and that's all I know' defense from Higginbotham's standpoint, and from co-defendant's, a 'I didn't do it, and he didn't either' defense. So far as we can see, these defenses dovetail perfectly, or to borrow a musical analogy, the defenses are contrapuntal, not dissonant. We discern no conflict, and it is little wonder that counsel did not move for severance.

Higginbotham, at 142-43, 273-74. Notably, Judge Smith clearly indicated an understanding that incriminating codefendant statements and antagonistic defenses are separate, distinct categories.

528 27 Ill.App.3d 569, 327 N.E.2d 51 (Apr. 23, 2975) (Hallett, J.).
529 Id. at 575-76, 578-79, 55, 57.

So although *Braune* reappeared in *Brown*, it ironically was not yet recognized to constitute authority on antagonistic defenses.

People v. Davis (1976),[530] a non-fatal stabbing case that came a century after *White* and forty years after *Braune*, was the first case in which a court attempted to carefully define the meaning of "antagonism," and recognized the lack of a proper definition, after so many decades in which courts had used the term more cavalierly. The *Davis* court, of course, came too late, and was only a mid-level appellate court, so its efforts to clarify the situation were hamstrung by earlier decisions that could not be harmonized properly, and *Davis* inevitably rested on the same shoddy precedential foundation as earlier Illinois cases.

The *Davis* court cited *Canaday* on discretionary severance, *Gendron* on severance where fairness requires it, and *Brooks* and *Henderson* for "Separate trials are required when the defenses of the several defendants are so antagonistic that a fair trial can be assured only by a severance."[531] Davis' trial motion for severance was based only on a bald, conclusory allegation that codefendant Huff's defense was antagonistic, and the trial court denied the motion after the prosecution agreed to delete any inculpatory statements from Huff regarding Davis.[532] On appeal, the *Davis* court explained that Huff's statement had in no way implicated or prejudiced Davis, citing *Brooks* and *Clark* (1959).[533] Thus *Davis*, like so many earlier cases in the antagonism lineage, was a codefendant statement case involving no antagonism.

Returning to the "rule," the court stated, "Our supreme court has said numerous times that in determining whether a severance should be granted, the primary question is whether the defenses of the defendants are so antagonistic that a fair trial can be assured only by a severance. [Citing *Canaday*, *Yonder*, *Gendron*, *Henderson*, *Brinn*, and *Betson*.]"[534] The court added,

> Although we have found no Illinois case defining the term 'antagonistic', Webster's Third New International Dictionary defines it as 'characterized by or resulting from antagonism: marked by or arising from opposition, hostility, antipathy, or discord'. Huff testified and was available for cross-examination by defendant. Huff testified that neither he nor defendant stabbed Negron. Huff also denied making any statement to Eshoo. On the

---

530 43 Ill.App.3d 603, 357 N.E.2d 96 (Oct. 26, 1976) (Downing, J.).
531 *Id.* at 608, 100.
532 *Id.* at 609, 100-101.
533 *Id.* at 609-10, 101.
534 *Id.* at 610, 101.

> other hand, defendant testified that Huff stabbed Negron. Though the defenses contradicted, Huff was helpful to defendant, not antagonistic. To be antagonistic there must be a showing of true conflict in the several defenses; for example, where each defendant attributes the cause of an accident to the wrongful actions of the other [citing *Clark* (1972)]; where each defendant condemns the other and each declares the other will testify to facts exculpatory of himself and condemnatory of his co-defendant [citing *Braune* for the second time since 1942 in the antagonism lineage]; where the co-defendant's confession implicating defendant is received into evidence with only an instruction to the jury limiting its admissibility to the maker of the statement [citing *Sweetin* for the first time since 1959 in the antagonism lineage[535]]; and where each co-defendant makes an admission or confession orally and the references to the co-defendant applying for the severance are not eliminated from the testimony [citing *Barbaro*].[536]

Finding no prejudice, the court analogized to the one-sided antagonism in *Minnecci*, where Minnecci accused a codefendant of the murder but neither codefendant accused him, so Minnecci, like Davis, experienced no antagonism or prejudice.[537]

Thus the *Davis* court earnestly endeavored to illuminate a murky, muddled situation. Its invocation of the general definition of "antagonistic" in Webster's dictionary was problematic, however, in that the appropriate legal definition of antagonism in the antagonistic defenses context—unlike the joint representation context—required a very strict, strong meaning. Although the dictionary's mention of hostility and antipathy may have been strong enough to strike the right tone, other terms such as opposition and discord were not and opened the door to a looser, more liberal definition of "antagonism" as mere disagreement or contradiction. The court's requirement of "true conflict" did not help much, either, since "conflict" also could be watered down to mean mere contradiction. In citing its four examples of true conflict, the *Davis* court was properly inclusive, not exclusive—"for example"—but the court followed earlier authorities in improperly lumping purely codefendant statement issues together with antagonistic defense situations as in *Braune*. For all its conscientious efforts to research the issue, even reaching back to mostly forgotten cases such as *Sweetin*, *Betson*, *Minnecci*, *Barbaro*, and above all, *Braune*, the *Davis* court remained a prisoner of the garbage in the system that by then had muddled the meaning of

535 Five other cases cited *Sweetin* strictly regarding codefendant statements or other issues between 1959 and 1976.
536 *Id.* at 610-11, 101-02.
537 *Id.* at 611, 615, 102, 105.

antagonistic defenses in Illnois case law for almost fifty years. Ironically, the facts in *Davis* also were evidently clear-cut enough that the court could have reached its conclusion with much less effort. Notably, the *Davis* court gave an entirely separate, lengthy discussion of an alleged *Bruton* violation, again citing *Brooks* and *Clark* (1972) along with *Clark* (1959) and clearly recognizing this as a separate issue.[538]

People v. Miner (1977)[539] was a rare example of an Illinois case that involved some degree of actual antagonism beyond conflicting codefendant statements. The case involved a pair of codefendants who sought to steal gasoline from a local mine and wound up killing a mine guard with a shotgun blast to the face.[540] Before trial, the defendants moved for a severance based only upon somewhat differing statements.[541] Although the defendants' statements differed regarding why they went to the mine, both statements agreed that appellant Miner was holding codefendant Ledbetter's shotgun when it discharged, killing the victim.[542] The trial court denied the motions, finding they raised a mere apprehension of antagonistic defenses; the appellate court agreed.[543] At trial, however, both defendants testified. Miner claimed he was innocently holding the shotgun and " 'playing'" with the hammer of the weapon while chatting non-threateningly with the victim.[544] The court recounted: "Paul Ledbetter's testimony, however, clearly indicated that defendant was brandishing the shotgun and demanding gasoline from Starnes when the weapon discharged. Ledbetter's testimony was obviously antagonistic to defendant's defense."[545]

Confronted with this situation, the *Miner* court stated the various relevant rules, citing *Brown* (1975) regarding joint trial; *Brooks* for "Separate trials are required only when the defenses of the defendants are so antagonistic that a fair trial can be assured only by a severance"; *Rhodes* (1969) on a pretrial showing of prejudice from joint trial; *Davis* and *Yonder* for the need for specific grounds and the insufficiency of mere apprehension of antagonism; and *Pulaski* (1959) regarding the trial court's discretion to deny severance absent a showing of prejudice.[546]

---

538 *Id.* at 611-13, 102-04. That the United States Supreme Court did not treat the *Bruton* situation as antagonism might have helped some Illinois courts to rediscover that codefendant statements and antagonistic defenses were actually separate, distinct issues.

539 46 Ill.App.3d 273, 360 N.E.2d 1141 (Feb. 28, 1977) (Karns, J.).

540 *Id.* at 275-78, 1143-45.

541 *Id.* at 283-84, 1149.

542 *Id.*

543 *Id.* at 284, 1149.

544 *Id.*

545 *Id.*

546 *Id.* at 283, 1149.

Although the court accepted that Ledbetter's actual testimony was antagonistic to Miner's defense, the court distinguished *Braune*, where "evidence was presented, prior to trial, indicating that each defendant would take the witness stand and testify to a set of facts which would be exculpatory of the witness and condemnatory of his codefendant."[547] Although Miner contended that "a showing of antagonistic defenses may be made either prior to or during trial[,]" the court concluded that such a proposition "contradict[ed] several supreme and appellate court opinions which clearly state that a showing of antagonistic defenses must be made prior to trial."[548]

The court also concluded that notwithstanding the antagonistic testimony from Ledbetter, Miner had received a fair trial.[549] The only evidence admitted at trial that would have been inadmissible in a separate trial was a witness' testimony regarding a statement by Ledbetter.[550] The court noted that although Miner was not denied his confrontation rights as to this statement because Ledbetter testified and was thus available for cross-examination (citing *Bruton* and its progeny), that alone did not make the statement admissible unless all references to the non-declaring codefendant were deleted.[551] Because a state's witness testified regarding a similar extrajudicial statement from Miner, though, the court followed earlier authority in holding that "the admission of a codefendant's statement inculpating the defendant was harmless error where the defendant had made substantially similar statements and where the other evidence against the defendant was convincing and adequate to support a guilty verdict."[552] The court similarly held that Ledbetter's counsel's cross-examination of Miner concerning a prior conviction for burglary was also harmless error "[i]n light of the overwhelming evidence of [Miner's] guilt[.]"[553]

A TRIFECTA OF PRECEDENTIAL CONFUSION: *PRECUP*, 1977

People v. Precup (1977)[554] involved three jointly represented codefendants all convicted of armed robbery of a tavern.[555] On appeal, two of the defendants alleged plain error from the trial court's failure to sever their trials sua sponte based upon their differing alibis in statements they made to police, particularly

547 *Id.* at 284, 1149-50.
548 *Id.* at 284, 1150.
549 *Id.* at 285, 1150.
550 *Id.*
551 *Id.*
552 *Id.*
553 *Id.* at 286, 1151.
554 50 Ill.App.3d 23, 365 N.E.2d 1007 (Jul. 5, 1977) (Trapp, J.).
555 *Id.* at 25, 1008.

where they were jointly represented.[556] Thus, it appears that the appellants wove together the issues of antagonistic defenses, codefendant statements, and joint representation in a jumbled, haphazard fashion that the court then had to try to pick apart—frequently a recipe for trouble.

The court noted that "no defendant undertook to inculpate another, each denied participation in the robbery[,]" and the codefendants' alibi defenses were "consistent" and "compatible."[557] On sua sponte severance, the *Precup* court distinguished *Wheeler* (1970), an anomalous case that never mentioned antagonism and is a extremely rare example of an appellate court finding error in the trial court's failure to sever defendants sua sponte,[558] and cited *McCasle* and *Merritt* (1973) in rejecting the appellants' argument.[559] The court cited authorities, including *Miner*, holding that the severance issue should be raised pretrial and not for the first time on appeal.[560] The court also rejected the appellants' contention that their differing statements "create[d] 'a basic antagonistic relationship,' " declaring, "Antagonistic defenses in the context of severance have been confined to those instances where one or more co-defendants testifies implicating the other. [Citing *Ware*, *Johnson* (1970), *Augustus*, and *Halluin*, ironically all joint representation cases.]"[561] Quoting *Davis*' four examples of "true conflict" from *Clark* (1972), *Braune*, *Sweetin*, and *Barbaro* for good measure, the court agreed with the trial court's finding that no defendant had implicated another.[562] The court apparently was unaware that its brief, summarizing statement that antagonistic defenses required that defendants testify against each other went against a wide array of earlier Illinois authorities, namely, all those involving only codefendant statements. Notwithstanding this, *Precup*'s loose language regarding defendants testifying and implicating each other spawned a substantial sublineage of its own.[563]

556 *Id.* at 27-30, 1009-10.

557 *Id.* at 27, 1009-10.

558 121 Ill.App.2d 337, 339-40, 257 N.E.2d 587, 588-89 (Mar. 10, 1970) (Burke, J.).

559 *Id.* at 28, 1010.

560 *Id.*

561 *Id.* at 29, 1010.

562 *Id.* at 29, 1011.

563 See People v. Moore, 65 Ill.App.3d 712, 719, 382 N.E.2d 810, 816 (Nov. 2, 1978) (Boyle, J.); People v. Jones, 81 Ill.App.3d 724, 727, 401 N.E.2d 1325, 1328 (Mar. 12, 1980) (Green, J.) (recognizing *Precup*'s language as dictum, but following it); People v. McMullen, 88 Ill.App.3d 611, 613, 410 N.E.2d 1174, 1176 (Sept. 24, 1980) (Mills, P.J.); People v. Murphy, 93 Ill.App.3d 606, 609, 417 N.E.2d 759, 761-62 (Feb. 20, 1981) (Mejda, J.) (citing *Precup* and *Jones* and losing *Jones*' observation about dictum); People v. Griggs, 104 Ill.App.3d 527, 530-31, 432 N.E.2d 1176 (Feb. 22, 1982) (McGloon, J.); People v. Sanchez, 110 Ill.App.3d 893, 904, 443 N.E.2d 252, 260 (Nov. 29, 1982) (Mejda, J.); People v. Brophy, 96 Ill.App.3d 936, 946, 422 N.E.2d 158 (May 28, 1981) (Linn, J.); People v. Poree, 119 Ill.App.3d 590, 595, 456 N.E.2d 950, 954 (Nov. 18, 1983) (Mejda,

The court then turned to the appellants' ineffective assistance argument, noting that it "incorporates similar considerations and is essentially the reverse side of the coin."[564] In a thorough review of relevant authorities, the court cited *Husar* (1974), *Barren* (1975), *Falconer* (1975), *Robinson* (1969), *Brown* (1976), and *Holman* to reject the appellants' proposed rule finding conflict per se in the joint representation context and reaffirm the rule that "an actual existing conflict of interest in defenses must appear."[565] The *Precup* court discussed and accepted *Holman*'s garbling of the proper distinction between the rules on severing antagonistic defenses and appointing separate counsel, observing, "Since there was no implicating of any defendant in the offense, the defenses were not antagonistic and it was not error to deny a motion for severance or to fail to appoint separate counsel," and citing *Brooks*, a non-joint representation case, as further support.[566] Thus, as so often happened, the *Precup* court only got itself into trouble and added to the overall confusion by attempting to conscientiously and completely answer the appellants' basically bogus arguments.

Justice Craven further added to the confusion in a dissent, agreeing with the majority that "an attorney is placed in a conflict situation by the representation of two defendants only when the defenses of those defendants are antagonistic. [Citing *Smith* (1974), which merely referred to antagonistic defenses, and *Dickens*, which repeated the unfortunate rule-lumping language from *Chapman*.]"[567] Craven, however, concluded, "The alibi defenses here were antagonistic and mutually exclusive."[568] He cited and quoted *Bopp* as an example of inconsistent alibis requiring separate counsel, not recognizing that *Bopp* was considering an entirely different question from antagonistic defenses.[569]

J.); People v. Edwards, 128 Ill.App.3d 993, 1000, 471 N.E.2d 957, 963 (Nov. 26, 1984) (Lindberg, J.). The joint representation cases cited by Precup were all very brief, and none had anything to do with antagonistic defenses outside the joint representation context. Seemingly the only other case that mentioned codefendants defending by implicating each other and called it "a classic example of conflicting and antagonistic interests which would justify a severance," though it certainly did not call it the exclusive ground for severance and was not considering that issue, was yet another joint representation case, People v. Bass, 101 Ill.App.2d 259, 262, 243 N.E.2d 305, 307 (Sept. 19, 1968) (Sullivan, J.) (cited in *Halluin*).

564 *Id.*

565 *Id.* at 30-32, 1011-1013.

566 *Id.* at 32, 1013.

567 *Id.* at 32, 1013 (Craven, J., dissenting).

568 *Id.*

569 *Id.* at 32-33, 1013.

Thus, *Precup* was a hopeless mess of a case. Nevertheless, it was cited in more than a dozen later opinions.[570]

ACTUAL ANTAGONISM?: *JONES*, 1980

People v. Jones (1980)[571] involved two African American male defendants, Cedric Jones and Anthony Newbern, convicted of felony theft of roughly $350 from an Urbana pizza shop.[572] At trial, the pizza shop manager and an employee testified that one afternoon as they were preparing to open the shop, first one, then another black man entered the shop. Each requested and was given a glass of water. At around the same time, the manager brought the previous night's cash receipts to a cutting table behind the shop counter at the front of the store for the employee to count, then went back to his office. One of the visitors asked to apply for a job, and the shop employee went back to tell the manager. The manager talked with one visitor, whom he later identified as Newbern, then returned to the back. The shop employee testified that he heard sounds like someone jumping over the counter, ran back to the front of the shop, and found the visitors and part of the money gone. He rushed out into the parking lot and saw two black men in a 1968 white Buick with a black top driving away. Approximately $350 was missing from the previous evening's receipts ($149 of an estimated $500 remained on the cutting table). A woman who was driving by the shop that afternoon testified that she saw two black men run from the store and enter a light-colored car with a dark top. The employee testified that while driving with police a short while later, he saw Newbern in the same Buick in Champaign, and later saw at Newbern's house what appeared to be the same hat Jones had been wearing.[573]

Newbern testified that he drove to the shop to get a job application and found Jones already there. He said he talked with the manager, but had to leave before filling out the application because his mother's dog had escaped from his car, and he ran out of the shop to try to catch the dog. He drove around for a while seeking the dog, unsuccessfully, then went home. Jones was still in the shop when he left. Newbern admitted that he gave a different statement to police before trial.[574] Jones testified that he was not there when the theft occurred.[575]

---

570 These included Meng (1977), Moore (1978), Jones (1980-1), Jones (1980-2), Lee (1980), Stevenson (1980), Murphy (1981), Griggs (1982), Lumpkin (1982), and two cases after 1985, People v. Davis 142 Ill.App.3d 630, 491 N.E.2d 1285, and People v. Bramlett, 211 Ill.App.3d 172, 569 N.E.2d 1139 (1991).

571 81 Ill.App.3d 724, 401 N.E.2d 1325 (Mar. 12, 1980) (Green, J.).

572 *Id.* at 725, 1326.

573 *Id.*

574 *Id.* at 725, 1327.

Although the court rejected Jones' argument that the evidence was insufficient to convict him, it agreed the joint trial had proved problematic. The court repeated the language in *Yonder* that a "defendant is entitled to a severance upon making a clear showing that a codefendant will rely on a defense which is 'so antagonistic that a fair trial can be had only by severance[,]' " as well as *Yonder*'s requirement of a sufficient showing of antagonism in the pretrial severance petition, not on mere " 'apprehensions of antagonism"' or what later happened at trial.[576]

The *Jones* court then made two fairly sophisticated observations: that actual Illinois case law directly holding that defenses were antagonistic was scarce and hard to find, and that the *Bruton* situation involving codefendants' extrajudicial statements was a separate, distinct category from antagonistic defenses.[577] The court noted that no Illinois opinion directly "holding that defenses were 'antagonistic' has been called to our attention."[578] The court also distinguished *Miner* regarding mere apprehension and correctly observed that the language in *Precup* stating that "'Antagonistic defenses in the context of severance have been confined to . . . where one or more co-defendants testifies implicating the other"' was dictum.[579]

Turning to the case at hand, the court described how the two severance hearings indicated that there would be a strong inference that the money was taken by one of the two visitors, Newbern would testify that he and Jones were both there but he did not know what happened after he left, and Jones would testify that he was not there.[580] The *Jones* court held that notwithstanding *Yonder*, courts properly "may also consider the representation of counsel made at the hearing on the petition."[581] Here, representations of counsel indicated that there would be a dispute over Jones' presence at the scene, "and that in view of the nature of the circumstantial evidence, the issue would likely be determinative."[582] The court distinguished the alibis in *Precup* as being only conflicting but not " 'implicating the other.'"[583] The court turned to Webster's New World Dictionary (2d Ed. 1974) to define "to implicate" as ' "to show to have a connection with a crime * * * .'"[584] The court continued, "Here, although defendant's presence at the scene would not of itself have been enough to convict him, his counsel showed at the hearings on

575 *Id.*
576 *Id.*
577 *Id.* at 727, 1328.
578 *Id.*
579 *Id.*
580 *Id.* at 728, 1328.
581 *Id.*
582 *Id.*
583 *Id.*
584 *Id.* at 728, 1328-29.

the severance motion that, when combined with the circumstantial evidence, it would infer his guilt. Thus the Newbern defense testimony implied defendant's guilt."[585] The court added, "Indeed, it was apparent that the likely testimony of Newbern would be only slightly more damaging to defendant if he were able to testify to actually having seen defendant take the money." With yet another flash of rare insight, the Jones court noted, "We are unable to discern any hard and fast rule as to when severance should occur in a criminal case and believe that each situation should be judged on its own facts."[586] The court concluded, "In the instant case we believe the defenses were shown to be 'antagonistic' and the trial court should have granted a severance."[587]

Jones was thus an unusual case where, based on the facts rather than a formula, severance was probably the best choice. It is similar to the formulation of the antagonistic defenses doctrine that arose in certain federal jurisdictions: that severance is necessary when at least one of two codefendants must be guilty, and for the jury to believe one, it must convict the other.[588] The *Jones* court was perceptive in deciding the case on its facts rather than mechanistically on some supposed pre-existing legal rule, in recognizing that the severance decision is necessarily fact-dependent, in distinguishing the *Bruton* situation from the antagonistic defenses context, and in recognizing the *Precup* "rule" as dictum (although the court then followed that dictum as though it were more than dictum). *Jones*' acceptance of pretrial representations of counsel was a salutary move away from the mechanistic petition requirement from earlier cases. Its adoption of the dictionary definition of "to implicate," and its embrace of the *Precup* dictum requiring that one defendant implicate the other, however, set perhaps too liberal a standard for finding antagonism by stretching the earlier concept of "pointing the accusatory finger" to include potentially almost anything that connected a codefendant with a crime incident. It also left a situation where a defendant could force a severance by offering a conflicting alibi, however implausible. Because the *Jones* court could find no earlier cases finding antagonistic defenses, it offered a relatively new and independent source of law on the issue.

THE EARLY 1980S

People v. Lee (1980)[589] involved four codefendants who perpetrated a home invasion armed robbery that led to murder. Defendants Lewis and Chase were

---

585 *Id.* at 728, 1329.

586 *Id.*

587 *Id.*

588 *See* Dewey, *supra* note 58, at 171, 176-80.

589 86 Ill.App.3d 922, 408 N.E.2d 335 (Jul. 21, 1980) (O'Connor, J.).

convicted only of multiple counts of armed robbery and burglary; defendants Lee and Trosclair were also convicted of murder, attempted murder, aggravated battery, and battery.[590] The defendants, purportedly seeking a particular individual, forced their way into an apartment at gunpoint and forced the occupants to lie on the floor on their backs. Trosclair then said, "Kill them all." A pregnant woman in the apartment pleaded for their lives. Trosclair said not to shoot her. Lee replied, "I have to shoot, I have to kill someone," and indicated that he needed to kill at least two people. As Lee and Trosclair talked, Chase and Lewis took the apartment's stereo system out the front door. Lee then shot, apparently more or less at random, one victim, then another, as Trosclair watched. They then fled. One shooting victim later died; the other survived with a serious abdominal wound. One apartment occupant who had been able to flee out the back door when the defendants forced their way through the front door flagged down a police squad car and identified the fleeing defendants as three of them were attempting to join two other men waiting in an Oldsmobile sedan parked in a nearby alley. She and another victim later identified all four defendants from a 15-man lineup; two others identified Lee, Trosclair, and Chase. A revolver with Lee's fingerprints was found near the Oldsmobile.[591]

Lewis testified that he was with the others and another person, Larry, that night in the Oldsmobile; that he and Chase went to a different apartment to pick up Chase's suitcase; and that as they were returning to the Oldsmobile, they heard gunshots, then saw Larry running toward them with a stereo, Trosclair running close behind. Chase adopted Lewis' testimony.[592] Lee testified that Trosclair was the leader of the gang he was a member of when he was in school; that on the night of the crime, Trosclair entered the apartment with the gun, then apparently at some point gave the gun to Lee and ordered him to kill everyone in the apartment; that Lee said no; that Trosclair poked the gun barrel into Lee's stomach; that Lee said he could not shoot the pregnant woman, so Trosclair then said not to shoot her, but instead " 'Shoot them two'"; that Lee feared Trosclair and thought that he might have another gun and might shoot him if he didn't follow his orders; and that Lee fired two shots from near the door, then fled.[593]

On appeal, Lee and Trosclair asserted, inter alia, that the trial court erred in denying their respective severance motions, which were filed several months apart, and that Trosclair's counsel was not present when Lee's motion was argued.[594]

---

590 *Id.* at 924, 338.
591 *Id.* at 925-926, 338-339.
592 *Id.* at 926-27, 339.
593 *Id.* at 927-928, 339-340.
594 *Id.* at 928-929, 340-341.

The court reviewed the Illinois severance "rule" at length, citing *Jones* (1976) for the general rule of joint trial unless fairness required otherwise; *Henderson* for the trial court's discretion on severance; *Precup* for the requirement of a pretrial motion for severance; *Miner* for the requirement that any facts not in the record be supported by an affidavit; *Rhodes* for the defendant's duty to demonstrate prejudice; *Brinn* for the requirement that this demonstration be specific; *Nickson* (1978) for mere apprehension of conflict being insufficient.[595] The court, citing *Yonder*, observed, "Of paramount concern is whether their defenses are so antagonistic that a severance is imperative to a fair trial";[596] the court also noted *Yonder*'s requirement that the reviewing court focus on defendants' pretrial petitions, not subsequent happenings at trial.[597] The court added, however, "Nonetheless, the trial court has a continuing duty at all stages of trial to grant a severance if prejudice appears. [Citing *Clark* (1979)."[598]

Applying these concepts, the court held that Lee's pretrial severance motion, directed at the anticipated testimony of Lewis, was properly denied, because the motion was unclear as to what defense he would use, presented only the "mere apprehension of a conflict," and included no affidavit.[599] Nor was Lee prejudiced at trial, because his compulsion defense was not antagonistic to any other defendant's defense.[600]

The court also held that Trosclair's pretrial severance motion was properly denied, where Trosclair offered only mere apprehensions of conflict with no supporting affidavit.[601] The court, however, found that Trosclair had been prejudiced at trial by Lewis' testimony that Trosclair had been dropped off from the Oldsmobile near the crime scene plus Lee's directly implicating testimony on what happened inside the apartment.[602] The court concluded, "Co-defendants' testimony was patently antagonistic to Trosclair's defense. This was not apparent until trial. They placed Trosclair at the crime scene, indicated his responsibility for the crimes charged and inferred that he was fleeing with stolen property. Co-defendants' testimony may have necessitated Trosclair's decision not to testify."[603] On that

595 *Id.* at 929, 341.
596 *Id.*
597 *Id.* at 930, 341.
598 *Id.*
599 *Id.* at 930, 342.
600 *Id.*
601 *Id.*
602 *Id.* at 931, 342.
603 *Id.*

basis, the court held, "The cumulative effect of co-defendants' antagonistic defenses prejudiced Trosclair."[604]

People v. Dorsey (1980)[605] involved two men, Ben Dorsey and Leon Harris, convicted of killing a cab driver. Each defendant made a statement to police that was read into evidence at trial, but edited to delete references to the codefendant.[606] Each defendant also made pretrial motions for severance that were denied based upon the prosecution's promise to edit out references to codefendants.[607] Dorsey's statement indicated that he saw two people, Harris and another man named Curtis Nelson, engage in the shooting, but his statement was edited to delete any reference to Harris, so the edited statement read as though Dorsey claimed to have seen only one person, Nelson, do the shooting.[608] Harris' original statement described how Dorsey planned to rob the cab driver and later shot the cab driver as Nelson stood on the other side of the cab, but in the edited version, all references to Dorsey were replaced with "he."[609]

On appeal, Dorsey claimed antagonistic defenses.[610] The court cited *Miner* on joint trial and severance "only when the defenses are so antagonistic that a fair trial can be achieved only through severance."[611] The court noted that redaction of Dorsey's statement that removed any mention of Harris and mentioned only one shooter made his statement appear unbelievable, given that a witness who was in the back of the cab when the shooting happened testified that there were two people involved, one shooting from each side of the cab.[612] Rejecting the prosecution's argument that Dorsey's severance motion did not adequately spell out the prejudice he would suffer, the Dorsey court cited *Jones* (1980) at length for its holding that a court should also consider representations of counsel made at a severance hearing, noting that Dorsey's counsel had warned that redaction of the statements would not avert prejudice.[613] As to Harris' statement, the court found a clear *Bruton* violation, explaining that replacing "Dorsey" with "he" had not eliminated prejudice where "he" clearly implied "Dorsey."[614] On these grounds, the court held that Dorsey and Harris had antagonistic defenses that were clearly

---

604 *Id.*
605 88 Ill.App.3d 712, 410 N.E.2d 1132 (Sept. 18, 1980) (Johnson, J.).
606 *Id.* at 715-716, 1134-1135.
607 *Id.* at 714, 1133.
608 *Id.* at 716, 717; 1134, 1135.
609 *Id.* at 717, 1134-1135.
610 *Id.* at 717, 1135.
611 *Id.*
612 *Id.*
613 *Id.* at 717-718, 1136.
614 *Id.* at 718-19, 1136-37.

disclosed before trial, so their trials should have been severed.[615] Thus, *Dorsey* clearly involved exclusively codefendant statements, but the court characterized the issue as antagonistic defenses, in addition to lumping *Bruton* problems together with antagonism.

In *People v. McMullen* (1980),[616] two mentally handicapped high school students were charged with lewdly fondling a fellow student.[617] The appellant's counsel moved for severance before trial based upon the codefendant's statement to police implicating the appellant, which the prosecutor promised not to use to prevent *Bruton* problems, but the defense counsel warned that there still would be prejudice if the codefendant testified in keeping with his statement.[618] At trial, the appellant presented a witness who testified that the appellant never got out of his seat; the appellant also testified that he never arose from his seat, but that his codefendant was standing near the victim while the teacher was out of the room.[619] The codefendant testified that both he and the appellant left their seats while the teacher was absent and touched the victim on her breasts and legs, but he claimed that he believed the victim was 16 years old or older.[620] On cross-examination, the prosecutor impeached him with his pretrial statement stating that both he and the appellant had fondled the victim's breasts and legs.[621]

The court noted the appellant's invocation of *Strayhorn*, "where the supreme court noted in dictum that a motion for severance should be allowed where it appears that defenses of codefendants are antagonistic."[622] Citing dictum from *Precup*, the appellant contended that "such antagonism existed here since one of the defendants testified implicating the other."[623] Apparently also on the basis of the *Precup* dictum, the State conceded that the defenses were antagonistic, but cited *Yonder* regarding the need for prejudice to be demonstrated specifically in a pretrial severance motion.[624] The court, however, reviewed its holding in *Jones* (1980) regarding representations of counsel at the severance hearing and held that the *McMullen* trial court had sufficient notice of antagonism from counsel's warning.[625] Because both defendants actually testified and strongly implicated each other,

615 *Id.* at 719, 1137.
616 88 Ill.App.3d 611, 410 N.E.2d 1174 (Sept. 24, 1980) (Mills, P.J.).
617 *Id.* at 612, 1175.
618 *Id.* at 612, 1175-1176.
619 *Id.* at 613, 1176.
620 *Id.*
621 *Id.*
622 *Id.*
623 *Id.*
624 *Id.*
625 *Id.* at 614, 1176-77.

McMullen appears to be another rare example of actual antagonism in Illinois case law. The court, however, in deciding to remand, focused exclusively on the existence of conflicting codefendant statements and did not mention any indications either of defenses the defendants planned to offer or of the intent of either defendant to testify.[626]

People v. Murphy (1981)[627] involved two men, Danny Murphy and Kenneth Bell, convicted of armed robbery for holding up Mae Maxwell at gunpoint outside Perry's Chicken Shack.[628] The victim testified that Bell had a gun and demanded her purse and car keys, while Murphy stood nearby yelling, " 'Don't move or I'll shoot.' "[629] Murphy and Bell then drove away in Maxwell's blue Chevrolet Malibu.[630] Police later pulled Murphy over in the Malibu for various serious traffic infractions, and the next day, Maxwell identified him from a police lineup as one of her two assailants.[631] Two weeks later, she identified Bell as the other assailant.[632] Bell, who admitted he was a friend of Murphy, testified that he was at home with his family on the night of the crime, and his brother and grandmother corroborated that alibi.[633] Before Murphy testified, Bell's attorney requested that Murphy, who had requested a bench trial, testify outside the presence of the jury, because the testimony would implicate Bell and contradict his alibi.[634] The court denied the motion, and Murphy testified that he and Bell were both outside Perry's Chicken Shack that night, that he saw Bell approach Maxwell and speak to her, and that Bell then gave him keys to the Malibu and they then drove off.[635] Bell's counsel then moved for a mistrial, claiming the defenses were clearly antagonistic and prejudicial to Bell; the court denied the motion.[636]

Considering the matter on appeal, the *Murphy* court, like the *Davis* court, made an impressive effort to summarize all relevant authorities in stating an exclusive version of the rule:

> The general rule is that persons jointly indicted should be jointly tried and separate trials are only required when the defenses are so antagonistic that

626 *Id.* at 614, 1177.
627 93 Ill.App.3d 606, 417 N.E.2d 759 (Feb. 20, 1981) (Mejda, J.).
628 *Id.* at 607, 760.
629 *Id.* at 607-608, 760.
630 *Id.* at 608, 760.
631 *Id.*
632 *Id.*
633 *Id.* at 608, 761.
634 *Id.*
635 *Id.*
636 *Id.*

> a fair trial can be achieved only through severance. [Citing *Barbaro*, *Dorsey*, *Miner*, and *Davis*.] However, it is incumbent upon the defendant moving for a separate trial to demonstrate prior to trial how he would be prejudiced by a joint trial. [Citing *Stevenson*, *Miner*.] The decision to grant severance rests within the sound discretion of the trial court. [Citing *Clark* (1979).] However, this discretion should not be exercised arbitrarily, capriciously, or in such a way as to work an injustice. [Citing *Barbaro*.] The mere apprehension that defenses may prove antagonistic without a showing that such apprehensions are well founded is an insufficient ground for severance. [Citing *Moore* (1983), *Davis*.] Nevertheless, the court has a continuing duty at all stages of trial to grant severance if prejudice appears. [Citing *Lee* (1980), *Clark* (1979).] Antagonistic defenses have been confined to those instances where one or more co-defendants testify implicating the other. [Citing *Jones* (1980), *Precup*.] The verb "to implicate" has been defined as "to show to have a connection with a crime * * *." [Citing *Jones*; Webster's New World Dictionary (2d ed. 1974).] Antagonistic is defined as "that which is characterized by or resulting from antagonism; marked by or arising from opposition, hostility, antipathy or discord." [Citing *Davis*.] In sum, where there is more than one defendant and the defenses are antagonistic, and one defendant accuses the other, making it impossible for defendant requesting severance to have a fair trial, the severance should be granted. [Citing *Lindsay*, *Minnecci*.][637]

As so often happens when a court attempts to collect all relevant authorities, internal inconsistencies were revealed in the court's own summary of the law: for instance, for defendants to testify and implicate each other is different from defendants accusing each other. Also as usual, the diligently summarizing court did not notice the inconsistency.

As to Murphy, the court, citing *Davis* and *Minnecci*, explained that although Bell's alibi defense was inconsistent with Murphy's, it was not antagonistic to Murphy—Bell did not implicate Murphy.[638] Murphy did, however, clearly implicate Bell, even if he did not accuse him of any overt wrongdoing, and on this basis, the court concluded that Murphy's defense was antagonistic to Bell.[639] The court discussed *Jones* (1980) at length and analogized to *Jones* in explaining how, given that Murphy's self-exculpatory testimony contradicted Bell's alibi and not only placed Bell at the scene of the crime but also had him talking with the victim and giving Murphy her car keys, "It is apparent that Murphy's testimony could only be more

[637] *Id.* at 609, 761-762.
[638] *Id.* at 610, 762.
[639] *Id.* at 611, 762-763.

damaging to Bell, if he had testified that he saw Bell rob Ms. Maxwell at gunpoint."[640] The court held that Bell's attorney had given sufficient warning of antagonism, and that the trial court should have granted Bell's motion to have Murphy testify outside the jury's presence.[641]

People v. Powell (1981)[642] basically concerned the requirement that defendants file severance motions before trial. For various reasons, both defendants moved for severance only orally, after the jury was sworn, and did not then clearly indicate what the alleged antagonism would be.[643] The following day, after opening arguments, "both defense counsel were very specific in outlining to the trial judge what the antagonistic testimony of [codefendant] O'Neill would be. As it turned out, the defenses of the two were clearly antagonistic."[644] Notwithstanding that, the court, citing *Yonder* and *Rhodes*, held that the defendants were obliged to disclose the other side's "damaging testimony to the trial court at the earliest opportunity" and concluded, "[W]e cannot say that the trial court abused its discretion with what it had to consider prior to trial."[645] *Powell* was thus an example of *Yonder*'s chickens coming home to roost, and courts elevating the pretrial motion rule above the fundamental requirement that trials be fair.

In *People v. Lee* (1981),[646] the Illinois Supreme Court reversed the appellate court's earlier finding of antagonism causing prejudice to appellant/defendant Trosclair after the State successfully sought higher review.[647] The court summarized relevant law, citing *Rhodes* for the requirement of a pretrial severance motion, *Yonder* for the defendant's burden to demonstrate prejudice from joint trial beyond mere apprehensions, *Canaday* and the Illinois Revised Statutes for the trial court's discretion, *Lindsay* for the general rule of joint trial unless fairness demands otherwise.[648] The court then observed that "[a]t least two varieties of prejudice can be readily identified": first, the *Bruton* variety involving codefendants' extrajudicial statements, which did not apply here, and second,

> *Prejudice may also occur when a codefendant takes the stand to point a finger at the defendant as the real perpetrator of the offense.* No confrontation problems exist because the defendant is free to cross-examine the new accuser. But the

640 *Id.* at 611, 763.
641 *Id.* at 612, 763.
642 95 Ill.App.3d 93, 419 N.E.2d 708 (Apr. 9, 1981) (Webber, J.).
643 *Id.* at 98-99, 711-12.
644 *Id.* at 99, 712.
645 *Id.*
646 87 Ill.2d 182, 429 N.E.2d 461 (Nov. 13, 1981) (Simon, J.).
647 *Id.* at 184, 186; 462, 463.
648 *Id.* at 186-187, 463.

> procedure may be unfair. For example, as the court observed in People v. Braune (1936), . . . "The trial was in many respects more of a contest between the defendants than between the People and the defendants. It produced a spectacle where the People frequently stood by and witnessed a combat in which the defendants attempted to destroy each other." A severance may be ordered where the defendants cannot realistically be aligned on the same side, but care must be taken in such cases to insure that the nature of the defenses are truly inconsistent. [Citing *Brooks*.][649]

The court thus identified the *Bruton* situation and antagonistic defenses as two separate categories. It also appeared to set a fairly strict standard for what would constitute antagonistic defenses—namely, a defendant *testifying and implicating a codefendant*. Although the court tended to avoid using the term "antagonism," it clearly linked the second variety of prejudice to *Braune*, the classic example of true antagonism.

Noting that Trosclair claimed the second variety of prejudice, the court cited *Gendron* for, "The paramount inquiry in such cases is whether the defenses are so antagonistic that a severance is imperative to assure a fair trial"—again, identifying the second variety as the antagonistic defenses situation.[650] The court determined that Trosclair's pretrial motion made no such showing and gave the trial court no reason to sever at that point: "The conclusions set forth in his petition for a severance were no substitute for a detailed recitation of what his defense would be, what the codefendant's defenses would be, and how the two conflicted. [Citing *Braune* again.]"[651] The court, again noting *Gendron*, then considered the appellate court's determination that the trial court should have seen the need for a severance as the trial developed, even if the basis for severance was unknown before trial. The court observed that a strict rule requiring a pretrial motion might make more sense regarding the *Bruton* situation than in the antagonistic defenses context, where a defendant's counsel might not know for certain either a codefendant's anticipated defense or whether that codefendant would take the stand and implicate the defendant.[652] Even granting that, though, the court explained that Trosclair had never detailed antagonisms or inconsistencies between his and codefendant Lee's defenses to the trial court; instead, his stated defense was insufficient evidence.[653] Moreover, codefendant Lewis' placing Trosclair near the scene of the crime, and Lee's testimony as to what happened at

649 *Id.* at 187, 463-464 (italics added).
650 *Id.* at 187-188, 464.
651 *Id.* at 188, 464.
652 *Id.* at 188, 464.
653 *Id.* at 189, 464.

the crime scene, were merely cumulative to the testimony of several crime victims.[654] The court noted that the situation might have been different had Trosclair offered an alibi, as his counsel promised to do in opening statements, but that never happened, so the record showed no antagonism between Trosclair's defense and those of his codefendants.[655] The court quoted *Meisenhelter*: " 'It is incumbent upon a defendant, moving for a separate trial, to show to the trial judge how he would be prejudiced by a joint trial. If he fails so to do, he cannot, on review, complain of the action of the trial court in denying his motion.' "[656] The court reversed the lower appellate court.[657]

People v. Lumpkin (1982)[658] was another case in which the appellant unsuccessfully invoked *Wheeler* to argue that the court should have severed his trial sua sponte when the codefendant's out-of-court statement was admitted at trial.[659] The court cited *Precup* for the general rule that severance motions must be made before trial—though acknowledging the holding in *Clark* (1979) that "a trial judge has a continuing duty to grant such a motion if prejudice appears during . . . trial"—and *Appold* for its holding that prejudice may not be raised for the first time in a post-trial motion.[660] Lumpkin pointed out that like the appellant in *Wheeler*, he had notified the court that there might be prejudice from a joint trial.[661] The court replied that *Wheeler* appeared to be the only Illinois case ever to impose a sua sponte severance obligation upon a trial judge, and added that even under *Wheeler*, any sua sponte severance would have to occur before trial to avoid serious double jeopardy problems.[662] Lumpkin's counsel had only indicated before trial that a motion to sever then would be premature, and the *Lumpkin* court, citing *Precup*, determined that the *Wheeler* holding did not apply where the need for severance was not apparent before trial.[663] Citing *Davis*, *Precup*, and *Holman*, the court also rejected Lumpkin's parallel ineffective assistance argument because the codefendant's statement did not implicate Lumpkin, was merely contradictory rather than antagonistic to his defense, and thus "was not of such a prejudicial nature as to render a fair trial impossible in the absence of a severance."[664]

---

654 *Id.*
655 *Id.*
656 *Id.*
657 *Id.*
658 105 Ill.App.3d 157, 433 N.E.2d 1369 (Apr. 1, 1982) (Jones, J.).
659 *Id.* at 164, 1375.
660 *Id.* at 164-165, 1375.
661 *Id.* at 165, 1375.
662 *Id.*
663 *Id.*
664 *Id.* at 165-66, 1375-76.

People v. Sanchez (1982)[665] involved two defendants accused of raping a woman who drove with them in a pickup truck to an Indiana lake. Both defendants admitted being there in the truck, but denied having done anything wrong or having seen the other defendant do anything wrong, though both said they had fallen asleep for a time and so did not see everything.[666] The court reviewed various authorities, citing *Lee* (1981) for the defendant's burden to specifically show antagonism and resulting prejudice, *Murphy* on the trial court's discretion to sever, and *McMullen* and *Jones* (1980) on reviewing only the sufficiency of the petitions plus representations of counsel.[667] The court also stated, "The general rule is that separate trials are required only when the defenses are so antagonistic that a fair trial can be achieved only through severance. [Citing *Murphy*.] Antagonistic defenses have been confined to situations where one or more codefendants testify implicating the other. [Citing *Murphy* and *Jones* (1980) (and, notably, not *Precup*).]"[668] The court, citing *Allen*, rejected the appellant's reliance on a supposedly antagonistic statement that was never introduced at trial.[669] The court also reviewed and distinguished *Jones* (1980), noting that there, the circumstances indicated that one of the two defendants had likely committed a single act of theft, and the "determination that the defenses were antagonistic stemmed largely from the fact that the codefendant contradicted *Jones'* defense of *alibi*. [Citing *Murphy*.]"[670] In *Sanchez*, by contrast, the allegations were that each defendant had committed separate acts, and neither had a particularly viable alibi.[671] The court noted the *Jones* court's recognition that "there are, indeed, no hard and fast rules as to when severance should be granted in a criminal case, and that each situation should be judged on its own facts[,]" but held that its careful review of the facts in *Sanchez* indicated that the defendants never made a showing of antagonism sufficient to require severance.[672] *Sanchez* is chiefly notable for its exclusive definition of the severance rule—severance only for antagonistic defenses—further narrowed by the dictum, originally from *Precup*, that antagonism entailed defendants testifying and implicating each other.

People v. Columbo (1983)[673] involved a pair of cohabitants, Patricia Columbo and Frank DeLuca, convicted of murdering and soliciting murder of Colombo's

---

665 110 Ill.App.3d 893, 443 N.E.2d 252 (Nov. 29, 1982) (Mejda, J.).
666 *Id.* at 904-905, 260.
667 *Id.* at 904-905, 260.
668 *Id.* at 905, 260.
669 *Id.*
670 *Id.* at 905-906, 260-261.
671 *Id.*
672 *Id.* at 906, 261.
673 118 Ill.App.3d 882, 455 N.E.2d 733 (Jun. 24, 1983) (Wilson, P.J.).

parents.[674] Although Columbo admitted that she and DeLuca gave police " 'basically consistent'" statements prior to their arrest, she contended that his post-arrest statements to police and others inculpated her, placed her in a position where she would blame him entirely for the murders, negated her alibi, and made it inevitable that any defense of his must be "in conflict with, inconsistent and antagonistic toward hers."[675]

The court ran through the antagonistic defense litany, citing *Brooks* for the general rule on joint trial, *Lindsay* for the court's discretion to sever to avoid prejudice, *Rhodes* for the defendant's duty to demonstrate prejudice before trial, *Earl* for the abuse of discretion standard for reversal, *Yonder* for the court's duty to consider only the defendant's severance petition, *Brophy* (1981), *Cart* (1981), and *Powell* for the court's duty not to consider subsequent happenings at trial, and *Henderson* for "the primary question is whether the defenses of the defendants are of such an antagonistic nature that a severance is imperative to ensure a fair trial."[676] The court further cited *Miner* for the defendant's obligation to specifically show prejudice, cited *Davis* for the rule that "In order to be antagonistic, there must be a showing of true conflict between the defenses[,]" and quoted *Davis* along with *Murphy* for the Webster's dictionary definition of "antagonism."[677] The court also borrowed and summarized the *Davis* court's inclusive list of examples of true conflict while discarding any note of their origins:

> Examples of true conflict are: (1) each defendant attributes the cause of the offense to the wrongful acts of the other; (2) each defendant condemns the other and declares the other will testify to facts exculpatory of himself and condemnatory of his co-defendant; (3) a co-defendant's confession implicating the other would be received into evidence with only a jury instruction limiting its admissibility to the maker of the statement; or (4) each co-defendant makes an oral admission or confession and the references to the defendant requesting the severance are not eliminated from the testimony.[678]

Turning to the facts of the case, the court noted that Columbo merely informed the trial court during the severance hearing that, contrary to her earlier statements about her anticipated defense, "she could not vouch for DeLuca's whereabouts at

---

674 *Id.* at 886, 740.
675 *Id.* at 939, 775.
676 *Id.* at 939-940, 775.
677 *Id.* at 940-941, 776.
678 *Id.* at 940, 776.

the time of the murders."[679] The trial court wearily observed, in words that many trial judges faced with the issue have doubtlessly felt through the years, " 'Now we come down to the trial of this case and sure enough, lo and behold, we're faced here now with antagonistic defenses. One has to wonder.' "[680] The *Columbo* court explained that Columbo gave no further specifics to the trial court as to what her "new" defense would be, and that to change her tune to say she did not know where he was on the night of the murders was quite different from saying he committed them, while DeLuca never abandoned his alibi that he and Columbo went shopping, returned home, and went to bed that night.[681] As such, neither defense was antagonistic to the other, and the court, citing *Yonder*, concluded that "Columbo's mere speculation that the defenses would be antagonistic is an insufficient ground for severance."[682]

The court then proceeded to also reject Columbo's arguments based on alleged prejudice from DeLuca's extrajudicial statements—suggesting that both the court and Columbo's counsel recognized that this was an issue separate and distinct from antagonistic defenses. At any rate, the court never mentioned antagonism again through its whole lengthy discussion of DeLuca's statements, the Confrontation Clause, and *Bruton*.[683] It did, however, dip further into the antagonistic defenses lineage to cite *Mutter* (1941) to declare, "The mere fact that some evidence is only admissible against one defendant is not justification for a severance";[684] *Barbaro* for, "It has been clearly stated that a severance need not be granted where any reference to the codefendant applying for a severance is eliminated from an inculpatory confession";[685] *Williams* (1981) to state that "where a statement introduced at trial is not inculpatory of another, there is no error in its admission";[686] and *Strayhorn* and *Lindsay* for "the well-established legal principle that a severance is not required if, in the confessions of the codefendant, all references to the party seeking a severance are eliminated"[687]—further suggesting the court's realization that those cases were about codefendant statements, not about antagonistic defenses. The court also cited *Wilson* (1973) and *Williams* in holding that any possible slight mishandling of DeLuca's statements constituted

679 *Id.* at 940, 775.
680 *Id.* at 940, 776.
681 *Id.* at 941, 776.
682 *Id.*
683 *Id.* at 941-944, 777-779.
684 *Id.* at 942-943, 777.
685 *Id.* at 942, 777.
686 *Id.*
687 *Id.* at 942, 777 n.11.

harmless error beyond a reasonable doubt "in view of the overwhelming evidence of Columbo's guilt."[688]

MISREADING *BRAUNE*: *HARGIS* AND *DAUGHERTY*, 1983-1984

People v. Hargis (1983)[689] was a murder and armed robbery case in which defendant Hargis moved for a severance before trial because his codefendant, Daugherty, had made "an exculpatory statement which implicated [Hargis] in the crime" that in turn made their defenses " 'so antagonistic as to result in an unfair and prejudicial trial if they were tried together.'"[690] Hargis' counsel thus apparently lumped codefendants' statements and antagonistic defenses together as one and the same, like so many attorneys and courts before had done. At the severance hearing, counsel could not describe any specific prejudice resulting from a joint trial "but indicated his belief that each defendant would try to shift the blame to the other."[691] The prosecutor then "vowed not to use 'any statement made by either defendant Mr. Daugherty or * * * Mr. Hargis in this case[,]'" and the trial court denied the severance motion.[692]

The *Hargis* court, finding no abuse of discretion, held that Hargis' severance motion lacked sufficient specificity.[693] The court cited *Ruiz* (1982) for the "primary question" formulation of the severance rule from *Henderson*.[694] The court also reviewed the discussion in *Lee* (1981) regarding "at least two possible sources of prejudice" from joint trial: the "use of inculpatory statements made by codefendants in violation of *Bruton* . . . , and the possibility that the trial will become a contest between defendants as opposed to a contest between the State and the defendants. Such a state of affairs was condemned in *People v. Braune* (1936)[.]"[695] The court concluded that the prosecution's non-use of the codefendants' statements cured the first potential problem, and that "since neither defendant took the stand, the case did not become a contest between the defendants. *Ergo,* the second possible source of prejudice was also eliminated."[696] In short, the *Hargis* court followed *Lee* (1981) and other courts in concluding that by definition, no testimony meant no antagonism.

---

688 *Id.* at 944, 779.
689 118 Ill.App.3d 1064, 456 N.E.2d 250 (Nov. 3, 1983) (Mills, J.).
690 *Id.* at 1074, 255.
691 *Id.*
692 *Id.*
693 *Id.*
694 *Id.* at 1074-1075, 255.
695 *Id.* at 1075, 256.
696 *Id.*

Hargis also raised a related but slightly different argument in support of severance: "that he was unable to put on a full defense since he had no way to elicit from the testifying officer that the statement he gave to police prior to leading them to the body and murder weapon inculpated his codefendant," presumably, the court surmised, because Daugherty's counsel could have prevented Hargis' counsel from eliciting that statement on *Bruton* grounds.[697] The court, in confronting this argument, noted that it was basically a *Bruton* issue for which Hargis offered no supporting authority, but the court sidestepped *Bruton* analysis because "our disposition of this issue rests firmly on alternate grounds and we need not speculate about one defendant's right to successfully make *Bruton* objections to prevent a codefendant from fully explaining statements which are introduced against his interest."[698] The court then returned to *Lee* (1981) and discussed how the trial court there had noted there was a possibility of adverse testimony by a codefendant based upon that codefendant's alleged extrajudicial statements that the State would offer into evidence, but the trial court denied severance, and the state supreme court upheld that ruling based upon the lack of various factors the *Lee* (1981) court required from defendants seeking severance based on antagonistic defenses, including " 'a detailed recitation of what his defense would be, what the codefendant's defenses would be, and how the two conflicted.' "[699] Because Hargis presented "no such detailed allegations[,]" his motion and petition for severance were insufficient.[700] Thus, ironically, even after acknowledging in effect that codefendant statements/*Bruton* and antagonistic defenses are different categories, the *Hargis* court fell back on antagonistic defenses to sidestep a vexing *Bruton* issue.

People v. Daugherty (1984)[701] was a companion case to *Hargis* that went straight to the Illinois Supreme Court as a death penalty appeal.[702] Randy Daugherty and Clarence Hargis were convicted of the armed robbery and murder of Richard Dark, for which Daugherty received the death sentence, Hargis life in prison.[703] The two defendants were seen with Dark the last day he was seen alive, including at a tavern where the bartender noticed that Daugherty and Hargis, after finishing a pool game, sat at a separate table from Dark talking quietly with each other and grew silent whenever she approached.[704] The next day, both defendants were seen

[697] *Id.*
[698] *Id.* at 1076, 256.
[699] *Id.*
[700] *Id.* at 1076, 256-257.
[701] 102 Ill.2d 533, 468 N.E.2d 969 (Jun. 29, 1984) (Simon, J.).
[702] *Id.* at 535, 970.
[703] *Id.*
[704] *Id.*

in Dark's car, without Dark.[705] A witness later testified that when he gave them a ride to where Dark's car was parked, Dark's car would not start, so the defendants then took a gray sweater and two pairs of jeans, all with bloodstains, out of the back of Dark's car, put them in a paper bag, and moved them to the trunk of the witness' car.[706] Another witness later saw Daugherty soaking the gray sweater.[707] When police later learned Dark was missing and towed in his car to investigate it, they found bloodstains in the car, plus two of Dark's checks, one made out to Hargis.[708] After interviewing witnesses to the defendants' interactions with Dark and his car, the police searched for Hargis and Daugherty.[709] Hargis talked with officers several times, and ultimately drew a map and accompanied officers to a remote field on a gravel road where Dark's body and wallet were found at the bottom of a well—with no sign of the proceeds of a social security check he had received shortly before his disappearance.[710] The police and Hargis continued down the road to a bridge where an officer recovered a closed folding knife from the creek bed below.[711] A witness later testified that he had seen Daugherty with the same knife earlier that summer.[712] An autopsy showed that Dark had five stab wounds to the chest and abdomen, only one of them fatal.[713]

The *Daugherty* court then turned to discussing the sentencing phase of the trial, at which both defendants waived a jury.[714] The defendants' statements to police were admitted, with the trial court stating that it would consider such statements only as against the declarant to avoid confrontation clause concerns.[715]

In Daugherty's first statement, he admitted driving with Dark and Hargis on the date of the crime and said that Hargis asked for his knife "because he intended 'to stab or kill * * * Dark and get his money.'"[716] Daugherty gave Hargis the knife, not thinking he was serious.[717] Later, when they stopped to urinate, Daugherty, from a distance away, heard Hargis yell, then saw Dark bend over clutching his stomach and fall to the ground.[718] Hargis dropped the knife, found it again, stabbed Dark

705 *Id.*
706 *Id.* at 535-536, 970.
707 *Id.*
708 *Id.* at 536, 970.
709 *Id.*
710 *Id.* at 536-537, 970.
711 *Id.* at 537, 970.
712 *Id.*
713 *Id.* at 537, 971.
714 *Id.*
715 *Id.*
716 *Id.* at 537-538, 971.
717 *Id.* at 538, 971.
718 *Id.*

several more times, then said, " 'Didn't think I'd do it, did you?'"[719] Daugherty said there was no preconceived plan to kill Dark, and that he never stabbed him, but split half the money ($13) from Dark's wallet with Hargis, helped dispose of the body and knife, and changed clothes.[720] In a later statement to a polygraph examiner, Daugherty mostly repeated this story, except that he admitted " 'poking'" Dark after Hargis dropped the knife, though he insisted he had not " 'killed'" Dark.[721]

In his first statement Hargis also admitted that he and the defendant were with Dark on the date of the crime.[722] Hargis said that he and Daugherty had a "serious argument" over their pool game, and when Dark later stopped the car, Hargis and Daugherty began quarreling again, Dark attempted to break up the fight, and Daugherty stabbed him.[723] In his first statement, Hargis said that Daugherty put the body in the car, disposed of it in the well, and discarded the knife in the creek.[724] In a second statement made to the polygraph examiner, Hargis said instead that after Dark stopped the car, Daugherty got into a scuffle with Dark, and Hargis, attempting to stop the quarrel, accidentally stabbed Dark in the side, after which he and Daugherty disposed of the body together.[725]

The trial judge noted that although he could not determine which defendant struck the fatal blow to Dark, he nevertheless concluded that both defendants had " 'actually killed'" Dark and were eligible for the death penalty.[726] The judge observed that each defendant " 'seem[ed] to point the accusing finger at the other person stating well, he really did it[,]'" but their statements indicated that both had participated in the events leading to Dark's death, including wielding the knife, whether it was characterized as an accident, "poking," or whatever.[727] The judge added, " '*We cannot get into a situation where when both participate that the intent of the* [Illinois death penalty] *Statute is denied because of multiple participation.*'"[728] At the second phase of the death penalty hearing, the trial court heard testimony concerning Daugherty's prior conviction for the unrelated murder of a parole officer who was stabbed seventeen times, plus evidence of an unrelated conspiracy

---

719 *Id.*
720 *Id.*
721 *Id.*
722 *Id.*
723 *Id.*
724 *Id.* at 538-539, 971.
725 *Id.* at 539, 971.
726 *Id.* at 539, 972.
727 *Id.*
728 *Id.* at 540, 972 (italics in original).

between Hargis and Daugherty to rob and murder another victim shortly after Dark's murder.[729]

Noting that each defendant had moved for severance before trial, the *Daugherty* court declared, "We agree that the cases should have been separated for trial."[730] The court cited *Ruiz* for no right to a separate trial, *Lee* (1981) for the default of joint trial absent prejudice and the defendant's duty to demonstrate prejudice beyond mere apprehensions, and *Canaday* for reversal only for abuse of discretion.[731] Along with those Illinois Supreme Court precedents, the *Daugherty* court dipped into mid-level appellate court precedent, citing *McMullen* for the trial judge's duty to consider "the papers presented, the arguments of counsel, and any other knowledge of the case developed from the proceedings[,]" an expansive reading of *McMullen*, which basically only followed *Jones* (1980) in allowing the trial court to consider representations of counsel along with the petitions at a severance hearing.[732] The court then explained the "two common forms of prejudice" justifying severance: first, "when a codefendant has made hearsay admissions that implicate the defendant" [citing *Lee* (1981), *Bruton*, and *Clark* (1959)]; and second, "when defenses of the various defendants are so antagonistic that a severance is imperative to assure a fair trial. [Citing *Lee* (1981).]"[733] The court continued,

> The classic example of antagonistic defenses arose in *People v. Braune* (1936) . . . , where each defendant "was protesting his innocence and condemning the other." . . . In *Braune* it was apparent "that an actual and substantial hostility existed between the defendants over their lines of defense. * * * Criminations and recriminations were the inevitable result." . . . In *Braune* each defendant attempted to discredit the witnesses of his codefendant. "The trial was in many respects more of a contest between the defendants than between the People and the defendants. It produced a spectacle where the People frequently stood by and witnessed a combat in which the defendants attempted to destroy each other." . . . This court held in *Braune* that to guarantee a fair trial to both defendants the motion for severance should have been granted.[734]

---

729 *Id.*
730 *Id.*
731 *Id.* at 540-541, 972-973.
732 McMullen, 88 Ill. App. 3d 611, 613-14, 410 N.E.2d 1174, 1176-77.
733 *Id.* at 541-542, 973.
734 *Id.* at 542, 973.

In so identifying *Braune* as the "classic example of antagonistic defenses," the *Daugherty* court neglected to mention how *Braune* had been entirely forgotten by the antagonism lineage for more than thirty years, and almost entirely forgotten for nearly forty years, while numerous other courts and opinions had tossed the term "antagonistic defenses" around regarding entirely different situations from that in *Braune*.

The court described how Daugherty and Hargis had alleged both forms of prejudice—*Bruton* and *Braune*:

> They each had made the statements to law-enforcement officers that were later admitted in evidence at their sentencing hearing. [More significantly, though, the statements were not admitted at trial.] In his statement, Hargis accused the defendant of stabbing Dark when Dark tried to break up an altercation between the defendant and Hargis. [Ignoring Hargis' second statement to the polygraph examiner, in which he said that he stabbed Dark while trying to break up an altercation between Daugherty and Dark.] Hargis claimed that the defendant alone had disposed of the body and the murder weapon. [Ignoring Hargis' second statement to the polygraph examiner, in which he said he and Daugherty disposed of the body together.] The defendant, on the other hand, accused Hargis of planning to rob Dark and stabbing him in the chest several times. [Thus, notably, only Daugherty implicated Hargis in committing murder during the course of armed robbery, the charged offense; Hargis, in each of his statements, indicated that the stabbing was more or less an accident, and in one version he alone did the stabbing—though that of course does not explain the other four stab wounds.] Although the defendant admitted helping Hargis dispose of the body, he vigorously maintained that he had not planned with Hargis to rob and kill Dark, nor had he stabbed the victim during the murder.[735]

The court noted that the trial court had been apprised of these "conflicting claims" at the preliminary hearing, even before the severance motions:

> The judge said: "Let me say that the Court heard the preliminary hearing, the evidence adduced, and we had a situation where one said no, I didn't do it; he did it. That's what they both said in fact." The prosecutor then stipulated that he would not use either of the codefendants' statements at trial. Although this eliminated the source of any problem under the

[735] *Id.* at 542-543, 973.

> confrontation clause, it did nothing to alleviate the codefendants' concerns about their antagonistic lines of defense.[736]

The court added, without bothering to cite any authority,

> The trial court's denial of the defendant's motion for severance was an abuse of discretion. When codefendants have each made statements implicating the other but professing their own innocence, it is almost inevitable that their lines of defense at trial will become inconsistent and antagonistic and severance is necessary to forestall that result and ensure a fair trial. In such cases, the hostility between the codefendants is likely to surface at trial whether or not they each take the stand themselves. An unacceptable spectacle occurs in which the trial becomes as much a contest between the defendants as it is a contest between either defendant and the prosecution.[737]

Here, the *Daugherty* court, by sleight of hand, did what earlier opinions had tended to do more by accident or oversight and basically defined conflicting codefendant statements and antagonistic defenses as one and the same thing, always subject to severance automatically. Even if courts and prosecutors could appropriately address *Bruton/Buckminster* issues in the handling of codefendant statements—even by not using them at all—the *Daugherty* court seemed to be declaring that the mere existence of such statements required severance. Moreover, rather than letting defendants spell out what their defenses would be, the court second-guessed that process by proclaiming in advance that antagonism was "almost inevitable." In *Barbaro*, for example, although conflicting statements existed, the actual defenses were that those statements were extracted by coercion.[738] *Daugherty* also turned its back on various cases in Illinois' antagonism lineage that pointed out that where no defendant testified or offered any defense, by definition there could be no antagonistic defenses.[739] It is noteworthy that the court, in referring to lines of defenses at trial becoming "inconsistent and antagonistic," seemed to be suddenly setting a much lower standard for antagonism, given that "inconsistent" is obviously a much weaker term than "antagonistic" is or should be in the context of antagonistic defenses. Moreover, Hargis' statements, although they implicated Daugherty in being at the scene and participating in an altercation that led to Dark's death (and Daugherty's own statement placed himself at the scene), did not implicate Daugherty in armed robbery or premeditated murder and did

736 *Id.* at 543, 974.

737 *Id.* at 544, 974.

738 *See* discussion *supra* at notes 403 and 404.

739 *See, e.g.*, Betson (1936) at 507; cases cited at note 564, *supra*.

not particularly profess Hargis' own innocence—Hargis obviously admitted being at the scene and one way or the other participating in the altercation that led to Dark's death. Thus Hargis' statements were, in effect, as self-inculpatory and exculpatory to Daugherty as they were self-exculpatory and inculpatory of Daugherty.

The court then distinguished *Lindsay*, a pre-*Bruton* case purely involving codefendant statements, because the statements there, though incriminating of codefendants, were not self-exculpatory to the declarants.[740] It distinguished *Yonder* because the codefendants expressed " 'mere apprehensions'" that they would incriminate each other "without specifying how their defenses were antagonistic."[741] Justice Simon, author of *Daugherty*, also distinguished his own earlier opinion, *Lee* (1981): "Likewise, in *People v. Lee* . . . , one defendant moved for severance claiming "that he believed the codefendants would testify on their own behalf and implicate [him]. The court was not informed of what the substance of such testimony would be" . . . , nor how it would be antagonistic to the defendant's defense."[742] Rather, the court continued, "This case is more like the situation in *Braune* than like *Lindsay, Yonder* or *Lee;* the circuit court was apprised that each defendant was incriminating the other while asserting his own innocence, and the court was informed of the statements of each defendant to that effect. It should have been apparent to the trial judge that the danger of prejudice and confusion caused by these antagonistic defenses was great, and the motion for severance should have been granted."[743]

The court added that consistent with *Yonder*, it would not consider subsequent happenings at trial, but it could not help pointing out that "what actually took place in this case dramatically illustrates the risk of prejudice involved in permitting the joinder of defendants in a case based wholly upon circumstantial evidence, where each defendant has accused the other of the crime while professing his own innocence."[744] The court quoted at length the closing arguments of the defendants' respective counsel, with Daugherty's pointing out that it was *Hargis* who showed police where the knife was, while Hargis' counsel reminded the jury not to discount the possibility that Daugherty could have done the murder alone and told Hargis about it later, pointing out that it was *Daugherty's* knife, and *Daugherty's* sweater that had blood on it.[745] Hargis' counsel also pointed

740 *Id.*
741 *Id.*
742 *Id.* at 544-545, 974.
743 *Id.* at 545, 974.
744 *Id.* at 545, 974-975.
745 *Id.* at 545-546, 975.

out that the stab wound on Dark's abdomen looked as though it was done by somebody left-handed, and Hargis was not left-handed, but Daugherty was.[746] The court declared resoundingly, "The prejudice that the motion for severance was designed to prevent actually occurred in this case. The closing arguments in this case 'produced a spectacle where the People * * * stood by and witnessed a combat in which the defendants attempted to destroy each other.' (*People v. Braune* (1936) . . . .) Based on the information available to the trial judge the risk of prejudice inherent in this situation was apparent, and severance should have been granted. The defendant's convictions must therefore be reversed, and the cause remanded for a new trial."

Here it is necessary to point out—it is frankly laughable to compare *Daugherty* to *Braune*, and indeed, it is only possible to do so if one abstracts the language from *Braune* (as, admittedly, legal treatises and the whole process of law formation and distillation tend to do), takes it entirely out of context and divorced from its original meaning, and wholly ignores the actual facts of *Braune*. To illustrate: in *Braune*, both defendants testified aggressively and at length against each other. Not so in *Daugherty*, where neither defendant testified. In *Braune*, both defendants announced before trial that they would testify, and what their defenses and specific conflicting testimony would be. Not so in *Daugherty*. In *Braune*, counsel for each defendant aggressively cross-examined the other defendant's witnesses throughout the trial. In *Daugherty*, the court could only point to some rather feeble and implausible finger-pointing in closing arguments, which are, of course, not evidence.[747] In *Braune*, counsel brought out extraneous testimony regarding

---

746 *Id.* at 546-547, 975.

747 *Id.* at 545-547, 975. To justify its claim of a spectacle in which the prosecution could sit back and watch the defendants destroy each other, the Daugherty court reported:

In his closing argument, the defendant's attorney stressed that the jury should make an independent determination of the elements of the offenses proved against each defendant. In support of this argument the defendant's counsel argued that the evidence established that Hargis was the killer:

"I'll * * * emphasize my client's connection to the whole transaction that involves this particular knife that was-remember, shown to the People not by Randy Daugherty. It wasn't Randy Daugherty who showed that knife, where that knife was. It was Edward Hargis. Edward Hargis is a separate defendant in this case. * * * Billy Clark said that that was Randy Daugherty's knife. * * * They're not saying that it was continually Randy Daugherty's knife because the last time that * * * Billy Clark had seen that it was sometime last summer. He couldn't remember exactly when he had seen it, but it was quite a bit of time before the offense that we were talking about supposedly when it occurred here. * * * It wasn't Randy Daugherty who took the police out there where it was. That was done by Edward Hargis, and the conduct of Edward Hargis should be considered separate."

codefendant Dale's Jewish heritage, as well as Dwyer's attempted suicide, to attempt to inflame the jury against Dale. There is no indication of anything similar occurring in *Daugherty*. *Braune* was a salacious, scandalous media circus involving illicit cohabitation, miscegenation, attempted suicide, and abortion in the 1930s.[748] *Daugherty* was a run-of-the-mill murder case in the 1980s that drew no media attention. The attorneys in *Braune* performed their antics before a jury at trial; in *Daugherty*, only the judge heard about the codefendants' pretrial statements during a non-jury sentencing phase. All in all, to say that *Daugherty* "produced a spectacle where the People . . . stood by and witnessed a combat in which the defendants attempted to destroy each other" as in *Braune* is ludicrous. *Braune* is about as similar to *Daugherty* as the city of Chicago is to a Cuban fishing village: they're both on the water, but otherwise have nothing in common. Yet comparison to *Braune* was the only basis for treating *Daugherty* as anything other than the codefendants statement case it essentially was, as the Appellate Court treated *Hargis*.

This raises the question: what were Justice Simon and the *Daugherty* court doing? To what extent did they realize they were pulling a new rule out of a hat, and to what extent was this deliberate? It is of course possible that the whole magic trick was done entirely through accident, oversight, and over-abstraction, as with most of the rest of the history of the Illinois antagonistic defenses doctrine. Yet that seems at least a little harder to believe with *Daugherty* than with some earlier

---

Later in the closing argument Hargis' counsel argued that the evidence supported the conclusion that the defendant was the murderer:

"What they * * * have is what Eddie Hargis did and that is he knew where Dickie Dark's body was. And he knew where the knife was and he showed the cops that was where it was. After that they want you to find him guilty of murder. * * * And they want you to discount any other reasonable possibility, any other reasonable way that he could have known about that, that Randy Daugherty could have done it. And Randy Daugherty could have told him later. The body wasn't discovered for three weeks and only when Eddie Hargis told him. Peculiar for a murderer lead them straight to the body, very peculiar. It's Randy Daugherty's knife. Randy Daugherty is the one that had the blood on the sweater testified to by Billy Clark. * * * You've got evidence that it was in the bathtub being soaked. You can draw inferences from there but it wasn't Eddie Hargis's. They didn't find any blood at any time on Eddie Hargis."

Hargis' counsel observed that the killer probably was facing Dark when he stabbed him, and the wound in the lower abdomen was on the left as the victim faced the killer, "as if it was done by a person that was lefthanded. I've been able to watch both Eddie Hargis and Randy Daugherty this whole time, and Eddie Hargis is not left handed. Randy Daugherty is." Hargis' counsel argued that the only reason Hargis was on trial for murder was because of his association with the defendant: "Eddie cooperated fully. * * * [B]ecause he knows Randy Daugherty, and he was with him that night, he gets accused of murder."

748 *See* note 347, *supra*.

opinions, given its dramatic revival of the long mostly forgotten *Braune* as the "classic example of antagonistic defenses" even as the facts of *Braune* were wholly ignored. This raises the possibility that the *Daugherty* court, consciously or not, felt a need to bring the state of Illinois more into step with then-current practice in various federal circuits, notably the Seventh, which during the late 1970s and early 1980s were actively constructing their own expansive versions of the antagonistic defenses doctrine upon a similarly muddled, shoddy precedential foundation, as has been discussed at excessive length elsewhere.[749] One way or the other, suffice it to say that *Daugherty* came out of left field.

In *People v. Laboy-Rivera* (1984),[750] published the same day as *Daugherty* and hence oblivious to it, the appellant did not specify the nature of either the antagonism or the prejudice in his motion to sever, although counsel for one defendant warned that he would " 'point the finger' " at the other as the perpetrator of a robbery.[751] The court, rejecting the appellant's "conclusionary assertions,"[752] cited *Murphy* for the required specific showing of prejudice, *Lee* (1981) for the trial court's discretion to sever, *Guyon* for severance where defenses are so antagonistic that fairness demands it, and *Cart* and *Lee* (1981) for "truly conflicting and antagonistic defenses marked by opposition, hostility or discord," and not "mere apprehensions," being required.[753]

UNCERTAINTY: POST-*DAUGHERTY* CASES, 1984-1985

In *People v. Edwards* (1984),[754] a case involving a cocaine sale, the court reviewed earlier decisions from the Illinois Court of Appeal at length—and ironically (perhaps deliberately?) showed no awareness of *Daugherty*.[755] The court cited *Murphy* on joint trial and severance "only" for antagonistic defenses; *Columbo* for the court looking only at the petition and not subsequent happenings at trial; and *Jones* (1980) for, "Antagonistic defenses have been confined to those instances where one or more codefendants testify implicating the other" (clearly contradictory to *Daugherty*, in which neither defendant testified).[756] The *Edwards* court also quoted at length from *Guyon* (paraphrasing *Davis*): "There must be a true conflict; such as where each defendant attributes an offense to the actions of

749 *See generally* Dewey, *supra* note 58.
750 126 Ill.App.3d 197, 466 N.E.2d 1144 (Jun. 29, 1984) (, J.).
751 *Id.* at 201, 1147, 1148.
752 *Id.* at 202, 1148.
753 *Id.* at 201, 1147-1148.
754 128 Ill.App.3d 993, 471 N.E.2d 957 (Nov. 26, 1984) (Lindberg, J.).
755 There was a five-month lag between the publication dates of the two cases; doubtlessly the delay in courts getting news of higher courts' opinions was longer then than now.
756 *Id.* at 1000-1001, 963.

the other; where each defendant condemns the other and declares the other will testify to facts exculpatory to himself and incriminating to the other; where a codefendant's confession implicating defendant is received into evidence without instructions to the jury limiting its admissibility to the maker of the statement; or where each codefendant makes an admission or confession orally and the references to the codefendant applying for the severance are not eliminated from the testimony."[757] Notably, the statements regarding severance being allowed only for antagonistic defenses, and antagonistic defenses being limited only to situations where codefendants testify and implicate each other, conflicted with *Guyon/Davis*' "true conflict" litany, which included non-testimony situations relating to codefendant statements as grounds for severance. As usual, the court summarizing various different earlier authorities apparently did not recognize this inconsistency.

In his pretrial severance motion, Edwards stated that he would deny involvement in the cocaine sale, but a codefendant planned to testify, to admit his guilt, and to assert the defense of entrapment; that defense would be antagonistic to his; and allowing the jury to hear testimony from both of his codefendants would tend to incriminate him.[758] Citing *Lee* (1981), the court held that these "generalized statements" unsupported by facts failed to demonstrate how Edwards would be prejudiced.[759] The court also quoted *Laboy-Rivera*: "[C]onclusionary assertions * * * are no substitute for a detailed recitation of what the codefendant's defense could be and how they conflicted with his."[760] The court further noted that Edwards' severance petition also failed on the merits, because his assertion that the codefendant's entrapment defense was antagonistic did not establish antagonism, for the codefendant could have admitted the charge without implicating Edwards.[761] The rest of the discussion of the severance issue in the case concerned codefendants' extrajudicial statements, which the court notably treated as a separate matter from antagonistic defenses. The court discussed and distinguished *McVay* and Clark (1959) at length in rejecting Edwards' arguments.[762]

People v. Cole (1985) was a murder case in which both defendants accused each other in pretrial statements, but not in their respective trial testimony.[763] The *Cole* court cited *Lee* (1981) repeatedly for aspects of the general rule on joint trial and

---

757 *Id.*
758 *Id.* at 1001, 963.
759 *Id.*
760 *Id.*
761 *Id.* at 1001, 963-964. The codefendant's entrapment testimony ultimately was heard only by the judge in a bench trial. *Id.* at 1002, 964.
762 *Id.* at 1002-1004, 964-966.
763 131 Ill.App.3d 36, 39-40, 475 N.E.2d 620, 623 (Feb. 21, 1985) (Linn, J.).

severance, then offered *Daugherty*'s description of two (separate) grounds for severance: incriminating codefendant statements and antagonistic defenses.[764] Regarding codefendant statements, the court distinguished *Daugherty* because in *Cole*, both defendants testified and were free to cross-examine each other about their pretrial statements, and neither statement was self-exculpatory (each claimed to have been a lookout while the other did the killing).[765] As to antagonism, the court quoted *Daugherty*'s statement that " 'The second type of prejudice occurs when defenses of the various defendants are so antagonistic that a severance is imperative to assure a fair trial,' " then, perceptively, noted that that antagonism that developed "was not between the defendants' trial testimony but rather between each defendant's trial testimony and his codefendant's pretrial statement"[766]—clearly showing an understanding that antagonistic defenses, *at trial*, and conflicting pretrial statements are not the same thing, *Daugherty* notwithstanding. In addition, the defendants' pretrial severance motions were merely generalized, nonspecific, and hence inadequate claims of the existence of antagonism, and neither defendant accused his codefendant at trial or significantly contradicted the other's testimony—one claimed self-defense, the other claimed not to have seen what happened.[767] Thus, in affirming, the *Cole* court more closely followed the language of *Daugherty*'s new version of the rule than *Daugherty* did.

In *People v. Zambetta* (1985),[768] a cocaine-sale case, Zambetta moved for severance after opening arguments, contending that codefendant Irmen would offer a defense antagonistic to his.[769] Zambetta argued that his defense was that the State could not prove him guilty beyond a reasonable doubt, but Irmen would testify that he neither provided nor sold the drugs, but rather that Zambetta supplied the drugs and ordered him to transfer them to the purchaser.[770] At trial, Irmen did so testify, and claimed that throughout the drug sale, he did not know such a transaction was happening, but only followed Zambetta's orders.[771] Zambetta offered no testimony or evidence.[772]

The court cited *Lee* (1981) and *Braune* for the defendant's burden to make a "detailed and specific showing of antagonism, including a detailed recitation of what the defendant's defense would be[,]" *Yonder* and *Goodman* for " 'mere

---

764 *Id.* at 40-41, 624. The *Cole* court also cited *Braune* and *Sanford.*

765 *Id.* at 41, 624.

766 *Id.*

767 *Id.* at 42, 624.

768 132 Ill.App.3d 740, 477 N.E.2d 821 (Apr. 29, 1985) (Strouse, J.).

769 *Id.* at 744, 824.

770 *Id.*

771 *Id.* at 744, 824-825.

772 *Id.* at 744, 825.

apprehension'" of conflict being insufficient.[773] The court cited *Lee* (1981) as calling for severance "only when the defendants could not realistically be aligned on the same side" and disallowing severance absent "truly inconsistent and antagonistic defenses[.]"[774] The *Zambetta* court then made an honest effort to make sense of *Daugherty* in light of the rest of Illinois case law on antagonistic defenses, explaining,

> [*Daugherty*] suggests that antagonism exists when each defendant denies his participation while simultaneously blaming his codefendant. The facts in *Daugherty* reveal that in a case based wholly upon circumstantial evidence, severance should have been granted where each defendant accused the other of the crime while professing his own innocence. . . . The closing argument in *Daugherty* "produced a spectacle where the People * * * stood by and witnessed a combat in which the defendants attempted to destroy each other." . . . The supreme court in *Daugherty* concluded that based on the information available to the trial judge, the inherent risk of prejudice was apparent and severance should have been granted.[775]

The court was noticeably circumspect about both defining what *Daugherty* said and agreeing with its reasoning—"suggests," "[t]he facts . . . reveal," "[t]he supreme court . . . concluded." It appears that the *Zambetta* court was attempting to limit the relatively freewheeling, unmoored statements and reasoning in *Daugherty* and treat it as it frankly should have been, an unusual case decided on its facts. At any rate, the court distinguished *Daugherty* and emphasized the different facts of the two cases, observing,

> The facts compelling severance in *Daugherty* are dissimilar to the facts of the instant case. The conflict here bore no resemblance to the outright "finger-pointing" in *Daugherty*. While the codefendant's testimony implicated the defendant in the drug transaction, it did not exonerate his own participation. . . . The codefendant at no time pinned the blame exclusively on the defendant, nor did the defendant blame the codefendant. Meanwhile, the defendant argued as his defense that he was not guilty because the delivery of cocaine was made to Mannarino rather than to Fieroh as the information charged. He stressed that this fact precluded a finding of his guilt. The court in *Lee* held where a defendant relies solely upon the State's inability to prove him guilty, and the codefendant testifies the defendant forced him to commit the offense

[773] *Id.* at 745, 825.
[774] *Id.*
[775] *Id.*

> charged, the defendant has not been prejudiced by a joint trial and his motion for severance during trial is properly denied. [Citing *Lee* (1981).] Thus, following the standards expressed in *Lee* and *Daugherty,* the defendant's defenses are not "classically" antagonistic so as to warrant a severance.[776]

The court further noted that even if Zambetta's and Irmen's defenses were antagonistic, Irmen's testimony was "merely cumulative" to testimony from other trial witnesses, making denial of severance no error.[777] The *Zambetta* court was involved in a difficult dance, though, and its efforts to distinguish *Daugherty* appear slightly tortured.

People v. Trass (1985)[778] concerned several defendants found guilty of aggravated battery, home invasion, and armed robbery.[779] Codefendants Trass and Bryant appealed, arguing, inter alia, that the trial court erred by denying Bryant's motion for severance and denying Bryant his Sixth Amendment right to confront witnesses.[780] The victims identified Trass and Bryant at trial and in a post-arrest lineup.[781] Neither defendant testified. Trass presented alibi testimony from his girlfriend that he was with her the night of the crime; Bryant presented no evidence.[782]

The *Trass* court cited *Lee* (1981) for the general rule of joint trial unless fairness demands otherwise; *Laboy-Rivera* for the defendant's burden to specifically show prejudice; *Daugherty* for the trial court's obligation to predict the likelihood of prejudice based upon the motion papers along with "arguments of counsel and any other knowledge of the case developed from the proceedings."[783] Invoking *Daugherty*, the court explained that "[s]everance motions are generally granted based on two types of prejudice": first, "when defenses of the various defendants are so antagonistic that a severance is imperative to assure a fair trial[,]" and second, "when a codefendant has made hearsay admissions that implicate the defendant and such statement is likely to be admitted into evidence."[784] The court identified the latter situation as a *Bruton* problem, where the " 'defendant may be denied his constitutional right of confrontation if the codefendant's hearsay

776 *Id.* at 745-746, 825.
777 *Id.* at 746, 825-826.
778 136 Ill.App.3d 455, 483 N.E.2d 567 (Sept. 9, 1985) (Buckley, P.J.).
779 *Id.* at 457, 569.
780 *Id.* at 457, 570.
781 *Id.* at 458, 570.
782 *Id.* at 459, 571.
783 *Id.*
784 *Id.*

admission is admitted against him and the defendant is unable to cross-examine the codefendant because the latter does not testify.' [Quoting *Daugherty*.]"[785] The *Trass* court thus recognized, tacitly, that antagonism and *Bruton*/codefendant statements constituted two separate matters.

In his severance petition, Bryant alleged both forms of prejudice and indicated that he would testify at trial, exculpating himself and inculpating three codefendants by claiming that he tried to help protect the victims from his three codefendants.[786] This conflicted with Trass' statement to police, in which he said that he was present at the scene of the crime, did not participate in it, but saw Bryant approach one victim and demand money.[787] The State indicated at the severance hearing that it intended to introduce Trass' statement.[788] Over Bryant's objection, the trial court allowed that, provided that Bryant's name was redacted to "a male."[789]

The *Trass* court held that "even in its redacted form, there remained a clear implication that defendant Bryant was 'the male' referred to in Trass' statement"'—based in part upon the police officer who described Trass' statement testifying after one victim who testified that Bryant approached him and demanded money from him.[790] The court cited *Clark* (1959), *McVay*, and *Serritello* regarding situations where redacted codefendant statements nevertheless clearly implicated a fellow defendant.[791] Citing *Clark* (1959) and *Johnson* (1958), the court also held that a jury instruction limiting consideration of the statement to the declarant was insufficient to obviate prejudice.[792] Analogizing to *McVay*, the court concluded that in light of the other evidence, Trass' statement, even redacted, was incriminating and prejudicial to Bryant.[793]

The court added that even if Trass' statement had not been used, "the denial of the severance motion would still have been improper in view of the antagonistic nature of the defenses of Bryant and Trass. [Citing *Daugherty*.] In *Daugherty,* each codefendant made a statement to the police exculpating himself and inculpating the other. In remanding the cause for a new trial, the court noted that the prosecutor stipulated he would not use either of the codefendants' statements at

785 *Id.*
786 *Id.* at 459-460, 571.
787 *Id.* at 460, 571.
788 *Id.*
789 *Id.* at 460, 572.
790 *Id.*
791 *Id.* at 460-461, 572.
792 *Id.* at 461-462, 573.
793 *Id.* at 461, 572.

trial, but the court concluded '[a]lthough this eliminated the source of any problem under the confrontation clause, it did nothing to alleviate the codefendants' concerns about their antagonistic lines of defense."'[794] That this summary of *Daugherty* is all the *Trass* court said on the supposedly separate issue of antagonistic defenses, and that the court made no effort to apply the quite different facts of *Trass* to the analysis of *Daugherty*, suggests that the *Trass* court did not really clearly understand what the *Daugherty* court was driving at, which is understandable.

A NEW RULE PRETENDING TO BE OLD: *BEAN*, 1985

People v. Bean (1985),[795] like *Daugherty*, involved a direct appeal to the Illinois Supreme Court by Harold Bean, who was jointly tried, convicted, and sentenced to death along with codefendant Robert Byron for murder, armed robbery, home invasion, and conspiracy in the death of Dorothy Polulach.[796] In the joint trial, Wayne Walters testified that in 1979, he and his wife, Ann, were living in Florida. Ann's father, George Polulach, had divorced Ann's mother and was living in Chicago with his new wife, Dorothy, whom Ann hated. When George committed suicide later that year, Ann blamed Dorothy. After George's funeral, when Wayne and Ann were at Ann's friend's house, Harold Bean, the friend's ex-husband, said he would kill Dorothy if somebody paid him to do so. Bean said the same again down in Florida when he and Ann's friend visited Wayne and Ann in May 1980. The next month, Bean again flew to Florida to discuss burglarizing Dorothy's home; Wayne believed Bean was again suggesting killing Dorothy.[797]

Robert Egan testified that on February 17, 1981, he, his ex-brother-in-law Robert Byron, and Bean left in Bean's car to burglarize Dorothy's home, Bean wearing a priest's smock as a disguise. Egan dropped the others off a few blocks from Dorothy's home and waited there. Byron returned alone, got a gun hidden in the car, and left again. Egan drove down the street, then picked up Byron and Bean a few minutes later. They all went to Byron's home, where they sorted jewelry taken from Dorothy's home, then left in Bean's car and drove to a bridge, where Bean got out and threw the gun in the river below. They later drove to a restaurant, where Bean put the priest disguise in a garbage can.[798]

---

794 *Id.* at 461, 572-573.
795 109 Ill.2d 80, 485 N.E.2d 349 (Oct. 3, 1985) (Simon, J.).
796 *Id.* at 84, 351.
797 *Id.* at 84-85, 351.
798 *Id.* at 85, 351.

The next day, Wayne testified, Bean flew to Florida and asked Wayne for $10,000 to pay off his partners. Egan testified that he and Byron picked up Bean at the airport after his return from Florida, and Bean described how he entered Dorothy's home, then handcuffed and shot her. In March 1981, Bean returned to Florida, where Wayne and Ann paid him $5,000. Bean gave Egan $1,300.[799]

Chicago police investigating Dorothy's murder flew to Florida to interview Wayne and Ann, who gave statements. Wayne went to Chicago with the police officers, who promised reduced charges in exchange for his cooperation.[800] The police then went to Byron's home and took him into custody, but he did not admit participation in the crime and was later released on habeas corpus.[801] Byron's ex-wife told Egan and Bean that Byron had been arrested, and Egan and Bean left in a car with Bean's girlfriend, who testified that she drove them to Nebraska, where a police officer stopped the car for a traffic violation and arrested Egan for driving without a license.[802] Bean and his girlfriend then returned to Chicago, abandoned the car, and stole a truck and stole different license plates.[803] While driving the truck, Bean told his girlfriend how he killed Dorothy.[804] After returning to Chicago, Bean's girlfriend made a statement to police, which led to the discovery of the hidden truck and of Bean, who was hiding in the forest.[805] Byron testified before a grand jury and was arrested as he left the grand jury room.[806]

Byron's pretrial severance motion argued that the overwhelming evidence against Bean would inevitably prejudice him. Byron said he would offer an alibi, supported by two witnesses who claimed he was with them until 7 p.m. on the night of the murder. He noted that no one saw him with Egan and Bean, and that the only evidence against him came from the coconspirators Wayne and Egan, and from Bean's drug-addicted, emotionally unstable girlfriend. "He claimed that Bean was the murderer and that he, Byron, had never been involved."[807] Bean's counsel orally joined Byron's motion, and at the severance hearing warned that "Byron's attorney had indicated that Byron's defense would be 'an actual attack' on Bean, all the blame for the murder would be placed on Bean, and that Byron's

799 *Id.*
800 *Id.*
801 *Id.* at 86, 351.
802 *Id.*
803 *Id.*
804 *Id.*
805 *Id.*
806 *Id.*
807 *Id.* at 86, 352.

attorney was planning to 'unequivocally attack [Bean] in his opening statement.'"[808] The trial court denied both motions.[809]

In his opening statement, Byron's counsel repeatedly referred to Bean, stated that " 'the innocent remain and the guilty flee,'" and pointed out that Byron stayed in Illinois while Bean fled.[810] He suggested that Bean picked Byron as a scapegoat because they had done time in the state penitentiary together.[811] Byron's attorney also noted the trial court's instruction on the State's burden of proof and the defendants' right not to testify, but promised that his client would testify "[b]ecause an innocent man can't wait to tell his story,'" while " 'a guilty man will never take the stand'" . . . " 'The murderer will never take the stand.'"[812] The trial court overruled all Bean's attorney's objections and denied his motion for a mistrial "based on the 'highly prejudicial, antagonistic, and illegal' opening remarks by Byron's counsel[,]" commenting mistrustfully, " 'Now, I don't know if you and [Byron's counsel] decided you would have [him] do it or not."[813]

During trial, "[u]sing leading questions, Byron's counsel reiterated the theory that Bean was the murderer and that he perpetrated the crime alone, repeating details of acts which Bean allegedly committed."[814] For example, Byron's attorney asked Wayne, " 'Now when you first talked to Harold Bean it was Bean's idea to kill Dorothy, is that right? . . . And you discussed with him in detail how he was going to accomplish this, is that correct? . . . And he told you that he was going to get a disguise, right? . . . And didn't [Bean] say he would rather do it himself because there would be nobody around to testify against him, it is safer that way? . . . And that after all she was an old woman, wasn't she? . . . He didn't need help killing this old lady, did he?'"[815] He asked Egan, " 'Now, the purpose of a criminal wearing a disguise is so that he can't be identified readily by his victims, is that right? . . . [Bean] is telling you there is a lot of money, you are going to get a lot of money, right?'"[816] Byron's counsel asked five repetitive questions of a Chicago police officer to be sure to bring out that the police, when arresting Bean, viewed him as armed and dangerous.[817] In his direct examination of his own client, Byron, the attorney asked what police had told him when he was first questioned; Byron

---

808 *Id.* at 86-87, 352.
809 *Id.* at 87, 352.
810 *Id.*
811 *Id.*
812 *Id.*
813 *Id.* at 87-88, 352.
814 *Id.* at 88, 352.
815 *Id.* at 88, 352-353.
816 *Id.* at 89, 353.
817 *Id.* at 89-90, 353.

answered (apparently initially forgetting the first part of a scripted and memorized statement), " 'They told me that all I had to do was to-they knew-let me rephrase that again. They told me they knew that I wasn't the trigger man. They knew Bean pulled the trigger and killed the woman and they told me all I had to do was just tell them that I was driving the car and that would be all and I would be granted full immunity from any prosecution.' "[818]

Throughout the trial, Bean's counsel objected to Byron's counsel's attacks on Bean, but was overruled.[819] The court also rejected Bean's motion for a mistrial based on antagonistic defenses that forced Bean to " 'fight on two fronts' " against Byron as well as the State.[820]

During his closing argument, Byron's counsel continued attacking Bean, observing, for instance, that Bean never had told Wayne or Ann Walters that he needed assistance with the burglary/murder, and adding, " 'So, here he [Bean] is, a con man, a murderer, and now he becomes an extortionist.' "[821] Counsel reminded the jurors that Bean wore a disguise and stated, " 'You do know that Harold Bean went into that house.' "[822] He reemphasized that Byron stayed while Bean and Egan fled, and again argued that only the guilty flee.[823] Ultimately, Byron's counsel dramatically stated, " 'Now, Dorothy Pululach [*sic*] was murdered. There's no doubt about that. There's a doubt in my mind-strike that. I don't think there can be any doubt that Harold Bean is the one who killed her.' "[824] Bean's frequent objections were again overruled.[825] In the State's closing rebuttal argument, the prosecutor charged both Byron's and Bean's counsel with conspiring to derail the trial process, declaring, " 'It's a facade. . . . They have put on a show for you of being one opposed against the other in the hope that one would create reversible error for the other.' "[826] The court sustained both defense counsels' objections to the reference to error.[827] The prosecutor then adjusted the language slightly: " 'They have put on a facade of seeming to be at each other's throats, in the hope that you will get caught up in that.' "[828] The court denied Bean's objection.[829] Although Bean raised many errors, Justice Simon and the *Bean* court surmised,

818 *Id.* at 89, 353.
819 *Id.* at 90, 353.
820 *Id.*
821 *Id.* at 90, 354.
822 *Id.* at 90-91, 354.
823 *Id.* at 91, 354.
824 *Id.*
825 *Id.*
826 *Id.*
827 *Id.*
828 *Id.*

> It is only necessary for us to address three interrelated issues, the denial of the defendant's motion for severance, the denial of his repeated motions for a mistrial and/or for severance once the trial had begun, and the prosecutor's remarks during closing arguments. All three questions reduce to the same irremediable error. The comments by codefendant's counsel upon this defendant's failure to testify in his own behalf were prejudicial to his right to avoid self-incrimination under the fifth amendment to the Constitution of the United States, as applied to the State of Illinois through the fourteenth amendment. Byron's defense strategy was hopelessly antagonistic to Bean's constitutional rights. For this reason, the two should have been separately tried.[830]

Notably, the Court here lumped together both "comments by codefendant's counsel upon this defendant's failure to testify in his own behalf" and "Byron's defense strategy [that] was hopelessly antagonistic to Bean's constitutional rights"—potentially two separate grounds for reversal—as "the same irremediable error."

The court then ran through the litany on joint trial and severance in Illinois, citing *Ruiz* for no automatic right to separate trial, *Daugherty* and *Canaday* for the trial court's discretion to sever, *Daugherty* and *Braune* for the defendant's burden to demonstrate prejudice because "[m]ere apprehensions of prejudice are not enough[,]" and *Daugherty* quoting *Lee* (1981) regarding " ' "The general rule . . . that defendants jointly indicted are to be jointly tried *unless fairness to one of the defendants* requires a separate trial to avoid prejudice." ' "[831] The court noted,

> Two independent sources of potential prejudice are each likely to require that jointly indicted defendants be separately tried. The first is interference with the constitutionally guaranteed right of confrontation. [Citing *Bruton*.] This problem is cured either by severance or by the action taken by the trial judge in this case, removal of all references to the moving defendant. [Citing *Daugherty*; *Clark* (1959).) Removal of the names, however, does not address the second issue, that of antagonistic defenses.
>
> Illinois recognizes that when codefendants' defenses are so antagonistic to each other that one of the codefendants cannot receive a fair trial jointly with the others, severance is required. [Citing *Daugherty*; *Gendron*; *Wilson*

829 *Id.*
830 *Id.* at 92, 354.
831 *Id.* at 92, 354-355.

> (1963); *Braune*.] Actual hostility between the two defenses is required. [Citing *Daugherty*; *People v. Lee* (1981).] Here Bean alleges that Byron's strategy of comparing Byron's willingness to testify to Bean's unwillingness to take the stand deprived Bean of his fifth amendment right to remain silent and thus prevented him from receiving a fair trial. In addition, Byron's trial strategy of depicting Bean as the "murderer" and of producing testimony damaging to Bean which was not elicited by the State from its own witnesses unfairly placed Bean in the position of having to defend against two accusers, the State and his codefendant. [Citing *Braune*.][832]

Here, ironically, the *Bean* court seems to have been so committed to its by then standard two-types-of-prejudice-requiring-severance doctrine that it felt compelled to categorize the fifth amendment violation, which was also a violation of Illinois state law,[833] as an antagonistic defense.

The court found *Bean* to be more similar to *Daugherty* and *Braune* than to cases in which severance was held to be unnecessary, because, "In both *Daugherty* and *Braune* the trial became more of a contest between the defendants than between the State and an individual defendant. That is also the case here, and it is an unacceptable situation."[834]

The court explained, summarizing *Braune*,

> In *Braune,* the fountainhead of this State's jurisprudence in this area, the defendant was found guilty of manslaughter. Prior to trial, he filed a verified petition for severance, alleging that the two defendants' defenses were diametrically conflicting and antagonistic. Subsequently the other defendant filed a petition alleging that the first defendant would testify, and that the second defendant would be disadvantaged by being unable to cross-examine him; this motion was also denied. This court was especially concerned that one of the defendants, through cross-examination, brought out facts harmful to the other, just as occurred in this case. . . . Again, "the trial was in many respects more of a contest between the defendants than between the People and the defendants. It produced a spectacle where the People frequently stood by and witnessed a combat in which the defendants attempted to destroy each other." . . .

832 *Id.* at 93-94, 355.

833 *Id.* at 96, 356 (citing Ill. Rev. Stat. 1981, ch. 38, par. 155-1).

834 *Id.* at 94, 355.

> In this case, the People stood by while Byron's attorney tried repeatedly, in his opening statement, in his cross-examination of various witnesses, and in his closing argument, to destroy Bean's case. Byron's defense was that Bean was the murderer. He could only convince the jury of his own innocence by convincing them to convict Bean. Obviously, this strategy resulted in irreparable prejudice to Bean and could only have been avoided by the mechanism of a separate trial.[835]

In its effort to analogize closely to *Braune*, the *Bean* court implied that only one defendant in *Braune* brought out harmful facts against the other, when in fact both did. The court also gave the appearance of buying Byron's argument that his "only" defense was to attack Bean, when of course he had the option, which most defendants exercise, of relying on his alibi witnesses to say that he wasn't there when the crime was committed. There is no indication that Bean testified or claimed that Byron was at the scene of the crime.

The court also distinguished *Lee* (1981) at length:

> This case is distinguishable from *People v. Lee* . . . , in which this court held that severance was not required because the defendant's claim that he would be prejudiced by a joint trial was never made specific. The defendant in *Lee* moved for severance on the ground that a codefendant had made statements incriminating him, and also on the ground that one of the codefendants would mount an antagonistic defense by taking the stand and implicating the moving defendant. The motion was denied on the ground that there was only a possibility of antagonistic defenses. Even when the motion was renewed after the codefendant testified, the defendant never detailed the antagonism. The court believed that the codefendant's testimony that the defendant forced him to shoot the victim was not entirely antagonistic to the other defense.
>
> The situation in this case is different. Here, the codefendant's counsel specifically commented upon the defendant's refusal to testify, violating both the fifth and fourteenth amendments and an Illinois statute . . . . Defense counsel explained that Bean's right to avoid self-incrimination was being infringed. In addition, Byron's defense was clearly entirely antagonistic to Bean's. In a word, Byron's defense consisted of the contention that Bean was the murderer and Byron was not even there. Byron's counsel elicited admissions from witnesses which implicated Bean and were totally irrelevant to Byron. Finally, Byron's closing argument

[835] *Id.* at 94-95, 355-56.

> labeled Bean as a murderer. Unlike the situation in *Lee,* the motions for severance and mistrial were sufficiently specific to put the trial judge on notice that Bean's constitutional and statutory rights would be violated if he were tried jointly with Bean.[836]

The court's observation about Byron's defense—that Bean was the murderer and Byron was not even there—brings up an interesting conundrum: if Byron was not there, then he of course had no personal knowledge of what happened, so his defense was alibi and there was no logical reason for his counsel to be commenting on what Bean did at all. And, as the record indicates, outside of his reckless statements in his opening and closing statements, Byron's counsel only emphasized, to Bean's detriment, points already brought out by the prosecution. Thus the issue was really Byron's counsel acting as a second prosecutor, and second-prosecutorial excess or misconduct, rather than truly antagonistic defenses. Here, unlike earlier, the *Bean* court recognized that the fifth amendment violation was separate and distinct from the issue of antagonistic defenses. In discussing Byron's counsel's cross-examination and closing argument, the *Bean* court tacitly acknowledged that, as in *Daugherty*, the traditional nicety about ignoring subsequent happenings at trial was not in effect.

The *Bean* court then lengthily addressed the fifth amendment right against self-incrimination. Regarding comment by a codefendant's counsel on an accused's failure to testify, the court adopted the reasoning of *De Luna v. United States*,[837] a 1962 Fifth Circuit federal opinion that involved a similar situation.[838] Like the *De Luna* court, the *Bean* court concluded that a defendant may not comment on a codefendant's silence.[839] Yet the *Bean* court did not clearly answer the more difficult, controversial question whether a defendant has a right, or counsel a duty, to comment on a codefendent's silence—a question *De Luna* answered affirmatively and other courts generally have answered negatively.[840] On that issue, the *Bean* court stated elliptically,

> [A]s in *De Luna,* we point out that it is an advocate's duty to represent his client as vigorously as possible within the bounds of the code of ethics. Byron's counsel believed that he could best represent his client by

[836] *Id.* at 96-97, 356-57.

[837] 308 F.2d 140 (5th Cir. 1962).

[838] On *De Luna*, *see* Dewey, *supra* note 58, at 157-60.

[839] *Id.* at 97-99, 357-358.

[840] *See, e.g.*, United States v. McKinney, 379 F.2d 259, 265 (6th Cir. 1967); Hayes v. United States, 329 F.2d 209, 221-22 (8th Cir. 1964); United States v. McClure, 734 F.2d 484, 491 (10th Cir. 1984); United States v. Marquez, 319 F. Supp. 1016, 1020 n.11 (S.D.N.Y. 1970). *See also* De Luna v. United States, 308 F.2d 140, 155-56 (5th Cir. 1962) (Bell, J., concurring).

> contrasting the behavior of the two defendants. Byron, like Bean, was entitled to the best defense available, and Byron's counsel was duty bound to use the strategy most likely to achieve a just and fair result for his client. On the other hand, Bean's counsel was bound to assure a fair result for his client by protecting Bean's right against self-incrimination. The two defense strategies inexorably clashed. Severance was the only solution, the only way in which both counsel could fulfill their duties to their respective clients without at the same time violating Bean's constitutional rights.[841]

In saying all this, the *Bean* court appears to have sided with *De Luna* on counsel's right/duty to comment on a codefendant's silence—which, taken to extremes, would seem to make joint trial of codefendants impossible if one or both did not testify. The court also seemingly indicated that there would be no way to limit attacks on a defendant by a codefendant's counsel, however unreasonable, illogical, or irrelevant, if that was the strategy counsel selected. Most tellingly for our present purposes, in stating that the "two defense *strategies* inexorably clashed," the court indirectly pointed out that the two defenses didn't—raising the issue of whether it was defenses or defense strategies that courts were to check for antagonism in severance motions, given that a defendant could launch an attack on a codefendant totally unrelated to the defendant's defense, as Byron did.

The *Bean* court then sanctimoniously observed, "We do not decide the merits of this motion for severance based on subsequent events during the trial[,]" before launching into an extended review of those subsequent events "as in *Daugherty*" to "illustrate the prejudice which results when the motion for severance is not granted at the earliest possible point."[842] The court noted that the only evidence against Bean was the testimony of his alleged coconspirators along with Bean's unstable girlfriend, that the jury did not believe Byron's claim of non-involvement, and that there was no corroboration of Egan's testimony, making it "impossible . . . to ascertain how the jury would have evaluated Bean had he not been the object of the improper attacks by Byron's counsel."[843] On that basis, it rejected the State's argument that any error was harmless beyond a reasonable doubt and held that the "trial judge abused his discretion by failing to grant the motion for a mistrial at the earliest possible moment, which, at the latest, was when the motion for mistrial was made during opening argument."[844] The court also faulted the prosecutor's suggestion in the rebuttal closing argument that the hostility of Byron's and Bean's respective counsel at trial was "a subterfuge deliberately calculated to introduce

---

841 *Id.* at 99-100, 358.
842 *Id.* at 100, 358.
843 *Id.* at 101, 359.
844 *Id.*

reversible error" as being "without any basis" (though the trial judge clearly shared that suspicion).[845]

What is most striking about *Bean* is that it was fundamentally a straightforward case that could have been decided entirely on the ground of the Fifth Amendment violation (and hence upon subsequent events at trial) without ever reaching the issue of antagonistic defenses. Once the court decided, correctly, that Bean's constitutional right against self-incrimination had been violated, there was no need to do more—though it would have been useful to get a clear answer whether Byron's counsel had a right to comment on Bean's silence. Instead, *Bean* offered a definition of antagonistic defenses, expanded further beyond the mushy, confusing definition in *Daugherty*, that based the rule on defense strategies rather than defenses and allowed any enterprising defense counsel to force a severance by announcing, without specifics, an intent to attack a codefendant willy-nilly and without regard to her client's actual defense. There would seem to be no doubt that *Bean* required a reversal, based on the court's failure or constitutional inability to control Byron's counsel's excesses, even aside from the fifth amendment issue. Yet *Bean*, like *Braune*, was a remarkable case properly decided on its remarkable facts. The *Bean* court, though, unlike the *Braune* court, tried to pull the case within the antagonistic defenses lineage. Its efforts to do so were tortured at best. Yet it would become, along with *Daugherty*, one of the principal authorities in that lineage for the next twenty-five years.[846]

CONCLUSION: ARE WE HAVING *STARE DECISIS* YET?

Here, I must make another apology.

This article is excessively long.

A frustrated reader might reasonably ask, "Couldn't you have neatly summarized most of this and just told me what the point is?"

The answer, however, is no. Here's why.

First, a well-known quip from Woody Allen: "I took a speed reading course and read *War and Peace* in twenty minutes. It's about Russia."

---

845 *Id.*

846 *Bean* was cited in 42 of the 85 antagonistic defenses cases that followed *Bean* through the end of 2010; *Daugherty* in 46.

Legal analysis, unfortunately, frequently shows much of the same over-summarization and over-abstraction as Woody Allen's comment on Tolstoy's novel. All too often, if one carefully compares a particular case with how that case is later described and summarized in a later case or treatise, one may see that the later author's effort to neatly and succinctly extract a rule from the earlier case, by paring down many paragraphs to a sentence or two and ignoring most or all of the factual context of the earlier case, often effectively loses most of the meaning of the earlier case. That is what seems to have happened in *Fisher*, *Payne*, and *Lehne*, and in *Daugherty* and *Bean*.

A reader might protest that this is how the law works, and how it must work, because we of course cannot carry all the baggage from each old case forward into history; rather, their meaning must be distilled. To which I would answer: yes, but if that meaning cannot be distilled reasonably accurately and meaningfully, then there is no justification for a common law system based on precedent and *stare decisis*, and we might as well confront that fact forthrightly. Precedent is not supposed to be the blind leading the blind, or the wrong leading the misled; if it is, then there's no point to it whatsoever, except as a self-justifying myth for an overpaid legal profession.

Philosophizing aside, this article, if it has any meaning at all, is in large measure a study of the dangers of summarizing, abstracting, misreading, and rephrasing or paraphrasing, cumulatively over the course of time, gradually creating and entrenching a rule that never should have existed. That being so, it is especially important that I try to avoid the same faults of over-abstraction and over-summarization that bedeviled the Illinois courts. Moreover, if my own reasoning is incorrect, I want readers to be able to see that by having access to the relevant original language at issue, rather than hiding my own logical flaws hidden behind neat summarizations.

Precedent is supposed to be a way to help judges not to have to rethink and reopen every legal issue each time it reemerges in the ongoing stream of cases judges must decide. In this example, however, that process broke down. The strange career of the Illinois doctrine of antagonistic defenses shows the intertwined doctrines of precedent and *stare decisis* misfiring badly in practice. The misconceived doctrine, apparently originally a product of mere accident, of lawyers taking the magic word "antagonistic" out of context (*Sweetin*, *Nussbaum*), inserting it in their briefs, and trying to persuade courts that it had magical powers courts had never given it, and of courts being led gradually further in that wrong direction as they attempted to quickly summarize and dispatch the attorneys' arguments and the complex earlier opinions associated with them, added no real clarity to the thinking of Illinois courts during the decades in which it took shape. It did not meaningfully help to protect legitimate rights. Instead, it only added confusion and helped to gum up the work of the courts unnecessarily. There was no logical reason why mere references to antagonism in cases involving the entirely separate categories of joint representation (*Bopp*) or codefendant statements (*Rupert*) should spawn a new doctrine of antagonistic defenses. Nor was there any good reason why the new misbegotten doctrine should frequently subsume the older, better-reasoned independent category of codefendant statements or sporadically contaminate the category of joint representation. Yet both of these processes happened almost inexorably.

Ironically, even as the makeshift doctrine of antagonistic defenses was cobbled together haphazardly on an inappropriate foundation, *Braune*, a case that actually provided some support for such a doctrine, was ignored for forty years before it was abruptly rediscovered, labeled "the fountainhead" of Illinois jurisprudence on antagonistic defenses, and pulled into the sloppy mishmash of confused case law that was assembled entirely without it. Nor were the almost heroic efforts of courts in cases such as *Davis* and *Murphy* to pull together all the various strands of the misbegotten doctrine able to make sense of it; the material they were working with was already too hopelessly corrupted. *Davis*, notably, was the first opinion to recognize and try to do something about the fact that Illinois courts had been throwing around the term "antagonistic" for more than fifty years without having any clear definition of what it meant—a realization one might have expected or hoped would have come much sooner, and perhaps prevented some of the damage.

Most courts that were forced to address the doctrine clearly attempted to do so by dutifully following precedent, with no apparent intrusion of personal or political preference save the traditional jurisprudential preference for following settled rules. Yet this process was, in effect, merely the blind leading the blind, or lemmings charging toward the sea, as the conscientious, precedent-minded later judges by their diligent actions only helped, gradually and accretively, to increase the supposed legitimacy and hide the unsound origins of the erroneous precedent they were following. This overall process was driven by certain sudden leaps forward in the doctrine's evolution, like the punctuated-equilibrium path dependence that Oona Hathaway described.[847] Tragicomically, though, almost all these leaps forward were logically unfounded and broke all the rules of proper precedent-formation. For starters, there was simply no basis for the *Fisher* court to proclaim that "[i]n [*Sweetin*] the main ground for the motion was that the defenses

[847] *See* Hathaway, *supra* note 50, at 613-17, 635-45.

of the two defendants were antagonistic"; that was plain wrong—but it shaped the path of precedent.

There was similarly no sound basis for the *Payne* court's sudden announcement that "[t]he right to a severance depends upon whether the defense of one defendant is so antagonistic to the defense of other defendants that a severance is necessary to assure a fair trial"—even any elliptical statements pointing vaguely in that direction in cases that *Payne* (ambiguously and thus unhelpfully) group-cited, such as *Birger*, *Lawson*, and *Fisher*, simply could not add up to *Payne*'s implicitly exclusive statement of the "rule." Moreover, *Payne*'s statement of the new "rule" was clearly dictum, albeit state supreme court dictum. *Lehne* made matters worse by mischaracterizing *Rupert*, *Sweetin*, and *Rose* as all being antagonistic defenses cases when none of them were. *Betson* and *Barbaro* made matters still worse by making *Payne*'s implicitly exclusive rule explicitly exclusive—declaring that antagonism was the only basis for severance—and *Barbaro* furthered the confusion by following that unfounded rule to the logical if somewhat absurd conclusion that therefore, any codefendant statement issues justifying severance by definition constituted antagonistic defenses even if the actual defenses were not inconsistent. *Daugherty*, paying lip service to the by then entirely confused antagonistic defenses lineage and also stirring in *Braune*, did further violence to that tradition with an opinion that came out of left field to further collapse any logical distinction between defenses and pretrial statements. *Bean* used *Daugherty* to drag the Illinois antagonistic defenses doctrine further in the new direction when it could and should have been decided entirely on more limited grounds.

Other opinions that attempted to state the law accurately and responsibly as of when the cases were decided, such as *Minnecci* and *Lindsay*, compounded the problem of unsound precedent by inadvertently engaging in a process that might be called "precedent-laundering"—creating apparently thorough, well-reasoned, authoritative opinions that obscured the starting points of the unsound precedent at issue. Unlike *Betson*, which at least clearly cited *Payne*, *Lawson*, and *Fisher* as the basis for its exclusive statement of the rule, *Minnecci* did not even cite any authority directly in relation to its version of the rule, which apparently was derived from *Lehne*. *Lindsay*, like *Payne*, group-cited six cases, which were listed after a lengthy paragraph that had *Lindsay*'s version of the rule (borrowed from *Minnecci*) buried in the middle. Of the six cases—*Fisher*, *Albers*, *Minnecci*, *Meisenhelter*, *Tabet*, and *Varela*—the latter two were insignificant cases that barely mentioned the issue and added nothing to the doctrine, *Albers* and *Fisher* both just contained basically the same misstatements about *Sweetin* and *Rupert*, and *Meisenhelter* and *Minnecci* both stated a rule derived from *Lehne*. So *Minnecci* tended to cover the bad precedent's tracks by citing too few authorities; *Lindsay* by citing too many. Both cases tended to make it difficult for later courts to find out just what was said in which cases, had anyone cared to check.

Precedent-laundering was completed by the tendency of most courts to cite only recent authorities for the rule. For instance, *Lehne* (1935), one of the key problem cases, was cited only three times in the antagonistic defenses lineage and effectively ceased to be recognized as a relevant authority in that lineage after *Minnecci* (1936).[848] *Payne* (1935), another key problem case, also was only cited three times, and had limited independent life after being cited in *Betson* (1936).[849] *Betson* itself had limited impact, being cited only once (by *Barbaro* in 1946) before being rediscovered and cited an additional four times during the late 1960s-70s, usually clustered with other more recent authorities.[850] *Albers* (1935), in addition to the group cite in *Lindsay*, was only cited in the insignificant *Mosher* (1949). Even *Minnecci* (1936), cited eight times in the antagonism lineage, was largely forgotten after *Lindsay* (1952) until, like *Braune*, it was rediscovered and had a brief second act in the 1970s-80s.[851] *Fisher* (1930), one of the key authorities in the lineage from the 1930s, was cited twelve times, seven of them during the 1930s, then was largely forgotten after *Barbaro* and almost entirely forgotten after *Lindsay*.[852] So most of the bad or problematic authorities on antagonistic defenses from the 1930s pretty well vanished from the antagonism lineage by the 1950s if not the 1940s, replaced by *Lindsay* or the numerous *Grilec* (1954) progeny. *Braune* (1936), as noted, was mostly ignored up to 1942 and was then entirely forgotten in the antagonism lineage up to 1975, and thus had no role in the entrenchment of the misbegotten doctrine. As for even earlier cases, *Rupert*, more nearly (if wrongly) the "fountainhead" of Illinois antagonism law than *Braune*, quickly fell out of the antagonism lineage after *Lehne* (1935).[853] *Sweetin* (1927) had a more illustrious career, cited twelve times, half of them in the 1930s but including a second act after rediscovery in *Davis* (1976).[854] The remaining case from the early rogue's

848 *Lehne* was later cited in *Varela* (1950) and in *Clark* (1959), in each case for codefendant statements, not for the antagonism rule.

849 *Payne* was cited for the antagonism rule in *Mutter* (1941) and for the general severance rule in *Mosher* (1949).

850 *Betson* was cited by *Berry* (1967) and *Gendron* (1968) regarding a proper motion for severance, then as one among various authorities in *Davis* (1976) and *Clark* (1979).

851 *Minnecci* was cited in both *Meisenhelter* opinions (1942 and 1943), *Lindsay* (1952), *Clark* (1959), *Arnold* (1968), *Williams* (1976), *Davis* (1976), and *Murphy* (1981).

852 *Fisher* was cited in *Sullivan* (1931), *Hotchkiss* (1931), *Payne* (1935), *Albers* (1935), *Lehne* (1935), *Patris* (1935), and *Betson* (1936), and then in *Serritello* (1944), *Barbaro* (1946), *Varela* (1950), *Lindsay* (1952), and *Bracken* (1966).

853 *Rupert* was cited only five times: in *Sweetin* (1927), *Bolton* (1930), *Fisher* (1930), *Albers* (1935), and *Lehne* (1935).

854 *Giardiano* (1930), *Bolton* (1930), *Fisher* (1930), *Albers* (1935), *Lehne* (1935), *Patris* (1935), *Serritello* (1944), *Barbaro* (1946), *Clark* (1959), *Davis* (1976), *Colon* (1979), and *Guyon* (1983).

gallery, *Barbaro* (1946), was cited eleven times, more than half of them after rediscovery by *Davis* (1976).[855] For all these cases, the point remains the same: they were generally fairly soon forgotten or ignored, making any clear errors of precedent-formation much harder to find, especially in the days before online legal research. Through precedent-laundering, the "rule" took on a life independent of its own roots.

Just as it would be interesting to know exactly how certain cases later got swirled back up to the surface while others remained submerged, it would be fascinating to know just why certain courts, such as the *Davis* and *Murphy* courts, took the time and effort to try to sort out in detail just what exactly the antagonistic defenses doctrine really said, while most courts just recycled stock language. Was this all driven by attorneys' briefs that selected some cases and not others, seemingly largely at random? Whatever the reason, though, the fact sadly remains that the efforts of such conscientious courts were not as helpful as they might have wished, given both the already deeply entrenched nature of the precedential confusion as well as the status of most such courts as mid-level appellate courts that were not in a position to tell the state supreme court that its earlier opinions were wrong even if the appellate courts had recognized that to be so. Indeed, the efforts of a court such as the *Davis* court to offer an illuminating mini-treatise on the antagonistic defenses doctrine might have only added to the overall confusion by, for instance, offering a dictionary definition of "antagonistic" that was inappropriately weak and overly flexible for a legal doctrine demanding a strict definition, and by dutifully following earlier authorities in lumping codefendant statements together with antagonistic defenses, thus struggling to create harmony where it would have been better to recognize the fundamental disharmony. Although the *Davis* court was diligently and appropriately trying to do its job, it was also inadvertently digging the antagonistic defenses hole even deeper.[856]

Moreover, because the whole question of antagonistic defenses is by its very nature intensely fact-specific, it is by definition not a particularly suitable subject for a legal rule.[857] Justice O'Connor and the United States Supreme Court, in

---

855 *Varela* (1950), *Grilec* (1954), *Clark* (1959), *Brinn* (1965), *Ross* (1968), *Davis* (1976), *Cain* (1979), *Murphy* (1981), *Griggs* (1982), *Columbo* (1983), and *Guyon* (1983).

856 As a former judicial attorney who in my draft opinions was especially prone to try to write mini-treatises to straighten out and clarify, hopefully forever, confusing questions of law I had to struggle through so others would never have to again, I now better understand the gentle warning of a more senior, experienced judicial attorney colleague that "less is sometimes more," and that additional discussion and verbiage can inadvertently create new problems, open new questions, create doubts in the minds of other judges on the panel, or give enterprising lawyers additional words or ideas to take out of context to plague later courts considering later cases.

857 *See* discussion at notes 41-46, *supra*.

Zafiro, recognized this key point in rejecting various federal circuits' antagonistic defense rules and holding that the whole severance question ultimately rests on a fact-specific inquiry into whether or not a defendant suffers actual, incurable prejudice or faces a serious risk thereof.[858] In other words, in the case of antagonistic defenses, where it is appropriate and necessary to see each case as unique and consider its "thisness," Hobbes' idiot had the right idea.

In sum, the strange career of the Illinois antagonistic defenses doctrine shows how easily error injected and rooted itself into case law, and how the system had no effective mechanism to either identify or uproot that error. This would all be more excusable and ignorable if the error in the system was merely technical, procedural error but the technically unsound precedents were substantively sound and beneficial to the law and to justice. But they were not that, either. In some cases, defendants who probably deserved separate trials were denied them because of the part of the rule that focused on demonstrating probable prejudice before trial rather than showing actual prejudice at trial—what really counts, as Justice O'Connor's majority opinion in *Zafiro* understood. In other cases—an unknown number, since many grants of severance at the trial level would never leave a footprint to that effect at the appellate level—some defendants who did not deserve separate trials likely were given them, increasing the risk of inconsistent verdicts as well as causing duplication of judicial effort for voir dire, the presentation of witnesses, and such.[859] In most cases, much ink was spilled, confusion caused, and judicial time wasted answering bogus arguments that deserved more summary treatment (e.g., "Defendant has not shown that he was prejudiced at trial.").

This all leads to what I personally find to be a very unwelcome conclusion, and one that I did not expect to reach when I began this project.

I should explain: I was a humanities graduate student during the 1990s, a decade when various academic subjects were poisoned to varying degrees at varying institutions by the then-current morbid obsession with deconstruction within the academy. Ever since, I have nursed a sense of bitterness toward the high priests of deconstruction, postmodernism, and other radical linguistic relativism who preached the indeterminacy of language.

[858] Zafiro v. United States, 506 U.S. 534, 538-541.
[859] *See* note 332, *supra*.

Yet with regard to the legal arena, or certainly the Illinois doctrine of antagonistic defenses, I fear they might have been right.[860]

The whole muddled story clearly supports Justice Frank's observation that cases mean only what a judge in a later case says they mean—even when the latter judge's interpretation is unjustifiable. Yet Frank and other legal realists, and attitudinalists today, have tended to assume that those judges who defined earlier cases were steering them in some direction in keeping with the judges' personal or political predilections. Though it flies in the face of legal traditionalism and formalism and might be alarming on that score, the legal realists at least believed that somebody was driving the bus. And that belief might be comforting in comparison to the situation with the Illinois antagonistic defenses doctrine, where basically, most of the time, nobody was driving the bus—it was driving itself. That is, due to the indeterminacy of the various courts' language, the words in effect took on a life of their own, pulling in sometimes contradictory, sometimes absurd directions, seemingly effectively beyond the control of the system or individual human actors within it. There is some possibility that Justice Simon and the *Daugherty* and *Bean* courts, presumably with the best of intentions, actually did seize control of the steering wheel to drive the doctrine in a particular direction similar to the direction many other jurisdictions were veering around that time. But it's also possible they didn't. Throughout the rest of the doctrine's strange career, it appears fairly definite that courts and judges were attempting to dutifully observe precedent and act in entirely good faith as they let the doctrine drive itself in the wayward directions it took.

This raises the question whether there are attributes of the legal and judicial arena that make it particularly vulnerable to linguistic indeterminacy and drift. I believe there are. One such factor is the role of lawyers in an adversarial system. Whatever inherently indeterminate tendencies there may be in language, and to whatever degree ordinary individuals might have personal or intellectual interests in bending language in different directions, lawyers have in addition strong economic and professional incentives to bend and twist language in ways to suit their purposes. That's how they win motion decisions, cases, and damage awards. Lawyers are also notorious for taking language out of context in order to do so. Overall, they are rewarded, and generally not penalized in any meaningful way, for digging up any strange and possibly irrelevant precedent they can find (that has not been

860 For a good overview of theories of linguistic indeterminacy in the legal context that perceptively distinguishes the radical indeterminacy claimed by the high priests of deconstruction from the lower-level linguistic indeterminacy with which we all must and do cope in everyday life and law, see Timothy A. O. Endicott, *Linguistic Indeterminacy*, *in* LAW AND LANGUAGE 667-97 (Thomas Morawetz ed., 2000).

clearly overruled on the point in question), taking language out of context and twisting it into any grotesquely deformed shape they can imagine, throwing it all against the wall of the court, and seeing what if anything sticks.[861] Thus lawyers, as a group and over time, may tend to exert an unusual, hydraulic (one might say corrosive) force against any relatively determinate linguistic meaning. Within our system as presently constructed, that's their job. They are in the argument-making business, and are not limited to legitimate arguments. Although lawyers generally are concerned with winning the case at hand rather than shaping the law overall, their persistent bending and twisting of language case by case to attain short-term goals can gradually lead to a reshaping of the law, often in unforeseen and possibly unhelpful directions.

At the same time, judges—in theory the defenders of linguistic determinacy in the legal arena—typically have their time and attention fragmented and divided in various different directions at once. Whether at the trial or the appellate level, they usually are responsible for several, perhaps many, cases at any one time. Each of those cases might involve from a few to a dozen or more separate legal issues, let alone factual issues. On each issue, there might be lawyers seeking to twist the language toward their ends. The judge usually cannot focus on any one issue for very long. Such conditions favor overly brief, hasty summarizations of complex cases, as seen in *Fisher*, *Payne*, and *Lehne*. The hydraulic pressure from the lawyers also means that anytime a judge lets her guard down even briefly, she might wind up following their use of language or arguments more than their merits warrant. Although judges, especially appellate judges, must think about the overall shape of the law, in practice they must focus primarily on the cases in front of them and the discrete issues in those cases. All these present-minded pressures on judges probably tend to push toward convenient, plausible locutions that appear acceptable in the short-term, even if they might bear the seeds of trouble for the future. This, for instance, might help explain courts toggling between exclusive and non-exclusive statements of rules without knowing they have done so—such a distinction might seem minute, and easy to miss, among the many other things they must consider and decide.

Another problematic factor relates to the passage of time rather than the lack of time. For an individual judge, or for a court system as a whole, there may be long gaps of time between when a particular issue is considered and when it is

[861] A judge of my acquaintance once explained that California appellate courts hold court-appointed appellate counsel for criminal defendants to the "razor test"—whether counsel could look himself in the mirror while shaving on the morning before the hearing, deliver his appellate arguments, and not cut himself from laughing. I'll leave it to others to think of a female version of the same test.

reconsidered. From my own experience, I often had trouble remembering cases I had worked on more than a year (let alone two years) earlier, and I believe that was not so different for other judicial staff. Thus the creation and perpetuation of precedent does not happen in a neat, orderly, continuous process—it happens in sporadic fits and starts, scattered among many different courts. Along with the other factors described above, this, for me, calls into question Dworkin's idea of legal precedent as a chain novel in practice, though I confess I find the vision a charming one in theory. Unfortunately, courts are not working on a single novel with regular installments written at some degree of leisure and without outside pressures; they are working on umpteen different novels at once, submitting installments that are highly irregular in length or depth at infrequent and varying intervals and subject to all manner of outside pressures. Sometimes they even submit an installment suitable for one novel to a different, incorrect novel, as with antagonistic defenses reasoning injected into the joint representation lineage. Thus bodies of precedent, rather than coming out looking like the product of a single master literary craftsman, often may come out looking more like—the Illinois doctrine of antagonistic defenses.

In sum, because of these interrelated factors—lawyers' strong and persistent incentive to twist meanings of words, judges' practical inability to stop them, the chronic fragmentation of judges' attention and of the whole process of creating precedent, and the memory-eroding impact of time, together with the hyper-abstracting nature of the law—courts are inherently engines of linguistic ambiguity and indeterminacy, notwithstanding all good intentions to operate differently. And this, perhaps more than judges' personal and political preferences, helps to explain the proliferation of varying, sometimes inconsistent precedents surrounding any one legal issue.

Thus, ironically, the common law—in theory the one area of human activity above all others (other than perhaps treaties and legislation) where minute linguistic distinctions must be observed and controlled carefully because of their greater possible concrete impact on the rights, property, and lives of citizens—is in practice predisposed toward an unusually high level of linguistic indeterminacy. Judges, for all their good conscientious efforts, may be unable to prevent a lot of seemingly minor or subtle changes from slipping through and reshaping a body of precedent in unforeseen ways. Perhaps, in a strange way, this is even beneficial to the common law, introducing an unplanned additional flexibility into the system, a sort of secret trap door to avoid *stare decisis*. Perhaps it is only further professional mystification, allowing the law to appear to honor precedent while it actually doesn't.

Justice Holmes famously observed that "great" or "hard" cases make bad law.[862] What we have seen regarding the formation of precedent gives the lie to Holmes' quip, though. For as we have seen, no case really makes law in itself; rather, later cases make law out of earlier cases. So the phrase should be rewritten to say: later bad, erroneous, or ill-considered interpretations of great or hard earlier cases make bad law. For example, *Braune* did not produce bad law because other courts and judges avoided touching it, correctly recognizing it to be a very unusual, intensely fact-specific case not amenable to summarization in some neat legal rule. *Daugherty* made the bad law, not *Braune*, but this was not a forgone conclusion. *Rupert* and *Sweetin* should have been handled with the same care, but *Fisher*, *Payne*, and *Lehne* instead made bad law out of them, improperly summarizing them and extracting incorrect principles from them. That was not the fault of *Rupert* or *Sweetin*. But perhaps Holmes' statement is ultimately correct, if we assume what he meant was that sooner or later, inevitably, some judge will, or some attorney will persuade some judge to, grossly misinterpret some complex, problematic earlier case or extract an overly abstracted rule from it that ignores the specific factual content and "thisness" of the earlier case. Although such a result should be avoidable in theory, it might in fact be inevitable in practice. And if the creation of bad law by improper distilling of earlier cases is inevitable, as Holmes suggests, and if there is effectively no reliable way to clean out or correct that bad law, as the strange career of the Illinois antagonism doctrine indicates, then our system of precedent-based common law is and must remain fundamentally tainted.

Now, a confession: I originally had planned to follow an earlier article in listing various aspects of our common law that have led to confusion and contradiction in the antagonistic defenses arena (and, I believe, elsewhere), then proposing ways of improving the use of precedent to avoid those flaws. Most of the same flaws apply here as well, such as courts relying (as I used to) upon the latest glib, concise reiteration of a rule in passing rather than on an older opinion that actually meaningfully considers and works through the rule, so I won't review them in detail again.[863] I thought of offering various proposals to keep actual meaningful holdings and rules more pure, distinct, and checkable for error and prevent the clutter and static of unnecessary and largely meaningless paraphrasings from obscuring the actual rules and unnecessarily twisting their meanings. These might include, for instance, requiring clearer marker-language in cases distinguishing actual, meaningfully considered holdings from dicta or throwaway sub-holdings, so that it would be easier for later courts to trace the cases that actually say anything of value on an issue or rule and to cite only those cases, so that the relevant lineage would remain more finite, manageable, and relevant. I also

[862] N. Secs. Co. v. United States, 193 U.S. 197, 400 (1904).
[863] *See* Dewey, *supra* note 58, at 254-66.

considered advocating new mechanisms for catching precedential anomalies, detecting whether they arose from erroneous precedent, and cleaning out any such error.

But I have abandoned that lofty purpose, recognizing that pursuing such goals would require fundamental changes in the practices both of law and of judging as we know them. And that's about as useful as trying to hold back the tide by pissing in the ocean. Both lawyers and judges have long been comfortable enough working within an engine of linguistic indeterminacy; if they weren't, they would have done something about it already. Lawyers thrive, and profit handsomely, in that setting; judges, who are themselves former lawyers and are typically sympathetic to lawyers' way of thinking, suffer more within the system but accept it without complaining too much. As long as the apparent legitimacy of the legal system can be maintained by persuading the general public that the outcomes of the judicial process are not unmoored, it does not matter so much to legal professionals if those outcomes actually are frequently unmoored due to one or another shortcoming in our system of observing precedent. In short, there is no real constituency within the legal profession for straightening out the use of precedent as much as possible, and as usual, the lay public has no idea what's going on in a highly mystified profession. So although I remain a faithful believer in the theoretical potential of a properly regulated system of precedent to provide at least partial objectivity and regularity to judicial decisionmaking, in practice, I know that the significant flaws in the system that inject significant unintentional indeterminacy into the system will remain. So I'll content myself with pointing out that additional problematic aspect of precedent, and leave it at that.

To sum up the takeaway points from this overly long article: Is *stare decisis* useful? Potentially. Is it always useful as presently practiced? Definitely not. Does it always work right? No. Are there ways it could be made to work better? Certainly—at least in theory. Would these require more disciplined techniques by judges and lawyers in creating and using precedent? Yes. Are judges or lawyers likely to embrace the extra effort? No. Is the current system for creating and using precedent inefficient? Decidedly. Is an unimproved, uncorrected system of *stare decisis* a net benefit? Probably not. There has to be a reason why most other civilized nations do not use it, or at least use much more stripped-down versions. Judge Posner has pointed out that America has the most expensive legal system of any advanced modern nation;[864] the time and effort spent wrestling with confusing and contradictory precedent probably contribute to that relative cost and inefficiency.

---

864 *See* POSNER, HOW JUDGES THINK, *supra* note 6, at 264.

All that being said, even if precedent and *stare decisis* are somewhat mythical and time-wasteful in practice, and even if America's common-law justice system is inefficient in other ways as well, hopefully America's conscientious, hard-working judges are nevertheless operating a system that, on balance, produces just, sensible outcomes overall, most of the time.

But one has to wonder.

Made in the USA
Monee, IL
05 November 2026

67814350R00125